The
PAJAMA
PHILOSOPHER

The
PAJAMA
PHILOSOPHER

Making Sense of the Mystery of Christ

Brett Bonecutter

Published by Thought Partner Publishing
949-829-1371 | www.thoughtpartnerpublishing.com
ISBN-13: 978-0-692-25055-6
ISBN-10: 0-692-25055-7

Cover design by Fabrizio Romano
Illustrations by Le Mei Ren
Interior design by Valerie Anne Bost
Printed in the United States of America

14 15 16 17 18 19 20 21   10 9 8 7 6 5 4 3 2 1

This book is lovingly dedicated to my four boys:

Blake, Jordan, Luke, and Jason.

I write in hope that you will stand on the shoulders
of those who have gone before
to do great things for the kingdom of God.

Contents

Introduction 1

CONSIDERING VARIOUS
PHILOSOPHICAL FRAMEWORKS

Chapter One: The Great Philosophical Divide 13
  Wrestling With Religious Pluralism
  Cosmological Dualism
  Cosmological Monism
  Revisiting the Parable of the Elephant

Chapter Two: Mapping Major Philosophical Pathways 25
  Philosophy Self-Assessment
  Atheistic or Agnoistic Materialism
  Nature Mysticism
  Generic Spirituality
  Religious Adherence

Chapter Three: Mulling Over Monism 47
  To My Atheist and Agnostic Friends | *Is Occam's Razor always the best tool?* | *Are faith and reason mutually exclusive?* | *Is religion necessarily bad for society and science?* | *Have you fully grappled with the consequences of moral subjectivism?*
  To My Nature Mystic Friends | *Are you keeping your experience and your cognitive mind in balance?* | *A powerful and wonderful mind* | *Where East meets West* | *Does the mystery of life have shape?* | *How should we understand evil, suffering, and death?*

Chapter Four: Dueling Dualists 75

To My Generically Spiritual Friends | *Aren't we all exclusive in our own way?* | *Should you revisit your thinking about comparative religion and myth?* | *Do you have a higher calling on your life?* | *Does the hypocrisy of Christians disprove their faith?*

To My Non-Christian Religious Adherent Friends | *Does your religion's revelation strongly correspond to phenomenal reality?*

DISCOVERING THE
CHRISTIAN THEOLOGICAL TRADITION

Chapter Five: Crossing the Cosmological Chasm 95

How Is God Revealed? | *Natural Revelation—Creational Order and Beauty* | *Natural Revelation—Human Community* | *Natural Revelation— Human Conscience* | *Special Revelation—God Himself* | *Special Revelation—God's Messengers* | *Special Revelation—God's Message*

Science and the Scriptures | *Intelligent Design and Creation Science* | *Parameters of Genesis 1* | *History and Science* | *Epistemic Authority* | *Jailing Copernicus*

Chapter Six: Demystifying the Dusty Book 123

What Is the Bible?

What About All of the Different Bible Translations?

Should We Read the Bible Literally? | *Chiasms in Scripture* | *Scripture interprets Scripture*

Doesn't the Bible Contradict Itself Since It Is Man-Made? | *Narrative Discrepancies* | *Transcription Errors* | *Historical Correspondence* | *Thematic Inconsistencies*

Isn't the Bible Culturally Antiquated and Irrelevant?

Chapter Seven: The Bible's Big Idea(s) 149

The Governing Motif

The Nature of the Day Two Divide | *Already and Not Yet*

What Heaven is Like | *The Worship and Work of Heaven* | *But Where Is Heaven?*

Chapter Eight: Man in the Middle 181

God's Garden Model for Human Maturity and Civilization | Work at the Core of Humanity's Identity | Masters of Art and Science | The Two Teaching Trees | Food and Faith

The Communal Building Blocks of Humanity | The Reason for Marriage | The Representational Principle | The Glory of Women | Biblical Leadership and Headship

Sex, Nudity, and Human Destiny | Sex and the City | The Dehumanizing Potential of Sexual Power | The Nature and Gravity of Sin | Humanity's New Clothes

Chapter Nine: Christ's Heroic Framework and Backstory 223

Superheroes through the Ages | The Source of the Snake Myths

Defeating Satan to Save the World | Angels and Demons | Humanity's Global Mop-Up Operation

Christ's Extensive Backstory | A Family of Faithful Superheroes | God's Strategy for Raising Abraham's Family | Putting the Whole Backstory Together

God Becomes the Hero | Christ As the God-Man

Chapter Ten: The Heroic Work of God's Son 249

The Expected and the Unexpected

Premier Prophet | Mighty in (Kingdom) Word | Mighty in (Kingdom) Deed

Supreme High Priest | The Basis of a Right Relationship with God | Extinguishing Evil Humanity and Raising It to New Life | The Centrality of the Resurrection

Conquering King | A Global Monarchy | Four Common Views | Concerns about Utopianism, Triumphalism, and Power

EXPLORING THE PRACTICAL IMPLICATIONS
OF THE KINGDOM

Chapter Eleven: Christ's Kingdom Strategy 289

Christ's Kingdom Strategy: Christian Unity | Reflecting on Several Paradigms of Personal Change

Refashioning Our Humanity and the Organized Church | Ministry of the Word (Recalibrating Our Identity Narrative) | Ministry of the Sacraments (Rehearsing Identity Rituals) | Exercise of Discipline (Reinforcing Identity Boundaries)

Practicing Our Identity Narrative, Rituals, and Boundaries | *The Supremacy of Corporate Worship* | *Covenant Renewal*

Which Christian Tradition?

Chapter Twelve: Life in the Kingdom 319

Self-Government | *How Great a Salvation* | *The Path of Morality* | *Matters of Conscience* | *Sincerity* | *The Pattern and Power of Prayer*

Family Government | *Duties of Parents* | *Duties of Young Children* | *Duties of Grown Children*

Church Government | *The Institutional Form of the Church* | *The Keys to the Kingdom*

Civil Government | *Relationship between Church and State* | *The Problem with Natural Law and the Secular State* | *The Challenge of Conservatism* | *The Disciple State Vision*

Introduction

One of the greatest and most surprising privileges of my life has been the opportunity to raise four healthy boys with my incredible wife, Gina. When Gina and I were dating during college she gave me several opt-out messages, but perhaps the biggest one was that she was not ovulating and had been told by doctors that she would not be able to bear children. She was concerned that any potential suitor would want to know this in case it was a deal-breaking issue.

I must confess that I was so head over heels in love with Gina that the news didn't have the impact on me that it probably should have. Frankly, I thought it just cleared a path to do a lot more traveling to Europe in our twenties.

As a result of her diagnosis, Gina was put on an oral contraceptive in order to induce a normal monthly cycle. For all intents and purposes, it seemed like a foregone conclusion that we would never have children or would have to adopt.

One day Gina came to me in a deeply troubled state of mind. She wanted to be a mother so badly, but felt she would never know if it were possible as long as she stayed on the course prescribed by her doctors. She asked what I thought of going off the pill to see if God might open her womb. Without much thought, I said that seemed like a good idea. After all, if she hadn't been ovulating, what were the chances?

Evidently the chances were 100 percent. Within months of going off of contraception, Gina was pregnant with our first son. I was only twenty-four years old. Fourteen months later our second son arrived. Within several years we had sons number three and four. Let's just say it took scientific measures to stop all of the supposedly improbable procreation.

Due to certain convictions and massive responsibilities at a relatively early age, I have spent most of my vocational career in the business world. Despite my early plans to pursue seminary education or a law degree, my sagacious mentor, Jack Kistler, urged me not to go to graduate school solely on my wife's support. He told me to get a job to provide for my family, and so I did.

To supplement my relatively unmarketable bachelor's degree in biblical studies, I got an MBA from Pepperdine University while working full time. I hoped that it would bolster my ability to provide for my growing and voraciously hungry clan—and it did.

After working in several industries through my late twenties, I decided to take a risk and embark on an almost five-year tour of duty through vocational ministry. For various reasons, I could not sustain the effort emotionally or financially. Looking back, it is clear that I was not in a good position to wear the collar. Back to the business world!

But my passion for helping people encounter and know God has not waned. Despite being heavily invested and engaged as a father, husband, and businessman, it pains me when people reject or neglect Jesus Christ because they misunderstand Him. Christians who remain significantly ignorant about the faith they profess cause me almost equal heartache. Our faith is so profound that it embraces everything in heaven and earth.

I'm not saying that I've arrived or know everything there is to know about the mystery of Christ . . . or about anything else, for that matter. Not at all. However, I have spent significant energy puzzling over various philosophical and religious claims, and I think I may be able to offer some help to other people along the way.

Without a doubt, my greatest sense of responsibility is to my four boys. I am deeply convicted that they have been entrusted to Gina and me for a purpose greater than I am able to understand or imagine. I firmly believe there are many generations of Bonecutters at stake. My heart's desire is that my boys and their descendants after them would have a long, prosperous, and extremely productive life for the kingdom of God. I want to help them however I can, even if it is from a great distance of time and space.

One of the best ways I can share what I have learned with my progeny and others is to write a book about Christianity. What better way to pass on an enduring message to people that I love and to those I may never meet?

The trouble is that writing a book is a lot of work, and I have no particular platform to speak from. The only way to get this project done was in my pajamas.

Let me explain.

I don't have a doctorate in anything. I have often thought it would be worth pursuing a PhD just so people could legitimately call me Dr. Bonecutter, but I was never quite serious enough to act on it. (My name is awesome enough as it is, right?) I am somewhat of a theological and philosophical layman. Having had just a brief stint in the ministry, I'm like a guy who played minor league baseball for a few years. But I've got some legitimate background. I can't boast about being a truly seasoned pro from the big leagues, but I can throw a knuckleball and have been known to steal a base on occasion.

The bottom line is that I am not speaking from an officially sanctioned ecclesiastical or academic place of authority. I'm just a dad trying to make a difference in the lives of my family and friends. I'm simply writing this book as a guy in his pajamas.

I rolled out of bed at 4:30 a.m. every morning for the better part of a year to write this book. It was the only time I could get it done. And so, in my flannel pajamas, sitting at the dining room table with a cappuccino in hand, I set about my task. My self-bestowed title of The Pajama Philosopher wasn't simply meant to be cute. It was an accurate moniker.

Before we jump into the book in earnest, I want to put forth a broad disclaimer. Our faith commitments and belief systems are complex and multifaceted. There is no way that I can be as persuasive or profound as I would like to be merely through communicating the intellectual data in this book. I wish it were that easy.

To appreciate how difficult it is to address peoples' beliefs it is helpful to get a glimpse into the way we're psychologically and spiritually built. For the moment I will not attempt to defend my understanding of this dynamic—I will simply assert it for later consideration. If you're skeptical, that's okay. This is preliminary food for thought.

I believe that one of the ways humans are unique in the world is that we are composed of both a body and a soul. We are made up of physical stuff that can be quantified and spiritual stuff that cannot be quantified. Our body and soul interpenetrate each other and work together, but they remain distinct. Our brains are not our minds, but our minds are primarily seated in our brains, and our brains are seated in our bodies. (Have fun with that one.)

Human anatomy is pretty straightforward and relatively easy to observe, but the anatomy of our souls is harder to understand. Some of the most useful theological and philosophical thinking on the subject understands the human soul as having three faculties that function like a prism.

The three sides of the spiritual prism are intellect, emotions, and volition (will). Our intellect is our ability to know things, our emotions include our feelings and desires, and our volition makes conscious and unconscious choices influenced by the other two dimensions. The Bible often interchangeably refers to the combination of these capacities as our *minds, souls,* or *hearts.*

The Faculties of the Human Soul

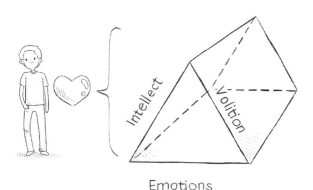

Emotions

None of the faculties is superior to the others, and none exists in isolation. However, the case could easily be made that our emotions and desires are naturally dominant by default. For instance, a guy may intellectually know that smoking is harmful and causes cancer, but it may not change his decision (volition) to smoke because he has an emotional affinity to smoking. The nicotine may make him feel relaxed or the social dimensions of smoking may help him fit into his subculture. Intellectual constructs are often overridden in this fashion, regardless of their significance. Mere knowledge is never enough to produce profound personal transformation.

A prism's usefulness depends on the integrity of its structure and the light source it is pointed toward. We orient ourselves toward what we love, and that becomes the light source. As that light shines into us, it refracts through our hearts to display its own character and quality in our thoughts, feelings, and actions. When our hearts are pointed to the pure God, an array of beautiful light shines through to color our intellect, emotions, and volition with graciousness and peace and joy. But when our hearts are pointed to false gods and cheap substitutes, a dull light refracts as selfishness and turmoil and discontentment.

In short, the object of our love and the complex interplay of our intellect, emotions, and will shape our lives. We orient our hearts toward what we love most—our God or our god or our "god"—and whatever it shines back at us comes through us, shaping the content and quality of our thoughts, feelings, and choices. To borrow a line from a great rock ballad, love is "more than a feeling"—it employs all of our soul's faculties.

The late King of Soul, James Brown, didn't quite have the same thing in mind when he sang about being a "loving machine," but we are, in a sense, all loving machines. We are uniquely made to function with love as the fuel driving us from the core of our being.

Love and worship (our expressions of delight and honor to what we love) are inescapable because they are what our souls exist to manufacture. We love and worship twenty-four hours a day, seven days a week, three hundred and sixty-five days a year. It is what we do because it is what we were made to do. In this sense, everyone is intensely religious by nature.

This dynamic is why the Bible places such emphasis on what we love as opposed to what we merely think or feel. Examples abound:

You shall have no other gods before me. (Ten Commandments, Exod. 20:3)

You shall love the Lord your God with all your heart and with all your soul and with all your mind .... (Jesus, identifying the greatest commandment, Mark 12:30)

If I speak in the tongues of men and of angels, but have not love, I am a noisy gong or a clanging cymbal. And if I have prophetic powers, and understand all mysteries and all knowledge, and if I have all faith, so as to remove mountains, but have not love, I am nothing. If I give away all I have, and if I deliver up my body to be burned, but have not love, I gain nothing. (1 Cor. 13:1–3)

The object of our love and the health of our soul's faculties determines the shape of our lives. When the faculties of our soul are focused on the faint glow of manufactured idols, the refracted result in our lives is distorted. If the broken and misdirected faculties of our hearts are oriented to money, sex, power, another person, an addictive substance, or anything else besides the Triune God, we will reap disastrous results. One theologian even remarked that our hearts are idol factories.

We are Loving Machines

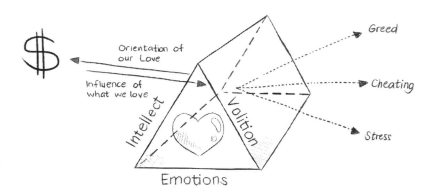

On the other hand, when our faculties are properly aligned and focused on God, a flood of beautiful light emanates from our innermost beings. Love—the dedicated orientation of our soul to the thoughts, passions, and will of God, results in a dazzling array of splendor in our lives and the lives of others. In fact, this love brings transformation beyond ourselves into the world around us.

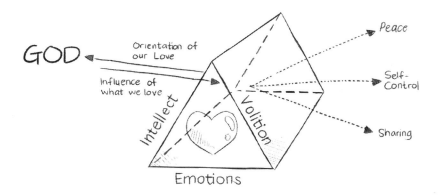

What does any of this have to do with making sense of the mystery of Christ and with this book project? In short, almost everything. It is very conceivable to have correct and compelling intellectual information about Jesus without having emotional feelings that support a volitional response of faith or trust.

You may have deep-seated feelings that rage against any intellectual advance in this arena. Perhaps you were abused or neglected by a hypocritical religious leader or domineering parent and cannot forget the damage it caused in your life. Maybe you are deeply connected to a community that is hostile to religion in general or Christianity in particular. You may have a strong attachment to a behavior or way of living that you simply don't want to give up. Without emotional and volitional engagement with the mystery of Christ, this book will be reduced to an exercise in academics and wasteful navel-gazing.

On the other hand, people who are emotionally committed to Christ but lack good intellectual instruction and knowledge may not refract the whole spectrum of available light. It is like their prism is aligned and pointed to the right source but is covered with smudges and scratches. Light gets through, but not at the potential brightness that we might expect. Solid information about Christ is critical to mature and abiding love.

In either case, changing our minds or making sense of something is far more complex than simply considering different rational propositions. If we truly thought knowledge was sufficient for personal transformation, we would turn high-security prisons into educational institutions. Information and right thinking have their place and are vital in their own right, but they do not stand alone or apart from other dynamics at work in our hearts.

Let's be honest—the intellect is a very tricky thing. Our emotions often use it as a tool for self-justification. We are incredibly efficient at rationalizing our behaviors and beliefs. It is not very hard for us to find various reasons to excuse ourselves, because our intellect is always ready to serve our emotions. Our capacity to self-manipulate and deceive with the full support of our intellect is an amazing and disturbing part of what it means to be human.

One of the advantages of having an intellect that is aligned to reality is that it can function as an anchor to our souls. To the extent that our hearts are like rowboats being tossed about on waves of emotion, our intellectual convictions and frameworks can prevent us from being shipwrecked. When we find ourselves emotionally pushed out to sea and adrift, our intellects can help keep us in safe harbor. It may not be primary or dominant, but it is critical.

Waves of Emotion

Intellectual Convictions

I recently heard a story about a pastor who would sit down for coffee with college students who came home between semesters. He would reach out to them to see how they were doing in their brave new world. Instead of asking them whether they were going to church or how they were intellectually surviving their philosophy classes, he would simply ask, "So who have you been sleeping with?" The approach might be very unsettling, but this pastor gets it. Our ultimate faith commitments and belief systems refract through the complex prism of our souls to what and how we love. Love is an affair of the whole person—of the whole heart.

In the spirit of total transparency, I want you to know that this book is fairly limited to the intellectual dimension of our identity. I'm not going to offer an altar call or a confrontation of particular sins and foibles. I will make a passionate case for Christ, but will not be explicitly attempting to elicit an emotional response. It is beyond the capacity of this work to try and tackle all of the dimensions of our beliefs.

In this respect and many more, this book stands as an extremely incomplete witness that may ring somewhat hollow in your soul. That should not be completely surprising. The mystery of Christ can fully make sense only in relationship and community with other people who are seeking to love God.

This book merely attempts to adjust the intellectual surface of the soul's prism so that it is more focused than before. My hope is that with a little more knowledge—a little clarification, perhaps a useful paradigm here and there—you will find more emotional and volitional energy to more fully seek and serve Christ.

It is important to confess at the outset that I have written this book to a broad audience—to Christians and to non-Christians. To conservatives and liberals. To young and old. And maybe I have bitten off more than I or you can reasonably chew or digest. However, I wanted to try to show the comprehensive arc of the Christian faith in a way that would provoke curiosity, discussion, and maybe even belief and renewed mission in the world.

With that said, I recognize that this is a rather large book. And in hindsight, perhaps it is regrettably large. And so I thank you ahead of time for understanding my burden to share a taste of the scope and sweep of the mystery of Christ.

To help you persevere through the journey, let me briefly explain the three-fold structure of the book:

Section One examines different worldviews and religions from a philosophical standpoint. My goal is to help people understand the large streams of thought that we all tend to derive our beliefs from. By laying out an overall philosophical framework, I hope to pique interest in the Christian witness about the nature of reality.

Section Two pivots away from abstract philosophy to an explanation of the underpinnings of the Christian faith. This includes a brief look at the structure and contents of the Bible itself and works toward a more specific argument for the identity of the person and work of Jesus Christ.

Section Three turns to a more intramural Christian discussion of the high-level practical implications of the Christian faith. In the final analysis, Christianity is not a mere abstraction and must not be understood in that light. Our beliefs are only profound insofar as they impact our lives.

I have broken the chapter outlines down in some detail in the table of contents. I would encourage you to peruse this to get a feel for the overall trajectory and perhaps to select topics that seem to be of most immediate interest. There is a definite logic and coherence that you will see by reading the book from beginning to end, but if that is too daunting then feel free to skip to the sections that are most relevant to you.

No matter where you find yourself in relationship to Christianity, I hope to provide a philosophical, theological, and practical perspective that stimulates thought and action. Life is too precious to live without deeply considering matters of ultimate significance.

And so from this pajama philosopher to other pajama philosophers near and far, I welcome you to a journey in making sense of the mystery of Christ.

With love,

BRETT BONECUTTER
The Pajama Philosopher

CONSIDERING VARIOUS
PHILOSOPHICAL FRAMEWORKS

CHAPTER ONE

The Great Philosophical Divide

Every man is born an Aristotelian or a Platonist.... They are two classes of man, beside which it is next to impossible to conceive a third.

—Samuel Taylor Coleridge

I've always been something of a believer. The minute—and I mean the minute—I got home from seeing the debut of Star Wars in 1978, I ran to my room, shut my door, and started to try to use the Force. I took a no. 2 yellow pencil out of my desk, sat in my chair, held out my hand and tried to make that pencil levitate. The first failure did not deter me. Surely, the Force had to be with me—even at five years old. Hand open, hand shut. Breathing slowly, not breathing at all. Squinting my eyes, pursing my lips. Iteration after iteration for hours on end I worked on becoming a Jedi. Luke Skywalker and I obviously had a lot in common and I would surely figure it out.

Spoiler alert—the Force was not with me. I never got that pencil to levitate, and I later learned about special effects and decided to abandon the notion of the Force entirely. Well, maybe not entirely. I have always sensed that there was much more to this world than immediately meets the eye.

What I failed to realize as a little boy was that not everyone believes that there is more to this world than meets the eye. Enter my best friend since fifth grade, Jason Rampelt. His family did not go to church because they didn't believe in God. In naive bewilderment I asked Jason how they could deny the existence of God and he said they believed in science and something called the big bang. I took this bit of information and brought it to my Sunday school teacher and parents—hoping they would have good answers for me about this radically alternative belief system. None were forthcoming. And so in sixth grade, I decided I would become an atheist too. I thought, "Who needs a god when you have science and the big bang?"

Fast-forward about thirty years. Jason and I have both become committed Christians with theological degrees. I have served as a pastor, and Jason went on to get a PhD in the philosophy and history of science at Cambridge University in England. Despite our early commitments to atheism and agnosticism, we both found Jesus. Or, to be more exact, Jesus found us.

What happened? There is obviously no easy or one-dimensional explanation. Each of us has formed beliefs about the nature of ultimate reality—or what I will call *cosmology*—of our own selves, other people, the material universe, and the existence of deity and the spirit. These beliefs are derived from a unique matrix of social, emotional, and cognitive influences. Almost by definition, our individual journeys toward spiritual understanding escape generalization—and this is one of the reasons we live in an age that celebrates religious pluralism.

As a freshman at Indiana University in Bloomington, I encountered an intense recognition of religious and spiritual pluralism within a week of my arrival. One of the mandatory orientation sessions we had to attend was diversity training. The ostensible point of this session was to break down personal prejudices that would inhibit the formation of community and academic freedom. I don't know that I will ever forget the Q&A panel led by Wiccans, lesbian and transgender activists, and Reform Jews. The point was very, very clearly made: there was a broad diversity of faith and practice on campus, and we must embrace that diversity to thrive at Indiana University and in the world at large.

Wrestling With Religious Pluralism

For the record, I have no particular beef with this kind of pluralistic principle. It is very good and right to acknowledge, understand, and tolerate different beliefs and how people have come to them. I don't mean to be combative, but I have a point of contention when efforts to recognize and tolerate a de facto plurality of views morphs from descriptive to prescriptive. As British theologian Alister McGrath has pointed out, it is one thing to observe that there are many points of view (descriptive) and another thing to posit that every view is therefore equally valid (prescriptive).[1] Descriptive pluralism is necessary and good, not to mention a pretty obvious reality, but prescriptive pluralism is a precarious non sequitur. It simply does not follow. Recognizing that there are many differences does not automatically mean that all the differences are equally valid.

Unfortunately, the non sequitur of prescriptive pluralism has become widely assumed as truth when it comes to matters of religion and faith. For those who adopt prescriptive pluralism, there is no particular need or means of discerning whether one religious belief is any better or worse than any other. Islam and Wicca may be radically different in their understandings of ultimate realities, but for the prescriptive pluralist there is no impulse to discern if either is more or less true, because faith commitments are assumed to be inherently subjective affairs. If a Muslim believes that there is one God who exists as a transcendent deity, and a Wiccan believes that *god* is a mere word that describes nature and its inherent energy, then they are both true for those individuals and equally valid. According to this point of view we should abandon any impulse to sift through faith commitments as true or untrue.

One of the classic illustrations that prescriptive pluralists advance in defense of their philosophical system is the parable of the blind men and the elephant. A group of blind men touch various parts of an elephant—its trunk, legs, tail, and so forth. When each man is asked what an elephant is, he describes it from his limited experience: "An elephant is a flexible, hose-like structure that can grasp things and even spray water," says the man who examined the trunk. "No, an elephant is a sturdy tree with leathery skin," counters the guy who touched the leg. And so on.

---

1   Alister E. McGrath, *A Passion for Truth: The Intellectual Coherence of Evangelicalism* (Downers Grove: InterVarsity Press, 1996), 178.

The point of the parable is obvious. God, spirituality, and religion are supposedly too large to be conceived by one group or one system of dogma. Therefore, in matters of faith we are all just experiencing spiritual realities from our own limited points of view. All religious beliefs are true from their own standpoints. Wiccans and Muslims are just seeing and understanding the same reality from vastly different and limited angles.

Tim Keller's book *The Reason for God* powerfully confronts the parable's fatal Achilles heel. Keller points out that it is internally inconsistent with its own conclusion. This parable assumes that the parable-teller is not blind in any way, but can see everything plainly and exhaustively—the very thing he is arguing against.[2] Prescriptive pluralists can't have it both ways. They can't have an omniscient and all-seeing parable-teller who is who claims that perfect knowledge and sight are impossible. While the story may look good on the surface, it doesn't play by its own rules, and therefore invalidates itself.

Of course, I do not want to erect a straw man by suggesting that this flawed parable is the primary motive people have for embracing prescriptive pluralism. The reasons for religious subjectivism are more complex and sophisticated. In the modern and postmodern West, subjectivism is rooted in the nineteenth-century philosophical works of Immanuel Kant. His greatest impact was in the philosophical area of epistemology, the theory of knowledge. This field of inquiry asks, "How do we know what we know?"

Kant promoted the idea that human knowledge is limited to the sphere that can be encountered physically through the senses, technically referred to as the *phenomenal* realm. According to Kant, so-called transcendent realities were beyond certain knowing because they are beyond our human senses and ability to directly observe. This approach advanced a cosmological duality between the two realms, with humans firmly restricted to the phenomenal.

Cosmological Dualism

We can map out this cosmological duality along a vertical spectrum of sorts. At the top of the spectrum is the transcendent and non-physical realm of spiritual reality. At the bottom of the spectrum are

2   Timothy Keller, *The Reason for God: Belief in an Age of Skepticism* (New York: Dutton, 2008), 138.

phenomenological realities accessible by our senses. The tear between the realms is courtesy of Immanuel Kant, and it suggests that the realms are distinct from each other and that phenomenal beings are rationally bounded to the material end of the spectrum.

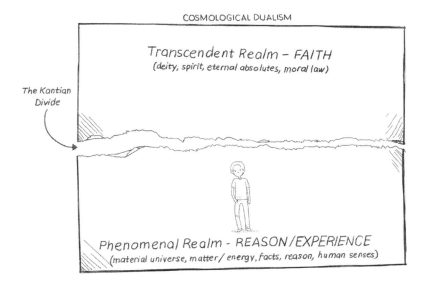

Kant's fixed duality between the transcendent-spiritual and the rational-phenomenological became the foundation for the notion that religious belief required a leap of faith—an irrational or even suprarational jump beyond the phenomenal realm. This in turn made faith and religious propositions entirely subjective affairs, meaning that they were dependent on the mind of the subject (subjective), not a truly observable object (objective).

Kant's philosophical influence exploded with the rise of Darwinian evolutionary biology that came on its heels. Suddenly the philosophical chasm between science and religion—between reason and knowledge—became vast beyond measure. Science and scientific knowledge existed in the phenomenal realm and could therefore be discerned and known with a measure of certainty. In contrast, religious propositions existed in the transcendent realm that could only be subjectively accessed by individual leaps of faith.

In truth, Kant's phenomenal-transcendent dualism was quite ancient. In ancient Greece, Plato and Aristotle represented two schools of thought that bore striking similarities to Kant's scheme. Plato believed that the world as we know it is derived from transcendent absolutes and Aristotle believed that the world as we know it is derived from worldly particulars.

One of the convenient examples to illustrate the difference between Plato and Aristotle can by seen through the consideration of the common dog. Plato thought that the different types and manifestations of dogs are based on an eternal canine archetype from which all dogs emanate. Aristotle's scheme rejected this and says that our concept of *dogness* does not come from an eternal blueprint, but is the amalgam of all of the different dogs we see on Earth. For Plato, the world was patterned after transcendent types, but for Aristotle, our concepts of types are patterned after our earthly experiences.

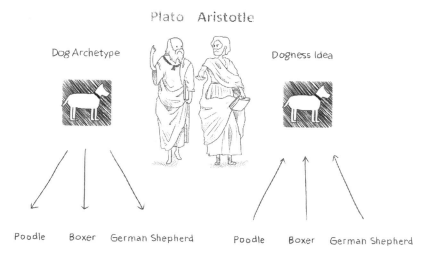

This over/under, above/below, transcendent/phenomenal distinction is therefore nothing new. Kant's philosophy simply influenced the way modern and postmodern people tend to reason through spiritual questions.

Cosmological Monism

Thanks to Kant, we can also clearly identify cosmological dualists from cosmological monists (mono =one). Cosmological dualists believe that both transcendent and phenomenal realms exist and should be distinguished. Cosmological monists deny the transcendent dimension and consider all things to be ultimately phenomenal—often using naturalistic reasoning to address spiritual concerns.

Keep in mind that the transcendent and phenomenal categories are not spatial, per se. It is not as if the transcendent realm occupies a different space or universe. It might be more helpful to think in terms of dimensions. We can make a distinction between nonphysical and physical realities that potentially exist alongside each other.

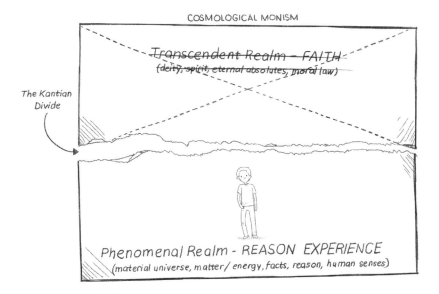

I believe that most people have simply defaulted to either cosmological dualism or cosmological monism without even knowing it because the success of Kant's philosophy and the reinforcement of Darwinism have been so pervasive. Faith and reason have been restricted to different spheres for well over a century in the West. Where does this great divide leave us? What are the options, if any, for believing with this structure?

Revisiting the Parable of the Elephant

Imagine that everyone in the world can see, but all suffer from significant visual impairment. Everyone wears glasses to help them function on a day-to-day basis, but there are only a handful of lens types available. Some people have very deliberately chosen the glasses they wear, and some have not. Many people have simply inherited a pair of glasses from family and friends. People are generally reluctant to discuss or to switch the glasses they wear because it can be extremely frustrating and disorienting. Glasses and lens types are taken so much for granted that people often forget they have them on.

One day a wide cross-section of people representing each lens type is invited on an African safari. They are asked to look out, describe, and discuss what they see and experience on the trip. On their first stop they are all led to a viewpoint looking down onto a broad field.

As the group squints through their glasses at the beautiful vista, a dark and relatively blurry object starts moving across their field of vision from east to west. Some of the people are frustrated by their inability to quantitatively measure it. Others are swept away by the beauty of the scene and are more focused on soaking in their experience of it. Another group is content to generally identify the object as a large animal, but will not speculate on the species. One group not only insists that it is an elephant, but that it is moving to the west for a specific purpose. A diverse discussion and heated argument breaks out:

> We don't have the necessary equipment to measure the properties of this image. Without precise and objective data we can't really afford to speculate on its identity. Let's focus on the things we can measure and know for certain.

> Don't worry about data! Look at how beautiful all of these colors are together! Have you ever seen such a stunning panorama? We must enjoy the drama of this moment together.

Well, it is probably a large animal of some kind – but it is really hard to tell. It doesn't really matter, does it?

Guys! That is an elephant – period! And it must be running to the west because a mouse is chasing it! How could it be anything else?

Show me exactly how you know it is an elephant and that there is a mouse – then I will believe you.

Everyone is missing the point! Breathe in the clean air and feel the breeze as the sun sets. That's what we're here for anyway!

Let's just agree that it's an animal of some kind and call it a day. Then we can all stop bickering and go to the next stop.

It's so obvious! What else could it be other than an elephant? And why would it be running unless it was afraid of something? There is a reason, people!

Within minutes, the large group quickly begins to break down into smaller groups according to lens type. Each of the smaller groups decides it will be a much more pleasant safari without having to debate about what they're seeing in front of them. It is simply exhausting to contend with the hubris and stubbornness of other people's opinions! The safari goes on with each group going its own way...

~

I believe this telling of the parable reflects reality much more accurately than the traditional elephant parable. We're all seeing and experiencing a common objective reality, but that reality is being subjectively interpreted through each mind's belief system. These systems act as imperfect prisms that screen out, highlight, and distort certain facets of experience and existence.

It has been said that there is no such thing as a brute fact. In other words, all inbound sensory and thought data that we encounter must pass through the prism of our intellectual paradigms, emotional biases, and volitional patterns. If we have an emotional block or cognitive distortion, we will interpret the information accordingly. As a statistician might say, "Garbage in, garbage out." Before we claim something to be a fact we should strive toward significant self-awareness of our own biases and mental paradigms.

My problem with the traditional parable of the elephant is that it presumes we are all experiencing and seeing completely different aspects of the same reality. I don't think our interaction with the phenomenal or transcendent truths works that way. It is not as if some of us encounter one piece of reality while some of us are encountering a different piece. The universe is not fragmented in this manner.

We all have bodies. We live on the same planet and are subject to the same gravitational pull. We have gustatory and psychological appetites. We experience joy and suffering. For all of our cultural and educational differences we still inhabit the same world together.

Therefore, the issue isn't that we each experience different kinds of realities, but that we each become so accustomed and attached to our particular prismatic focus that other perspectives often make little sense. Altering our belief systems is not an academic affair—it usually entails a totally different approach to life. It is intellectually, emotionally, and socially difficult.

Please note that in my retelling of the parable, each lens gives each person the ability to offer legitimate observations about the world. They can measure, see beauty, postulate about the nature of being, and so on. It isn't a matter of one group having the capacity to get everything right and every other group getting everything wrong; it is more about different lenses offering more or less clarity in certain areas.

I am a committed Christian who is attempting consciously to align the dimensions and focus of my soul's prism to Jesus Christ. I think it helps to see more clearly what other lenses tend to miss altogether or to perceive with considerable blur. However, I am happy and quick to acknowledge that non-Christians see things I might easily neglect or misunderstand because of my own foibles. My personal prism is surely out of focus in some respects.

To be clear, I am not a prescriptive pluralist in an ultimate sense. I believe that Jesus Christ is necessary, not optional, to fully enjoy and experience life as God intended. However, I don't think every other philosophical system outside of Christianity is necessarily wrong root and branch. That is simply not the case and not how Christianity works. C. S. Lewis wrote, "If you are a Christian you do not have to believe that all the other religions are simply wrong all through. If you are an atheist you do have to believe that the main point in all the religions of the whole world is simply one huge mistake."[3]

3   C. S. Lewis, *Mere Christianity* (New York: Macmillan, 1958), 35.

Before I advance a case for the Christian lens, I think there is tremendous value in getting a grasp of the different belief systems that are available. As hard as the task may be, we should attempt to understand the various philosophical glasses people wear. Perhaps we will find that this exercise helps us see things more clearly—even if it gives us headaches for a little while.

CHAPTER TWO

Mapping
Major Philosophical Pathways

The word philosophy sounds high-minded, but it simply means the love of wisdom. If you love something, you don't just read about it; you hug it, you mess with it, you play with it, you argue with it.

—attributed to Hugh Jackman

As a child growing up in the 1970s and '80s, LEGOs were a big part of my world. I loved models, and I spent hours building them as well as making my own designs—mostly spaceships outfitted with lasers, of course. I was the type of kid who had a gallery of finished masterpieces on the bedroom bookshelf. I was so proud and protective of my collection that some of the creations remained intact until my children inherited them almost twenty years later.

Early on I discovered that the best way to start a LEGO model was to sort all the different pieces by color and shape so that I could access what I needed quickly and easily. Looking back on it I sometimes wonder if the sifting and sorting were almost as fun as the creating itself. There is a certain joy to be found in categorizing and organizing because it often brings clarity.

Of course sorting through the maze of religious and philosophical beliefs is not quite the same as organizing piles of LEGOs. It is a far more complicated and sensitive task. No one I know comes to or maintains his or her beliefs in an emotional or social vacuum. We may be able to analyze a math problem in an emotionally detached way, but it is hard to examine our core beliefs without feeling a certain level of resistance, fear, or even anger.

Please understand, I do not intend to be glib with what follows here—especially when offering personal commentary. I have family, friends, and colleagues all over the cosmological map. I love and respect them all, regardless of their beliefs. The tricky reality is that any assessment like this is inherently biased by whomever is leading it. Rather than denying my biases and agenda for Christianity, I will just acknowledge them up front.

Philosophy Self-Assessment

Before we can effectively dive into an exploration of the mystery of Christ, it will be enormously helpful to recognize our own starting points and assumptions. Toward that end, I have put together a quick exercise to promote critical thinking and reflection on your philosophical-religious leanings. The assessment has two parts. Your results from Part 1 will determine which version of Part 2 you should take. Both parts consist of a list of questions. Each question has two options. Please choose the one that comes closest to expressing your opinion, even if you wouldn't say it quite that way. If neither option comes anywhere near to what you think, skip the question and go to the next one, buy try not to skip any, if possible, and do *not* pick both options.

∾

PART 1

1. **Does a higher power exist?**

    M. Even if a higher power did exist, humans wouldn't be able to know, so it is best not to believe it.

    D. I believe a higher power does exist.

2. **Is it important to believe in any God or higher power?**

    M. Believing in God or a higher power is totally unnecessary.

    D. Believing in God or a higher power is an important part of life.

3. **Is there a Creator?**

    M. Our origins are best understood by scientific theories such as evolution—there is no need to believe in a creator.

    D. Laws of physics do not exist on their own, but were set up and are sustained by a Creator.

4. **Where does the concept of morality come from?**
   M. The concept of morality does not ultimately depend on any religious deity.
   D. Without a higher power, there can be no compelling case for morality or moral behavior.

5. **What is your opinion about faith?**
   M. Faith is a mental crutch for ignorance.
   D. Faith and being spiritual are big parts of my life.

6. **Does the material universe have divine origins?**
   M. The material universe is eternal and does not require deity for explanations of its origin.
   D. The world shows signs of being created by a divine designer, and people should not deny it.

7. **What do you think about scientific facts versus spiritual faith?**
   M. Talk to me about facts, not about faith.
   D. Science and reason are valid, but they are not the only ways we know truth.

8. **What do you think about social structures such as marriage?**
   M. Marriage and other social structures are human conventions that help to propagate our species.
   D. Marriage and other social structures have been designed by God and are not man-made.

9. **What is your opinion of people who believe differently from you about the existence of God?**
   M. Religious people tend to be ignorant of science.
   D. When people deny a higher power in their life, they tend to be very cynical and selfish.

10. **What do you think about life after death?**
    M. Focusing on life after death robs people of fully living in the present.
    D. Pondering life after death helps give more meaning to the past and present.

11. **Are there moral absolutes?**
    M. It is technically valid to talk about morality, but not about moral absolutes that come from a deity.

D. There are some moral absolutes that everyone is subject to because God has designed the universe that way.

Self-Scoring for Part 1

of **M** responses: _____ *Cosmological Monist*
of **D** responses: _____ *Cosmological Dualist*

If the majority of your answers are Ms, you lean toward *cosmological
monism*. Please go to Part 2A and ignore Part 2B. If the majority of your
answers are Ds, you learn toward *cosmological dualism*. Please skip 2A
and go to 2B. Again, choose between the two options for each question.
Skip any that are truly not applicable, but try not to skip any if possible,
and don't select both answers to any question.

⌇

PART 2A

1. **Is the notion of deity helpful in our pursuit of truth?**
   A. There is no reason to ascribe "deity" or "god" to anything, because it gets in the way of reason.
   M. It is helpful to understand that, in some sense, all things are
   "god" or are infused with deity—people, animals, trees, sun-
   light, and so on.

2. **What is your opinion on meditation and meditative practices?**
   A. Meditation has many health benefits, but not because it helps
   people connect to any kind of spiritual dimension or reality.
   M. Meditation is one of many ways to connect our minds with the
   energy that unifies and animates the universe.

3. **How do you feel about Mother Earth?**
   A. The term Mother Earth comes from some nature religions and
   smacks of superstition.
   M. I believe that acknowledging Mother Earth is a way of affirming
   the life-giving force within our world.

4. **What is your understanding of the human mind or soul?**
   A. Our so-called minds are best understood from the vantage
   point of brain biology and psychological behaviorism.
   M. Our souls and minds are immortal because the energy is never
   lost or destroyed—it just takes new shape.

5. **What do you generally think of ancient spiritual beliefs?**
    A. Ancient spiritual beliefs are an intellectual relic of the past that should be abandoned.
    M. I think some ancient nature religions, such as Wicca, should be given more serious respect and attention.

6. **Do you believe in magic or miracles?**
    A. There are no such things as magic and miracles.
    M. Some magical or miraculous phenomena are real and are not mere illusions.

7. **Is it appropriate to think in terms of metaphysical reality?**
    A. Metaphysics is pseudoscience and is the product of overactive imaginations.
    M. Metaphysical realities are accessed by the alignment of our minds to the energy within and around us in the world

8. **How do you feel about the relationship between science and spirituality?**
    A. Self-help books that try to use the principles of physics to describe our personal lives and relationships are deeply misguided.
    M. I believe that universal laws such as the law of attraction apply to our relationships and the manifestation of our desires.

9. **What is your opinion of Jesus?**
    A. The teachings of Jesus were manufactured and provide false comfort to people.
    D. Jesus was a very spiritually enlightened person.

10. **What do you think about the afterlife?**
    M. There is no such thing as an afterlife.
    D. Reincarnation makes sense because when we die, the energy latent within us morphs into another physical form.

Self-Scoring for Part 2A

of **A** responses: _____   *Atheist/Agnostic* (Cosmological Monist)
of **M** responses: _____   *Nature Mysticism* (Cosmological Monist)

Feel free to read the questions in Part 2B, but there is no need to take that part of the assessment. You can now pick up after 2B.

~

PART 2B

1. How do we come to know God?

　　G. I believe we should all come to our own individual faith in our own way.

　　R. Deity breaks into the world, revealing itself so that human beliefs can have an objective basis for faith.

2. Do you regularly attend any kind of religious service?

　　G. I rarely attend religious worship services because I connect to God in my own way.

　　R. I go to religious worship services to praise God and to connect with people of my faith.

3. Should we seek to know specific doctrines about deity?

　　G. It is preferable not to be too dogmatic about religious issues because they are so subjective and everyone has to come to their own conclusions.

　　R. God has communicated though specially called prophets.

4. How do you try to learn more about God?

　　G. The divine is mostly discovered by looking inside ourselves and by experiencing nature.

　　R. My faith grows by studying the divine book of my religion.

5. Is it important to subscribe to a formal religion?

　　G. Religion, faith, transcendence, metaphysics—they're all pretty much the same. We each have to find our own beliefs.

　　R. I subscribe to a formal religion because I don't think we should make God fit whatever our imaginations come up with.

6. Are you willing to submit your mind to particular religious teachings?

　　G. Formal religion is usually too narrow-minded, and we should only believe the parts that resonate with us as individuals.

　　R. I am willing to submit my mind to the teachings of my religion, because that is part of what faith is all about.

7. How closely should we identify deity with nature?

G. I don't think it is quite right to say that everything is god, but I do believe in a higher power of some kind.

R. Belief systems that believe everything is god are confusing the creation with the Creator.

8. Are some specific religious practices spiritually helpful?

G. Specific religious practices often get in the way of helping people find God on their on terms.

R. When people seek God in their own way, they end up with a god of their own imagination.

9. What is your view of the afterlife?

G. I believe in an afterlife, but I don't know what to expect. Something like reincarnation seems like a legitimate possibility.

R. In the afterlife we will all be judged according to what we have done in this life.

10. How would you identify yourself, spiritually speaking?

G. I think spirituality is a good thing, but I don't subscribe to any formal religion.

R. If someone asks me what religion I am a part of, I can easily identify it.

Self-Scoring for Part 2B:

of **G** responses: _____ *Generic Spirituality* (Dualist)

of **R** responses: _____ *Religious Adherence* (Dualist)

~

If you followed the directions and didn't skip too many questions, you should have identified your beliefs as leaning toward one of the following macro groups:

1. **Cosmological Monist—Atheism/Agnosticism**
2. **Cosmological Monist—Nature Mysticism**
3. **Cosmological Dualist—Generic Spirituality**
4. **Cosmological Dualist—Religious Adherence**

Keep in mind that these groupings may have "fuzzy" boundaries, so don't be surprised if you score points in multiple areas. There is a certain danger in condensing such a diverse spectrum of views into a handful of categories, but I wanted to avoid being exhaustive or overly detailed in this analysis. These categories sketch a broad enough outline to allow us to see the pathways that emerge.

The logic of this sorting schema is simply that each of us begins with a denial or affirmation of the transcendent realm. We believe either that a realm or dimension of deity and eternal absolutes exists outside of the phenomenal realm or that it doesn't.

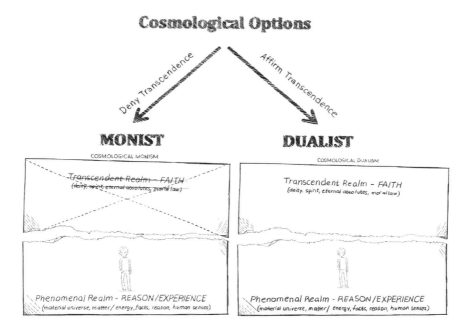

The monist group breaks into two groups—those who limit their knowledge to empirical methods, and those who ascribe mystical qualities to the phenomenal realm. These different approaches to the phenomenal realm are primarily what distinguish atheists/agnostics from nature mystics.

In a similar fashion, the dualist cosmology also breaks into two groups—those who believe that the transcendent realm is relatively inaccessible and more open to the subjective speculation of individuals, and those who believe the transcendent realm makes itself known to the phenomenal in objective and subjective ways.

Here is a brief summary of the four subsets:

1. **(Monist) Atheist/Agnostic**—Denies or refuses to subscribe to any religious or spiritual dimension or realm; prefers belief only in what can be proven or demonstrated by facts and science.

2. **(Monist) Nature Mysticism**—Spiritualizes the material world by identifying mystical spirits, energy, or universal laws that are embedded within the phenomenal realm.

3. **(Dualist) Generic Spirituality**—Does not subscribe to a particular religious revelation or dogma, but doesn't necessarily restrict a belief to facts or science; is often attracted to certain aspects of nature mysticism while acknowledging the transcendent in a highly subjective and individualized manner.

4. **(Dualist) Religious Adherence**—Subscribes to a formal religion organized around some kind of transcendent deity or deities known through special revelation.

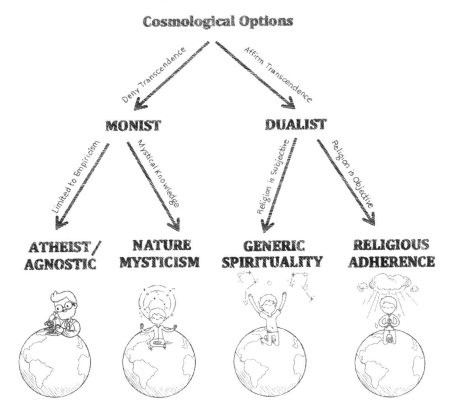

Cosmological Options

The next step in our thought experiment is to review each subset in light of the cosmology map. Feel free to skip to your own profile first, but take the time to understand all four. Let's look at them one at a time:

Atheistic or Agnostic Materialism

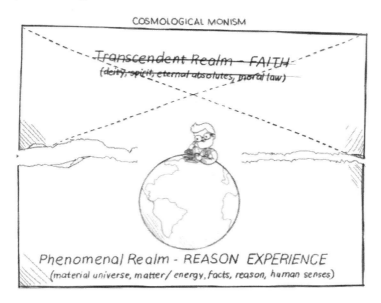

COSMOLOGICAL MONISM

Transcendent Realm - FAITH
(deity, spirit, eternal absolutes, moral law)

Phenomenal Realm - REASON EXPERIENCE
(material universe, matter/energy, facts, reason, human senses)

Atheists and agnostics are materialists in the strictest sense. They firmly deny the existence of or access to anything transcendent, and thus restrict themselves to the phenomenal realm of the cosmology map. While atheists and agnostics are somewhat different by definition, they are similar in their ultimate conclusions. Atheists (*a* + *theist* = without god) are more emphatic in declaring that a God or gods or the transcendent-spiritual do not exist. Agnostics (*a* + *gnostic* = without knowing) will not categorically deny transcendent reality, but claim it is impossible to know such things due to the cosmological divide and our human limitations.

Unlike nature mystics, atheists and agnostics do not attempt to spiritualize or personify scientific concepts such as the laws of physics. They see no justification in searching beyond or behind the inner workings of the phenomenal realm in a nonscientific fashion.

Admittedly, some of the smartest and most educated people I know are atheists and agnostics. Their thirst for discerning what is true is not easily satisfied. Philosophical-religious skepticism is not merely an

emotional bias; it is their life strategy for preventing intellectual ignorance and personal oppression.

An atheistic friend who grew up in Iran during the revolution of the late
1970s saw first-hand some evils produced by religion, and he is not interested in seeing them propagated. When he tells the story of his childhood
in Tehran, I sense that he suspects that religion is an excuse to persecute
and separate from others. I believe this is why the supposed neutrality of
data and the scientific approach are so appealing to him. In his experience,
religious fervor brings strife, but the impartiality of science can bring equality, justice, and peace. Whenever he and I talk about religion, he thanks me
for tolerating his disagreement, and I can totally understand why. Religious
adherents are often very intolerant of people who do not share their faith.

Atheists and agnostics believe that humans are very evolved animals
with brains large enough to be highly sentient. Our minds and emotions
are a byproduct of nature and nurture, but not of an immortal soul. Personality is a function of the mechanics of our brain chemistry and structure as
it develops within and reacts to its environment, not of a particular spirit.

The materialist concept of human personality is one of the reasons we
saw the rapid rise of psychotherapy and the use of psychotropic drugs
in the last century. Emotional and behavioral challenges are often diag-
nosed through the lens of biophysical dysfunction that can be amelio-
rated by manipulating body chemistry or structure. Personal transformation becomes more of a scientific endeavor than a spiritual journey.

Consider a couple of quotes from a committed atheist and one of the
fathers of modern psychology, Sigmund Freud:

> Religion is an attempt to get control over the sensory world, in which
> we are placed, by means of the wish-world, which we have developed
> inside us as a result of biological and psychological necessities.[4]

> Our knowledge of the historical worth of certain religious doctrines
> increases our respect for them, but does not invalidate our proposal
> that they should cease to be put forward as the reasons for the pre-
> cepts of civilization. On the contrary! Those historical residues have
> helped us to view religious teachings, as it were, as neurotic relics,
> and we may now argue that the time has probably come, as it does

---

4   Nandor Fodor and Frank Gaynor, eds., *Freud: Dictionary of Psychoanalysis* (Barnes & Noble
Books, 2004), 155.

in an analytic treatment, for replacing the effects of repression by the results of the rational operation of the intellect.[5]

Freud's point is painfully clear. Our personalities and minds are derived from biological mechanics and should be addressed accordingly. Religious approaches may have had some value in the past, but are nothing more than neurotic relics to be discarded in the modern era.

One of the most interesting aspects of the atheist/agnostic worldview is their various stances on the concepts of ultimate morality and meaning. Some atheists, such as Friedrich Nietzsche, have adopted a nihilism that denies them outright as mere illusions. Nietzsche famously said,

> The wisest sages of all time have reached the same judgment about life: *it's worthless.*[6]

In contrast, other atheists, such as Christopher Hitchens, have attempted to affirm a positive morality in terms of the common good that seeks the preservation of life and self-determination. The difference between right and wrong is not an absolute derived from transcendence, but a principle derived from our mutual need for self-preservation. In his best-selling book *God Is Not Great: How Religion Poisons Everything*, he wrote,

> Our belief is not a belief. Our principles are not a faith. We do not rely solely upon science and reason, because these are necessary rather than sufficient factors, but we distrust anything that contradicts science or outrages reason. We may differ on many things, but what we respect is free inquiry, open-mindedness, and the pursuit of ideas for their own sake.[7]

In an atheistic/agnostic construct of reality, social structures such as the nuclear family, marriage, and government are human conventions that may or may not serve self-preservation in their various expressions. So, for example, debating an issue such as gay marriage will be weighed in the pragmatic balance of whether it propagates the common good and self-determination of individuals, and little more. Religious traditions get in the way of practical reasoning because they absolutize principles beyond mutual preservation and self-determination. Atheists and agnostics believe it is imperative to keep the state

5 Sigmund Freud, *The Future of an Illusion.* (London: Hogarth Press, 1927), 56.
6 Friedrich Nietzsche, *Twilight of the Idols* (Indianapolis: Hackett Publishing Company, 1997), 12.
7 Christopher Hitchens, *God is Not Great: How Religion Poisons Everything* (New York: Twelve Books, 2007), 5.

separate from religion because religious scruples unjustly impinge on the liberties of individuals.

One of the key issues for the atheist and agnostic is that faith is, by definition, an irrational endeavor, a mental crutch for ignorance of the way things work, not another way of knowing or seeing. For the atheist, we only use the notion of faith as a way to explain things we may experience but don't fully understand in scientific terms. Some have referred to this as a "God in the gaps" strategy. Wherever we have a gap in our understanding, we use a god concept as an intellectual placeholder. Faith must therefore be eschewed in favor of reason and the scientific method. Other ways of knowing are superstitious ways of comforting ourselves in our ignorance and mortal hopelessness. Again, Hitchens articulates this perspective:

> To "choose" dogma and faith over doubt and experience is to throw out the ripening vintage and to reach greedily for the Kool-Aid.[8]

Other famous modern atheists are Richard Dawkins, Ayn Rand, Woody Allen, Ernest Hemingway, and Isaac Asimov. Well-known agnostics include the likes of Warren Buffett, Carl Sagan, and Ted Turner.

Nature Mysticism

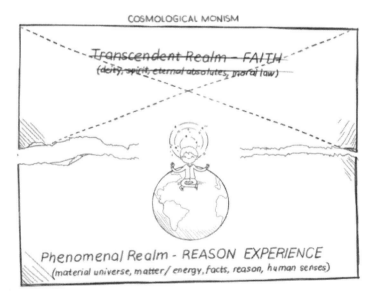

Nature mystics stress the phenomenal realm and do not subscribe to any deity or transcendent reality that might exist outside of it. For the mystic, the notion of deity is identified directly with or inherently within the physical. While mystics may frequently use terms such as *transcendence* or *metaphysical*, they do not believe in a transcendent reality or deity that is above, beyond, or apart from the phenomenal realm. When they use those terms they are speaking to the unseen energy, forces, and laws that are woven into the very fabric of the phenomenal.

The distinction between the cosmological monism of mystics and the dualism of transcendent religious systems can be difficult to distinguish. However, the difference is that mystics will not ultimately grant transcendent existence outside of the phenomenal. They are not comfortable with the austere and cool rationalism of the atheist or agnostic, but are equally uncomfortable with deity in a formal sense. Their solution is a mystical quality that is inherent in all things.

So, for example, you might hear a nature mystic talk about humans being god in a similar way that trees are god. Within this system, earth is often personified as a life-giving spirit of sorts—thus the concept of Mother Earth. More ancient versions of mysticism even believe that quasi-personal spirits animate animals. Practices of witchcraft and magic come out of this worldview.

Some modern manifestations of nature mysticism seek to avoid spiritual personifications and turn to scientific formulations such as Einstein's theory of relativity ($E = mc^2$) to buttress their belief that all matter is a form of latent energy. Some believe that we can perceive this energy through the mind or third eye—a metaphor for seeing beyond the dimension of material shapes and forms. They use practices such as meditation or induced trance, ostensibly to help them see the mystical dimension of the universe.

Modern mystics often emphasize the symbiotic relationship between our minds and our bodies. This is one of the reasons why nutritional-holistic health movements and practices such as yoga have become so important within this belief system. Eating organically grown foods and even avoiding meat becomes a way to facilitate greater health and harmony with the energy of nature.

Reincarnation also tends to be a popular strain of belief for mystics because it is consistent with the notion that when we die, the energy of our mind merely changes form and doesn't cease to exist. Our souls simply take new shape as nature morphs through the various phases of being.

One of the most popular examples of nature mysticism in our era can be found in the book *The Secret*.[9] According to this quasi-scientific system, the world has built-in universal laws such as the *law of attraction*, a belief that like attracts like—positive attracts positive and negative attracts negative. The thinking goes that all things are bound by and penetrated with different energy resonances. People participate and reverberate with these energy resonances through their minds and attitudes. Negative emotions with negative energy resonate with (attract) negative outcomes and positive emotions with positive energy attract positive outcomes. To become wealthy, one needs to have a mind reverberating with the *law of abundance*. This system takes the power of positive thinking to a whole new level.

I'm not sure if living in the western United States has anything to do with it, but I have quite a few nature mystics in my life. One of my friends, who grew up as a Roman Catholic, has decided to move toward an ancient strain of mysticism called *gnosis*, which comes from the Greek word meaning *to know*.

From a distance, my perspective is that her journey is rooted in a thoughtful disenchantment with certain aspects of Western culture and philosophy. Don't get the wrong impression here; she is not a wandering flower child passing out daisies at airports. She has been a successful entrepreneur within the organic food business. As she became more engaged in holistic health strategies while running her family and business, she started regularly practicing yoga and meditation, which strongly emphasize the mind-body connection. The composite of these experiences convinced her of a pervasive unity and synergetic interdependence between our bodies, our minds, and the world—a relationship that is often ignored and even denigrated in the West. She has become increasingly vocal about her experience of progressive enlightenment in hopes that others might share in the journey.

Each belief system has its own approach to cultural engagement and transformation. I recently read a quote attributed to the Dalai Lama:

9   Rhonda Byrne, *The Secret* (New York: Atria Books / Beyond Words Publishing, 2006), 7.

"If every eight-year-old child in the world is taught meditation, we will eliminate violence from the world within one generation."

This is a profound statement because it underscores what a prominent mystic believes about the world and our place in it. For the nature mystic, the means of self-transformation and world peace are not ultimately derived from specific social structures, transcendent morals, or the actions of deity. Instead, the path to peace is found when individuals collectively connect to the hidden and unifying dimension of light that is embedded in all things. Individual enlightenment is both the strategy and the goal.

It is hard to generalize the social constructs promoted by nature mystics. Their purpose in life is usually more focused on penetrating into the mystical aspects of physical realities than ordering them with a particular structure that will extend into the future. Because the world is believed to be in an eternal cycle of flux—ebb and flow—there is not a strong rational impetus toward organizing specific social configurations. I once heard of a nature mystic saying, "Our labors in this world are nothing more than plowing in the waves of the ocean."

For nature mystics, the meaning of life is not ultimately found in our lasting impact on the ever-changing world because in their view no such lasting impact is possible. Rather, meaning is found by fully entering into our experience of the present. This view on life is so profound that some have observed radically different orientations to the passing of time in cultures impacted by this religious outlook.

According to Craig Storti's book *Figuring Foreigners*, people in the United States and the United Kingdom tend to have a *monochromatic* view of time while people in China and even Mexico have a *polychromatic* view of time. In the monochromatic view, time is a limited resource that must be carefully allocated. In the polychromatic view, time is virtually unlimited, and plans are just general guidelines that can easily flex and bend. These views do not arise from a vacuum, but are rooted in totally different philosophical-religious belief systems.

Nature mysticism in its various forms is a very potent player in the philosophical-religious arena. As the postmodern West continues to be eclipsed by the rising powers in the East, we can expect its influence to continue growing.

Generic Spirituality

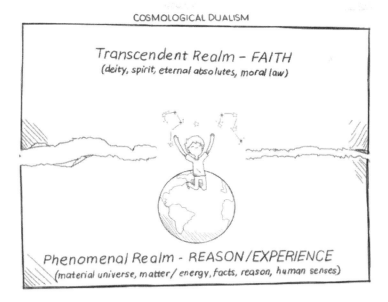

This is a catchall of sorts. I don't mean to be unfair by devising such a broad category, but I think it may be the fastest growing subset in the modern West. In my experience as a friend, family member, and former pastor, I consistently hear people say, "I am not at all religious, but I am definitely spiritual." In terms of our cosmological maps they are saying, "I am not a cosmological monist who restricts all reality to the material universe; however, I don't believe any particular transcendent reality can be known clearly enough to be exclusive. We can each come to our own beliefs in our own way."

This means that no monolithic belief system exists within this subset. It is a potpourri of doctrines based on individual experience and reasoning. The quality that seems to characterize this grouping is an emotional need to be open and inclusive to many spiritual possibilities. The irony, in my experience, is that generically spiritual people find dedicated nature mystics a bit crazy-extreme, atheists and agnostics too coolly rationalistic, and religious adherents narrow-minded and lacking epistemic humility.

My firm intellectual and emotional convictions are those of a religious adherent, but of the other cosmological options on the table, I am the most empathetic to the generic spirituality. Even though I flirted with atheism when I was young, it ultimately felt too reductionistic in its assumptions and approach. I sensed that to sustain that belief system I would have had to spend an immense amount of energy trying to remain skeptically dismissive to reality as I encountered it internally and externally.

On the other hand, nature mysticism never had much appeal for me because it feels far too subjective and amorphous in a world that has so many objective and distinguishable qualities. I appreciate much of the underlying sentiments and attitudes of many nature mystics, but I sense it is flattening out too many pieces of the intellectual dimension of these issues.

The generically spiritual position is attractive because it is not intellectually reductionistic or emotionally demanding, and it requires little to no commitment to a specific social organization. One of the difficult features of being a religious adherent is the need to interface with other religious adherents of the same stripe. Of course I am joking at one level, but I think everyone knows what I mean. Groucho Marx once remarked that he would never want to belong to a club that would accept him as a member—and I think many of us feel the same way. Sometimes the biggest obstacle with a particular religion is not its doctrines, but a social subculture that we don't want to be identified with.

Admitting to a dualist cosmology is not a particular problem for the generically spiritual. However, their thinking is that to whatever degree a higher power exists, we can subjectively ascribe almost whatever we would like to it because of our limitations as phenomenal-realm beings. Transcendent realities are vague and somewhat distant, so there is no sense in being overly dogmatic about a particular religious conviction. The important thing is to come to your own beliefs while respecting those of others.

Even though I haven't formally counted heads, I suspect that most of the people in my life are generically spiritual. Many of them also have a hybrid relationship of sorts with nature mysticism or specific religious views. I have personally found that a lot of generically spiritual people are disaffected religious adherents who witnessed rampant hypocrisy within their religious organization.

Many people also complain of religious teachings and practices that left them feeling emotionally empty and spiritually unsatisfied. Rather than being stimulated and positively challenged by their religious affiliations, they sensed that formal religion was just a way to find belonging in a particular subculture. Several of my generically spiritual friends maintain some relationship to formal religion but have divested themselves of any serious or regular engagement with their religious community.

I remember asking one of my acquaintances if he had been to church recently, and he told me that even though he hadn't been for a long time he worships God almost every week when he goes surfing. I have no qualms with worshiping while surfing, but my friend's point is poignant. For him and other people in the generically spiritual category, specific religious dogmas and practices are not terribly critical to being spiritual. The main purpose is to feel a sense of emotional connection to a higher power, however that feeling arises for them.

Examples of the generically spiritual system within our culture are ubiquitous, but the greatest proponent of this in recent times may be Oprah Winfrey. I enjoy Oprah and appreciate her philanthropy and zeal for life. I have no ax to grind with her personally, and I am sure she is as wonderful as she appears to be on the public stage. Nevertheless, she has been very open about embracing an all-inclusive spirituality that is largely self-discovered and self-directed. Her website even features a "Spirituality 101" page for people to consider these matters from a generically spiritual point of view.

Religious Adherence

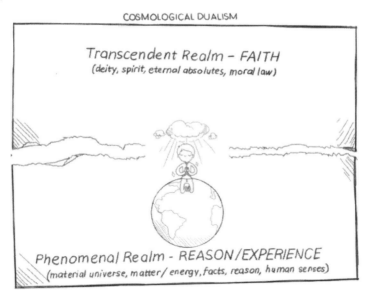

COSMOLOGICAL DUALISM

Transcendent Realm – FAITH
(deity, spirit, eternal absolutes, moral law)

Phenomenal Realm - REASON/EXPERIENCE
(material universe, matter/energy, facts, reason, human senses)

The ancient and pervasive religious adherent group believes that the transcendent crosses into the phenomenal in order to be known and that aspects of the phenomenal realm are reflections of the transcendent. Contrary to the claims of many atheists and agnostics, modern religious adherents are not generally hostile to the realities of the phenomenal realm as described through science. In many cases they believe scientific understandings of the phenomenal realm reveal the design of deity and function as a witness to deity. Whether the transcendent is a god, a group of gods, or a quasi-personal force, there is often a belief that the transcendent has crossed the cosmological chasm via revelation so that humans might believe.

The vast array of beliefs about the means and content of those revelations is beyond the scope of this book. Some have literary traditions and some have spiritual mediums. Some are monotheistic and some are polytheistic. And the variations go on.

I am befuddled when people say that all religions are basically the same. It betrays an indifference to the facts of the matter. Among the world's religions there are vast differences in understanding about the nature of deity, the identity of humans, our roles in life, and how social structures should be understood. With the possible exception of significantly overlapping moral codes, these religious systems have striking dissimilarities. It may be convenient to conceptualize all religions as basically the same, but it does not make such a claim true.

While not all religious adherents believe that their faith is exclusively and uniquely true, many do believe their religion contains absolute truth. They believe this, in part, because the revelation of the transcendent becomes objective and rises above total subjectivity.

For example, historic Christianity maintains that the Bible is a collection of divinely inspired books that tell the true history of God's people, Israel. The books of the Bible aren't the abstract philosophical musings of a singular sage, but represent the centuries-old story of an ancient community's experience with the Almighty. This kind of revelation embedded in a historical community has an objective quality that the meditation or experience of an individual does not have.

Atheists and agnostics, nature mystics, and generically spiritual people have a hard time swallowing this sort of reasoning from religious adherents because it defies their cosmological schemes and often offends their emotional commitment to their own view. For the other three philosophical-religious views that we have discussed, the transcendent may or may not exist, but it most certainly does not reveal itself in a universally objective fashion that can claim to be absolute.

One of the main problems people have with the concept of revelation is that it does not seem to be verifiable in ways that are normal within the phenomenal realm. How can a mere book like the Koran be confirmed or denied? If the answer is that revelation cannot be verified, the natural response is that it should not be trusted as absolute.

It is important to understand that many religions retreat from intellectual scrutiny by saying that belief in transcendent revelation is purely a matter of faith or an emotional "burning in the bosom" that intuitively serves as confirmation. I find that many within my own religion, Christianity, will seek shelter in an argument like this when the authority and authenticity of the Bible are challenged.

Faith certainly has its place in any religious system and is in some ways the final court of appeal. Nevertheless, faith shouldn't become or require a total disengagement of our need to think critically.

As a Christian, I am constantly asked how I can have a faith derived from a book, especially one with so many supposed contradictions. I will not hazard the answer until chapter five and following, but suffice it to say that many people find my commitment to the Bible as God's Word to be incredibly naive and unthinking.

For the record, I deeply appreciate their reticence and critical thinking at this point. As I will explain later, my belief in the Bible boils down to what I call a *reasonable faith*. In other words, I do not want to actively supplant or usurp reason with irrationality, but I see very convincing reasons for adopting a posture of faith in certain areas—the Bible being one of them.

The concept of faith is somewhat contingent on the particular religion that is using the term. For the sake of this discourse I will be advancing a very brief Christian understanding of it. Faith in its most basic sense is trust. It is not irrational, per se, but *suprarational*, meaning it functions on a different epistemological wavelength. Those who embrace faith as a way of knowing are not in the business of being explicitly irrational or prone to fits of fancy and imagination. Faith is simply understood as a different way of knowing something.

I would submit to you that even atheists and agnostics exercise a measure of faith. They take certain things as axiomatic (assumed) for the sake of their system. For example, in order to adhere to the scientific method, they must believe in uniformitarianism, the belief that so-called constants are uniformly unchangeable and have not and will not experience variation.

I am not suggesting that constants do not exist, nor am I begging the question by using an appeal to ignorance. But the fact is that every belief system, including the atheistic system, rests on certain axioms that are taken as matters of unexplainable presumption. People who embrace those may not call that *faith*, but it doesn't ultimately matter what the label is. Trusting in the fixity of a proposition outside of verifiable tests and proof lies strictly outside the scientific method and must be assumed. If it looks like a duck, walks like a duck, and quacks like a duck, it's a duck. This assumption of uniformitarianism is an example of the nature of faith.

$\sim$

We could go on and on with this global analysis, but the thought experiment has led us to a preliminary conclusion. We are faced with a cosmological chasm of sorts, and there are really only a handful of basic philosophical-religious responses to it:

1. Deny the transcendent and only know the phenomenal.
2. Deny the transcendent and ascribe mystical characteristics to the phenomenal.
3. Affirm the transcendent and come to our own individual subjective beliefs because we believe that it is closed to objective assessment.
4. Affirm the transcendent by receiving objective revelation to inform our faith of spiritual realities.

Even though I am a very committed Christian who is firmly rooted in the religious adherent subset, I empathize with the other points of view. Again, I have friends, family, and colleagues whom I dearly love across the entire spectrum. I have flirted with or occupied other parts of it myself. I understand the appeal of the other categories, especially if a robustly positive alternative has not been considered or understood. While I have ultimately found the other philosophical-religious views to be wanting because I don't believe they cohere to life as I believe we experience it, I heartily respect those with different conclusions.

Now that we have taken a fifty-thousand-foot view of the cosmological possibilities, I want to interact with each of the four subsets a bit more to see if we can take the discussion even further.

CHAPTER THREE
Mulling Over Monism

I did not marry the first girl that I fell in love with, because there was a tremendous religious conflict at the time. She was an atheist, and I was an agnostic.
—*Woody Allen*

I happen to be a man of several vices, and I take comfort in knowing that I'm in good company. Even President Abraham Lincoln once remarked that, "It has been my experience that folks who have no vices have very few virtues." One of my particular weaknesses is my tendency to get sucked into and become a devotee of various television series. I started young with *Sesame Street*, *The Electric Company*, and *Captain Kangaroo*. *Mister Rogers Neighborhood* wasn't quite my cup of tea, but I watched him, too.

And then one fateful day I discovered Lynda Carter starring as *Wonder Woman*. Fitting words to describe that blissful moment still escape me. She once appeared on the cover of some TV magazine, and I quickly hid it away as a personal treasure. It came close to surpassing the value of my LEGO spaceships. What a stunning spectacle of beauty, human achievement, and imagination.

A decade or two later, my tastes had matured. I loved and still miss *The X-Files*, starring David Duchovny as Fox Mulder and Gillian Anderson as Dana Scully. They played FBI agents who were assigned to investigate strange cases that had gone cold or seemed to defy explanation. Mulder was a student of ancient mythologies who often saw connections between the evidence and the paranormal, perceiving mystical, alien, or conspiratorial forces at work. As a counterpoint, Scully was a skeptical medical doctor and scientist who constantly tried to keep her partner in check by positing naturalistic explanations.

The contrast of mysticism and skepticism never ceased to interest me. As you might expect, the tension between the two characters became romantic and brought another level of entertainment value to the series. It was good stuff all around.

One of the icons of the show was a poster hanging in Agent Mulder's office. It was a picture of a UFO flying over a forest with the caption, "I want to believe." In many ways, I think that is what the show was about. It was about the struggle of a mystic and skeptic who both wanted to believe in something beyond the phenomenal realm.

When I speak with cosmological monists, whether they are nature mystics or skeptical atheists and agnostics, I am reminded of these characters. The dynamic of thinking and perceiving from a set of fundamental assumptions is palpable.

My goal in this chapter is to take a little sidebar with the mystics and skeptics of the world to talk about philosophy and religion. I can't take deep dives into the issues here, but I'm hoping to tease out some questions for you to chew on. My sense is that deep down, like Mulder and Scully, you want to believe.

To My Atheist and Agnostic Friends

I appreciate that you have hung in there with me this far. Your ongoing willingness to read is a testament to your intellectual integrity, curiosity, and patience. I suspect this brand of quasi-speculative endeavor is not something you are terribly fond of, and you are a good sport for wading through it.

Here's part of the dilemma as I see it: You want people with religious faith—in my case, Christians—to provide hard evidence for our beliefs. For the record, I don't blame you. I think that skeptical and empirical impulse is very good and right when rightly applied.

The irony is that I think the evidence for God is very close at hand. In fact, I think there is evidence pretty much everywhere. I would even go so far as saying there is a very real sense in which *you* are some of the strongest evidence for God that is on the table. Maybe for the sake of meaningful dialogue, we could leave aside the issue of specific evidence for a moment and see where we are philosophically missing one another.

Here are some of the big questions I would like to that I would like you consider:

1. Is atheism consistent with your own epistemology?
2. Is Occam's razor always the best tool?
3. Are faith and reason mutually exclusive?
4. Is religion necessarily bad for society and science?
5. Have you fully grappled with the consequences of moral subjectivism?

Is atheism consistent with your own epistemology?

You probably like to encourage skepticism as a way to keep everyone honest, including yourself. That is legitimate, but I worry that you are not holding yourself to the same skeptical standard you have for others.

For example, atheism in a literal sense pushes beyond the limits of your own epistemology. You could not make such an absolute claim about the absence of deity unless you also claimed to be omniscient, which of course, you don't and aren't. You aren't able to see or perceive everything from your limited point of view, so why would you make such a gratuitous cosmological leap of faith?

I realize that self-identifying as an atheist communicates that faith in a deity or the transcendent seems unwarranted at best and unhelpful at worst. However, I would like to suggest that the word *atheism* conveys too much and infers that there is absolutely no deity, period. I don't mean to engage in a semantic squabble, but let's try to be a little more precise about your position. Atheism, in a strictly unqualified sense, says more than you want it to say, because it is not consistent with your view of human epistemological limitations.

It seems to me that the term *agnostic* is much more intellectually defensible and appropriate because it literally means *not knowing*. According to your epistemology, people cannot know if there is a deity, and the very concept of deity itself breaks the scientific rules of the phenomenal realm, so we don't know or can't know. That seems much more reasonable because it doesn't infer any claims of ultimate knowledge on your part.

Most of the atheists I know strive to be brutally candid with themselves, so let's do that here. Please consider leaving atheism off the table as an epistemologically flawed term, and think about adopting the posture of an agnostic instead. Consider the words of Albert Einstein, who eschewed atheism in favor of agnosticism, saying that he preferred an "attitude of humility corresponding to the weakness of our intellectual understanding of nature and of our own being."[10]

Is Occam's razor always the best tool?

In the late Middle Ages, a Franciscan friar, William of Ockham, gained prominence as a philosopher who advocated for more efficient approaches to logic. He believed that the best theoretical explanations of certain phenomena are the ones with the fewest assumptions, causes, and variables. In matters of reasoning, less is more. This principle of cutting away unnecessary hypotheses has been aptly referred to as a philosophical "razor," thus, Occam's razor.

So, for example, if I can't find my wallet I can hypothesize about many things that could have happened to it. Aliens from a distant galaxy could have beamed it up. My dog could have buried it in the backyard. Maybe a neighbor kid decided to steal it and use my credit cards to buy video games. All of these are possible, but rest on a foundation of other assumptions. According to Occam's razor, the best explanation would probably be that I simply misplaced it, because that is the simplest theory with the fewest number of causal entities and assumptions.

---

10 Walter Issacson, *Einstein: His Life and Universe* (New York: Simon and Shuster, 2007), 390.

Atheists and agnostics tend to approach many matters of life and philosophy with Occam's razor firmly in hand. It would seem simpler to posit that the material universe is eternal, rather than theorizing about another transcendent realm of existence. Why insert transcendence and deity into explanations of life and philosophy if they are not necessary?

While the reductionist principle of Occam's razor is legitimate in many contexts, let's consider whether it should be universally applied across all spectrums of thought and being. Sometimes stripping away layers of causal entities diminishes our understanding, rather than amplifying it. Sometimes less really is less.

When we encounter thick realities like the subject of human personality and morality, we are going to end up with a complex multivariable analysis no matter how we slice it. I personally believe that the theories of evolution and natural selection alone are too thin to account for some of the complexities of human behavior. Consider our capacity for true altruism and self-sacrifice. If our biology is ultimately driven by instincts of self-survival, how can we adequately explain the willingness of people to martyr themselves for various causes? There is no simple way to deal with this sort of question because some things cannot be understood from a one-dimensional and elemental perspective.

One of the challenges of our Greek philosophical heritage is that we tend to look for the essence of a thing by breaking it down into atomistic parts. It is almost as if we try to describe a wristwatch by saying it is a mechanized construct of springs and gears. That may be what a watch is made of, but springs and gears don't give us perspective on what time is or why it is important. It doesn't tell us about how we have divided our day into seconds, minutes, and hours. Wristwatches exist in a very complex system that cannot be reduced to springs and gears.

In response to the challenge of theoretical reductionism, some have put forward an anti-razor referred to as *Bonaventure's beard*. If you were asked to describe the large beard of a mature man, would you approach it by trying to communicate its thick complexity or its thin elemental essence? Would you try to boil it down to one concept, or would you have to multiply concepts and perspectives? Ultimately, Bonaventure's beard cannot be properly understood as a hair follicle. That simply would not suffice.

Occam's Razor

Bonaventure's Beard

VERSUS

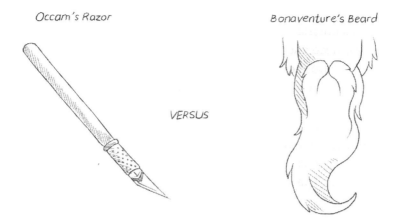

The same holds true for our philosophical attempts to grapple with this world. Simply cutting away philosophical and theological layers in an attempt to rest on scientific empiricism leaves too much out of consideration. We're not simply trying to find the atomistic essence of material existence, we're trying to wrestle with the sum total of existence. Try putting the conceptual razors down and see where it leads you.

Are faith and reason mutually exclusive?

Close to the root of your skeptical posture is your view that reason and faith are mutually exclusive categories of thought. Would you be open to considering the possibility that there are different grades of faith instead of lumping all faith claims into the same "irrational and naive" bucket?

In the same way that some water is not potable, some faith claims are not worth believing. If someone says that party fairies magically hold helium balloons aloft in the air, that faith claim should be rejected because it is unnecessary and specious. Does it therefore follow that every faith claim is as baseless as the "party balloon fairy" faith claim? I don't think so.

Faith is not necessarily anti-reason. Faith is a different way of knowing information that cannot be immediately reached by our own experience. It is often an extension of reason and of evidence to ends that we cannot directly sense or confirm. When juries convict someone "beyond a reasonable doubt," that is simply a negative definition for having faith in their verdict. They may not see the crime committed, but they can firmly believe who the criminal is and what he did. Faith is simply reasonable trust in the unseen.

Imagine that you have a friend, Bob, who died in a car accident. You went to Bob's funeral with some mutual friends, and there was no mistake that Bob was dead and gone—you saw his body in the casket. Now imagine that a few days later, the mutual friends who attended the funeral with you came to you with news that Bob was alive. They had even spoken to him and touched him before he ascended on a cloud and disappeared. They can't arrange a meeting for you with Bob because he has left, but they have a message from Bob for you and others to receive. Some of them were so impacted by Bob that they spent the rest of their lives talking about him and even suffered persecution and death to spread the message.

Such a faith claim is of a totally different nature and grade than the "party balloon fairy" faith claim. The party balloon fairy faith claim is intellectual filler for ignorance about the science of helium. The Bob rising from the dead faith claim is an assertion about an alleged historical event with multiple and supposedly credible eyewitnesses.

While I am obviously alluding to the Christian faith, this thought experiment doesn't have to be about Christianity, per se. Let's stay focused on the concept of credible evidence. The first point I am asking you to consider is that some faith claims are different and better than other faith claims.

Some of you may respond by saying that the example of Bob rising from the dead has possible naturalistic explanations. You may be right in the abstract, but do you recognize your own assumptions in this line of thinking? How do you know that all phenomena are restricted to naturalistic mechanisms? Isn't such a posture a form of trust and faith of its own? On what empirical basis can you make such a claim?

We can affirm the empirical method as the primary means of scientific discovery, but making it the primary foundation for knowledge is itself empirically improvable and unverifiable. An absolute claim like this cannot be validated by its own method. Such "scientism" is a circular faith claim of its own.

Please don't misunderstand. This is not an appeal to ignorance. I'm not saying that exceptions to naturalistic mechanisms exist because we can't prove the contrary. I am simply pointing out that an atheistic or agnostic epistemology should prohibit us from embracing universal axioms in an unqualified sense. The epistemological rules for those systems are just conceptual, pragmatic, and linguistic conventions, not hard and fast cosmological realities.

Agnosticism can only make probabilistic claims from its own epistemological standpoint. When agnostics extend such probabilities absolutely, they are exercising faith. Agnostics would be more internally consistent if they applied a certain amount of skepticism to their skepticism. This would help hedge some of their philosophical boundaries rather than being absolutist about them.

When we realize that even agnostics engage in a certain measure of faith, it starts to level the playing field a bit. When an atheist or agnostic says, "You have your faith, but I am content only with facts," that is superficially untrue and unfair. Where does your confidence in facts or your ability to interpret facts come from? We all exercise faith at different levels; that is not a question. The question is how we exercise that faith and in what we choose to trust.

The bottom line is that some faith claims are bogus on their face and should be dismissed. Some faith claims function almost like probability and are extensions of reason in places that reason and science do not and cannot function. Religious adherents like me are not interested in party balloon fairies. However, I would submit to you that the circumstantial evidence for certain religious faith claims is worth investigating because it coheres with so much of what we do know and experience.

Yes, some of the claims push beyond absolute naturalistic boundaries. Once you see that these absolute naturalistic boundaries are faith claims in and of themselves—and that we all exercise "reasonable faith" in some respects, some religious faith claims become less intellectually offensive.

Is religion necessarily bad for society and science?

Like my good friend who grew up in Iran, many atheists and agnostics feel that religion produces more harm and disharmony than good. Untold numbers of people have died and suffered at the hands of religious tyranny. Sadly, there is no arguing this fact. However, this does not logically negate the possibility that a particular religion could be true. It is merely evidence that there may be devoted followers of flawed religious systems or flawed followers of accurate religious systems.

And while there are many examples of religious people causing suffering and strife, there are also many examples of religious people bringing healing and aid to those in need. Think of the countless hospitals, orphanages, and educational institutions that have been supported by religious groups.

While some religions have good ideals, and some of their adherents fall far short of those ideals, it seems shortsighted to rule out all faith claims due to some of the evils that have been perpetrated in the name of God.

I am also aware that my atheist and agnostic friends express significant concern that religious commitments promote superstitious ignorance and discourage scientific inquiry that pursues truth. I share this very valid concern, but, as you might guess, not absolutely. In fact, there is abundant evidence that many of the greatest scientists and mathematicians in history have been very religious.

For example, Isaac Newton was a devout Christian man who profoundly influenced math and science. Many theists, like Newton, believe that the phenomenal order is discoverable precisely because there is a grand Designer who created and governs the universe. Rather than condemning all religion as having an anti-science ethos, it would be better to say that the wrong sort of religious faith can stunt the pursuit of truth and the right sort of religious faith can enhance it.

A noteworthy contemporary example is Dr. Francis Collins, who led the research team that successfully mapped the human genome for the first time. This remarkable achievement is widely recognized as one of the greatest feats of modern science. Some people might be surprised to learn that Dr. Collins is not only a committed Christian, but is also a staunch evolutionist. He is devoted to current scientific orthodoxy regarding the big bang and evolutionary mechanisms while simultaneously holding deep religious convictions.

As Dr. Collins mentions in his book *The Language of God: A Scientist Presents Evidence for Belief*, his religious and ethical orientation drove him to keep information about the gene sequence in the public domain.[11] At a time when private enterprise was trying to privately patent gene sequencing for profit, Dr. Collins fought to make sure that the data was widely available so that other important research around the world could go on. His religious beliefs didn't hamper the progress of science—they radically advanced it.

Michael Crichton's book *Jurassic Park* is a hugely popular treatment of the close and necessary relationship between science, philosophy, and ethics. If you have only seen or heard of the blockbuster movie

---

11 Francis S. Collins, *The Language of God: A Scientist Presents Evidence for Belief* (New York: Free Press, 2006), 121.

produced by Steven Spielberg, do yourself a favor and grab the book. It tells the story of a billionaire, John Hammond, who creates a remote amusement park based upon dinosaurs he has successfully cloned from preserved dinosaur DNA. Before opening the park, Hammond invites several renowned scientists to tour and review it in order to quell concerns about the safety of the project.

One of the dignitaries invited to review the park is Ian Malcolm, a mathematician who specializes in chaos theory. Throughout the book, Crichton uses Malcolm as a philosophical mouthpiece to challenge the wisdom of Hammond's venture. Malcolm's nagging apprehension is that complex biological systems cannot be fully contained or predicted by simple mechanisms. Unfortunately, his concerns are validated when the dinosaurs breach the park's security and wreak havoc on the park and its visitors.

The story of *Jurassic Park* is brilliantly entertaining while carrying a profound message. It not only confronts the commercialization of certain scientific endeavors, but also provokes questions about the ethical and moral boundaries of scientific exploration and implementation. Science that is untethered to ethics and morality breeds its own kind of tyranny. At one point, Malcolm says, "You know what's wrong with scientific power? It's a form of inherited wealth. And you know what assholes congenitally rich people are."

Religion and faith are not necessarily bad for science. In fact, when rightly applied they can help to stimulate and guide it.

Have you fully grappled with the consequences of moral subjectivism?

Finally, I must confess that I am deeply puzzled when some atheists and agnostics assert that the existence of evil and suffering in the world disprove the possibility of an infinitely good and gracious deity. Such a comment begs the question because it assumes the categories of *good* and *evil* out of nowhere. The so-called "problem of evil" requires the existence and identification of evil in the first place. How are atheists and agnostics able to posit the question without knowing what is good? And how can they know what is good without reference to an objective standard outside of themselves?

Perhaps atheists and agnostics are suggesting that the very existence of evil within religious systems demonstrates a ruinous inconsistency. It seems internally incoherent for a system to claim the existence of an all-good and all-powerful God while simultaneously believing in evil. In their view, the very postulate of evil proves that God is either tainted by evil, lacks omnipotence, or suffers from a combination of both, thus disproving any system that believes in a god. We must recognize that this is not a true philosophical problem or logical fallacy; it is a theological question. I would personally argue that the whole Christian system revolves around the story of God resolving the problem and existence of evil in the world.

It seems that some of the nihilists (who do not ascribe objective meaning or dignity to life) among you are more intellectually consistent and honest regarding the issue of good and evil. In an atheistic or agnostic system, the meaning of good and evil are ultimately self-derived and entirely subjective. In other words, there is no such thing as good and evil—they are only mental constructs.

Some atheists, such as Ayn Rand, author of *Atlas Shrugged*, have argued that the only real good or meaning we can pursue is our own self-interest and fulfillment. Consider this statement: "Man—every man—is an end in himself, not a means to the ends of others; he must live for his own sake, neither sacrificing himself to others nor sacrificing others to himself; he must work for his rational self-interest, with the achievement of his own happiness as the highest moral purpose of his life."[12]

Unfortunately, such a self-serving construct can never truly provide a rebuke or correction to individual or collective tyranny. Why shouldn't we sacrifice others to ourselves if it brings us happiness? By what authority, other than her own thoughts, does she make such a sweeping claim?

In this subjectivist system, tyrants and their minions are simply living out their own version of self-fulfillment. They may not explicitly articulate their ambitions this way, but there is nothing stopping them from applying concepts such as Darwin's "survival of the fittest" as an empirical justification for their brutality.

Believe me—I understand very well that the impracticalities and difficulties caused by a certain concept do not make the concept untrue. The fact that a subjective moral system is difficult does not necessarily disprove agnosticism. However, in the spirit of skeptical and brutal honesty, we should recognize its hazards for individuals and society at large.

I profoundly appreciate your resistance to certain personal scruples that parade as righteousness. When some people promote

---

12 Ayn Rand, "Introducing Objectivism" (*The Objectivist Newsletter*, Aug. 1962) 35.

fundamentalist-style prohibitions to promote the "good," you are right to be skeptical. The United States' ban of the sale of alcohol in the 1920s is a great example of personal scruples gone awry. However, reducing all morality to the level of petty personal scruple or mere social contract can be very dangerous.

Religious faith can produce abusive oppression, but so can exclusive self-interest and absolute subjectivity. The answer is not necessarily to declare all religion defunct. Such a conclusion lacks the logical nuance and rightly applied skepticism that you often apply to other fields of study.

Again, I realize that I am leaving out many other concerns you may have about religion in general. Perhaps some of these will be addressed for you later. My hope is that you can appreciate that many believers, including me, have wrestled with these matters from a philosophical standpoint and are not content with indulging our imaginations.

You may ultimately think that my faith or the faith of others is untrue, but I hope you will at least consider the possibility that some of these claims are not merely irrational flights of fancy. Just like you, we are seeking a high-grade "reasonable faith" that coheres with our world and ourselves.

To My Nature Mystic Friends

Almost every nature mystic I have ever met is a highly intuitive, empathic, and passionate individual—and I mean that as a very sincere compliment. Empathy and connectedness are not always my strong suits, so I admire people who are able to feel such a strong relationship to their neighbors and environment. I have a lot to learn from you.

With that said, I am deeply concerned that you may feel some resistance to me because of misperceptions you may have about my Christian faith. Don't get me wrong—I am a generally conservative guy in many respects and don't deny it—however, I am anything but a fundamentalist in a strict sociological sense. Let me give you some examples:

- In the context of our secular political system I lean toward libertarianism and preservation of our individual liberties.
- I enjoy non-religious yoga as a physical and mental discipline.
- I think that meditation is an amazing practice with huge benefits for health and self-mastery.
- If I could live at Whole Foods, I would.
- I am a believer in self-healing and alternative medicine.
- My wife and I own a hybrid electric car to cut down on gas consumption.
- My favorite way to pray is by walking a labyrinth.
- I think that the book *Eat, Pray, Love* by Elizabeth Gilbert is one of the great literary and religious works of our generation. (Even though I have very different religious convictions than the author.)
- I think we have a tremendous responsibility for protecting and cultivating a healthy planet and environment.

I do not intend to be silly or trite with this short list. I want you to know that I am trying to be engaged with life at a level that is beyond my left brain and frontal cortex. I do not want to put god or religion in a neat little cognitive box. That is not where I am coming from at all and I want you to know that.

The list of probing questions I would like to ask you to self-reflect on are:

1. Are you keeping your experience and your cognitive mind in balance?
2. Does the mystery of life have shape?
3. How should we understand evil, suffering, and death?

Are you keeping your experience and your cognitive mind in balance?
Several years ago I was feeling chronically ill for many months and finally went to my Western medicine doctor. After examining me, he said that nothing was wrong and that maybe I was depressed and should consider psychotropic drugs. This frustrated me because I didn't feel well physically and knew something was wrong. A good friend of mine recommended that I visit her alternative health practitioner, and I agreed to go out of sheer desperation. Needless to say, it was a very different experience.

When I arrived at the office, the alternative health practitioner had me remove all metal from my body. Then she sat in front of me with a tray of full of different vials in her lap. She closed her eyes and started to wave her hands around me and over the vials while doing some erratic finger snapping and counting. I'm not going to lie; I thought I might be on *Candid Camera* or something.

After a few minutes of the hand waving she got up, wrote down some notes, and then left the office to make a special concoction for me. She returned with a bottle of what I like to refer to as "dirt" that I was supposed to mix with water and drink for two weeks. To say that I was skeptical was an understatement. Nevertheless, I had gone this far, and the bottle of dirt wasn't dirt cheap, so I decided to play ball. I can't help confessing that I have lovingly referred to her as the "Dirt Doctor" ever since.

I'm sure it is no surprise to you, but the dirt-water worked. I felt totally better after two weeks on her alternative medicine. At first I was tempted to attribute this to a placebo effect, but my friend who is an M.D. changed my mind. When I told him what she did he said that she was probably trying to feel my "aura." I couldn't believe he would subscribe to such a quasimystical concept, but he said that after working with people's bodies for years he had developed a sense for bodily "energy" just by hovering his hands over people. He couldn't explain it and didn't know what to do with it, but he had consistently experienced it and didn't scoff at it whatsoever. Knowing his deep commitment to his practice and to science in general, I found it hard to doubt him.

I have no idea what the religious beliefs of the Dirt Doctor are. However, this strain of holism tends to derive from the nature mysticism system. Recounting this episode is important because I truly believe that nature mystics are experiencing and trying to articulate a significant piece of the cosmological puzzle. There really is more to this world than meets the eye, and there is an energy that animates life in this world—literally and metaphorically. I certainly don't pretend to understand it in all of its depths, and I don't think we will ever be able to fully articulate it, but I think there's something to it.

One of the concepts that many nature mystics embrace—especially in Eastern traditions—is the priority of seeking *balance*. I love that and think it is very powerful. I tend to articulate the concept slightly differently and speak in terms of *tension*. We need to hold certain things in proper tension to cognitively and experientially maximize our understanding of the world. It is no mistake that the best stories, music, and even culinary dishes exhibit just the right amount of tension between competing dynamics. Art, like life, is dull without the energy created by tension.

Dual priorities to optimize our perspective of reality

Experience   Cognition

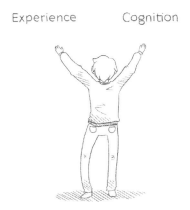

When I talk to nature mystics, I sometimes sense that they are not upholding the balance between rationality and experience as robustly as they could be. The cognitive end of the rope is often let down in benign neglect, and the dynamic tension between it and experience is lost. In fact, I have growing concerns that nature mystics try to suspend and suppress rationality as much as possible to seek true enlightenment.

If I could intellectually nudge nature mystics about their cosmological views, I would ask them to consider several things. First, we need to carefully examine the role of experience in our beliefs. Many people give their experience ultimate authority in their epistemology at the expense of balanced critical thinking and rightly applied skepticism.

There is a strong temptation for us to allow our experience to trump cognition in the formation of our philosophies.

The problem with a purely experientialist posture is that while our experience is vital and inescapable, it can easily be misinterpreted and mislead us. I remember taking my wife on her first trip to Las Vegas. After rambling through the strip for a couple of hours, we arrived at our hotel room feeling hungry and tired. I naturally asked her if she had seen any good restaurants on our walk. She glared at me and sharply retorted, "Have I seen any good breast jobs on our walk? Give me a break, pervert!"

Not only is this one of my favorite cocktail party stories, it also makes a crucial point. Somehow in the context of huge billboards and flyers strewn across the strip featuring scantily clad women, my wife heard me saying, "breast jobs" instead of "restaurants." While it is not totally unreasonable to think I could have asked such a question, her mind had distorted her experience of my words into something I never said. Her internal experience was completely undeniable, but it was not a direct reflection of the words that I uttered. Her mind had twisted objective reality to help fit the "breast job" context it was being overwhelmed by.

Experience is therefore something we must handle with a certain level of care. We cannot deny what we or others may experience, but those experiences may not be a direct reflection of an objective phenomenal reality and may not demand a singular interpretation. Experience needs cognitive and communal checks to truly inform our philosophical system.

Allow me to give an example of this from my own faith tradition before considering one more common to nature mystics. Since the late nineteenth century there has been a significant movement within Christianity to discover an immediate experience of the Holy Spirit. One of the ways this has manifested in certain communities is the phenomenon of speaking in tongues, that is, other languages that the speaker has never learned by natural means.

The experience of speaking in tongues is cited in several parts of the New Testament and is linked to the powerful moving of God. Many Christians believe tongues are a God-given angelic prayer language that individuals receive when they are specially blessed by the Holy Spirit. People who practice speaking in tongues periodically vocalize a unique and unintelligible babble-talk that is incomprehensible to the speaker as well. They believe that the Holy Spirit is mysteriously praying through them.

Without wading into my own take on the theological merits or demerits of this practice, I would like to point out a few things. First, an individual's experience of spontaneously vocalizing in this manner cannot be denied—it actually happens. There is an objective sense in which people demonstrate a totally unique system of speech and feel closer to God because of it.

However, I would maintain that this very real experience could be interpreted as something other than a spiritual gift from God. I personally believe this for specific theological reasons, but let's leave that intramural discussion aside for a moment. It is also possible that this experience is a culturally facilitated and self-induced behavior that provides emotional-psychological validation for those earnestly seeking it.

A powerful and wonderful mind

We all seek emotional-psychological validation for our views in various ways. A nonspiritual interpretation of the experience of speaking in tongues does not have to come from a posture of obnoxious cynicism. We should all want to understand our various experiences under the lens of cognition as a check on reality. When we look at speaking in tongues through this lens, we could view it as an intense form of self-hypnotic "confirmation bias" happening under the power of suggestion.

Let's try to break this cognitive perspective down piece by piece. I'm sure you would agree that our minds are incredibly powerful in ways we cannot totally grasp. We have underestimated the capability of our minds to make us sick or healthy. In an optimistic and hopeful state, our minds promote our sense of wellness—and can help to heal us. In a negative and hopeless state, our minds can make us sick to death.

Some practitioners of Western medicine have picked up on this reality and have intentionally altered the way they deliver diagnoses and prognoses to patients because of it. They have recognized that helping patients maintain a positive outlook is a huge component of the healing process. Our minds are often the source of the best medicine.

Part of our mental well-being is having the sense that our beliefs are congruent with our experience of the world. We want and need to perceive that our thoughts about the world fit our circumstances. One of the chief causes of depression occurs when our expectations about life do not match our experience of life. Our minds will go to great lengths to facilitate feelings of psychological congruence—even when it is ultimately self-destructive.

We often see this destructive dynamic in people who constantly identify themselves as victims. Almost everything in their life becomes interpreted through the lens of victimization—even where no victimization exists. Tragically, some people will enter into self-damaging relationships and environments that serve to further reinforce this belief about themselves. As perverse as it is, this belief stunts their ability to rise above challenges and embark on a journey of transformation. Even though this interpretive lens is ultimately destructive, it provides a level of congruence to their experience and becomes entrenched and self-perpetuating.

Self-hypnosis is an altered state of consciousness most of us experience from time to time as a means of cognitive rest in a non-sleep state. Some of us passively experience the sensation of "checking out" of certain low-level mental functions when we exercise strenuously or drive our cars. Many of us like to "vegetate" in front of our TVs or take on repetitive manual tasks like gardening or cleaning the house. I find that I can get into a trancelike state of consciousness when I play piano for long periods of time. Regardless of the ways we each achieve this state of mind, we all engage in self-hypnotic activities at some level.

Confirmation bias is a way of describing what our rational minds do to help us feel good about and reinforce our choices and beliefs. Many of us will try to find positive customer reviews for something we have bought after the purchase in order to feel good about the money we spent. We will often associate with those who make similar life choices to the ones we have made in order to feel better about ourselves. There are many reasons why people who choose to pierce and tattoo their bodies congregate together, but confirmation bias is one of them. In short, our minds are biased toward interpreting our behaviors, thoughts, and experiences in ways that bring emotional and psychological validation.

Finally, the power of suggestion needs to be taken into account. I find this aspect of our minds to be particularly fascinating. Our minds are built to filter information so that we can make sense of all the sensory inputs we have. Have you ever stopped to consider how many visual, auditory, tactile, olfactory, and taste sensations your body experiences at any given moment? It is beyond reckoning, and our minds cleverly screen out vast chunks of information so that we can mentally swim through this sea of sensory data without drowning in it.

Verbal and visual suggestion, particularly in an altered state of consciousness, become an incredibly potent way to help our minds filter information and feelings. One of the favorite exercises I participated in at a development seminar demonstrated the power of suggestion to impact our minds. I will try to replicate it here. If you're a speed-reader, try not to scan ahead too quickly because it will ruin the impact.

Try this exercise: give yourself ten seconds to find everything around you that is the color red. Go ahead—do this in a focused manner and pause for a moment before reading the next paragraph.

Now that you have those red objects in mind, close your eyes and think of everything you saw that was green. Identifying the green objects is incredibly difficult, right? The lesson is clear. Once we have applied a certain mental filter or lens through the power of suggestion, our minds start applying it with great force and focus.

This exercise demonstrates why so many self-help gurus like to emphasize the daily practice of verbalizing "positive affirmations." The idea is that when we repeatedly say certain things to ourselves out loud with conviction, our minds adopt a posture than interprets the world accordingly—to seek emotional-psychological congruence!

If I am told that I am a loser who will never amount to anything, and I mentally replay that comment over and over, my mind will adopt behaviors and interpretations of the world that are congruent with that assertion. If I say to myself, "I am a resourceful entrepreneur who can create wealth to bless my family and those around me," my mind will adopt behaviors and interpretations of the world congruent with that affirmation.

The cognitive key is that there is no need to posit a quasimystical and universal "law of abundance" that we resonate to when we use positive affirmations about entrepreneurship. Saying these things does not magnetically draw certain realities to my doorstep.

Our mental scripts, whether accidental or intentional, function exactly like the "red" and "green" visual filters. They tell our minds what to look for and what to toss out. If I believe that I can build wealth, my mind will look at the world for ways to confirm this, and vice versa. The power is not derived from a secret energy in the universe; it is in the power of our minds to shape our interpretations of reality and our resultant behaviors.

Many of us have applied filters to our minds that we are not re-motely aware of. We have mental models that sift through our body image, our relationships, our finances, and every other aspect of our lives. There is no magic, per se, only our minds sorting through inputs according to the suggestive programming we have received and pas-sively or actively reinforced.

Let's come back to the phenomenon of speaking in tongues. For the moment, it is important to simply recognize a few things:

1. The individual is experiencing an altered state of conscious-ness with physical and emotional consequences.
2. There are different ways to interpret the source and meaning of the experience.
3. Our minds are incredibly powerful and go to great lengths to create a sense of congruence between our beliefs, desires, and experiences.
4. Our experiences should not be exclusively authoritative and need external checks for interpretation and validation.

It is not particularly important at this juncture to come to a determina-tive conclusion about the nature of speaking in tongues. What is impor-tant is recognizing that we should carefully examine our experiences. We are not well served when we pit experience against cognition because they are meant to work together. We must be mindful of our minds if you will.

I am concerned that many nature mystics are often quick to grant mystical qualities to things that are actually evidence of our minds at work. Yes, there are deep mysteries in play that science and psychology may never be able to appreciate or explain, but this does not mean we should attribute quasimagical status to certain phenomena.

Consider the role certain healers play within various cultures. Some-times their seemingly eccentric methods work with great effect. Are we to immediately conclude that they have tapped into or personally pos-sess a mystical reservoir of healing power? Or are their methods trig-gering certain self-healing capacities of our mind and bodies?

Our discussion wouldn't be complete without briefly considering the practice and benefits of meditation. This is not an easy task because there are different approaches and schools of thought on meditation, but I think we can still take a bird's eye view look at it.

One of the great benefits to meditation is that it helps its practitioners to maintain a peaceful and calm state of mind on a more consistent basis. There is a reason the famous NBA coach Phil Jackson is referred to as the "Zen Master." His coaching style is influenced by Eastern philosophy and Native American spirituality, and he is unflappable and wise in the face of extreme competition and pressure. What is going on here?

We have all heard of the fight-or-flight response. The autonomic nervous system is wired to protect us from perceived harm. When triggered by perceived threat, this part of our brain will immediately get our bodies poised for action by releasing stress signals and hormones throughout our nervous system. In fact, brain scans have shown that under apparent or real stress, the brain sends a signal to dramatically raise our heart rate before our cognitive prefrontal cortex is ever engaged.

I think we have all experienced this stress response in our own bodies and minds. In the face of harm, we can feel our heart rate go up and our bodies tighten. Before we can thoughtfully examine our circumstances, our brains have taken over and put our bodies and minds in a high state of alert.

Brain scientists have recently discovered that the practice of meditation slows down our "heart rate variability"[13]—meaning it helps to interrupt the fight or flight response. Meditation can rewire our brains to allow our cognitive brain functions to engage before our alert system takes over. Practitioners of meditation are often able to experience more peace because they have effectively influenced their own brain function to slow down and think first.

Where East meets West

My mission is not to strip away all mystery in the name of science or skepticism. I'm not trying to reduce all healing to placebo effects or all inward experience to psychological self-delusion. Not at all. I think my trip to the Dirt Doctor probably provided something more than a mere impact on my psyche. Nevertheless, I don't feel compelled to attribute certain mystical powers to her. Her enhanced sense of my physiological energy (aura) and knowledge of my symptoms combined with an

---

13 Yunati, Monica, Vijaykumar Deshpande, and Anita Yuwanate. "Dynamics of Heart Rate Induced by Sahaja Yoga Meditation in Healthy Normal Subjects above 40 Years." *National Journal of Physiology, Pharmacy & Pharmacology* 4, no. 1 (January 2014): 80–85.

ancient understanding of herbal healing techniques probably played a huge role—and I'm glad for it.

I recognize that Eastern philosophical systems tend to emphasize practices like meditation and naturopathic healing in ways that Western systems do not. The Christian faith in particular has not had a strong record of incorporating these kinds of truths into its doctrine and practice. This cosmological "truth gap" leaves many nature mystics feeling that Christianity seriously misses the cosmological mark. This is a shame.

There is a very real sense in which Christianity should be the place where East meets West. Properly practiced and understood it is the great both/and of the cosmological options on the table. While certain forms of meditation and healing practice have often been neglected or downplayed in the church, that shouldn't be the case.

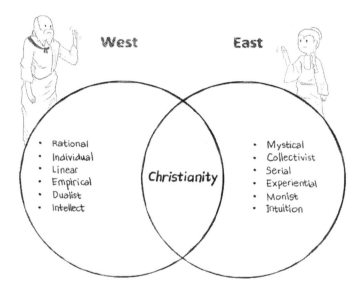

Many people would be surprised to learn that the Psalms of the Bible, the song-prayer book of the Old Testament, were written to be chanted. Granted, the chanting had a slightly different quality to it than you might experience in a purely Eastern system, but they are chants nevertheless. Even though vast numbers of Christians have relegated the Psalms to personal devotional material, they are supposed to be corporate chants that serve to call upon God and alter our state of mind and perception of reality.

I can't resist revisiting the example of speaking in tongues one last time. One of the reasons I think this phenomenon began resurging within certain parts of Protestantism in the nineteenth and twentieth centuries is that the church was not experientially engaging people with the means it had its disposal. In Christianity, the sacrament of the Lord's Supper is supposed to be one of the most central and powerful aspects of our corporate worship gatherings. Unfortunately, certain traditions, overreacting to Roman Catholicism, had suppressed the regular practice of the Supper and stripped it of significance. This contributed to an emotional and experiential vacuum that was waiting to be filled with tent revivals and phenomena such as speaking in tongues.

This small aside about the importance of the Christian sacraments is something we will focus on much more later. For the moment it is important to point out because I realize how emotionally arid and unbalanced many Christian traditions can be. They sorely lack any sense of intellectual and physiological tension, and that lack is palpable. No wonder my nature mystic friends do not resonate to Christianity.

There is more than enough intellectual and theological room in the Christian system to incorporate and in some cases reinterpret the best nature mystic practices. They would potentially be seen in a new light, but I think that is part of the balance and tension that promotes true life.

I hope we can agree that experience is very powerful and fundamental to the whole of our cosmology, but that it needs to be complemented by an objective witness to help evaluate and translate it. I believe we should seek as much balance as possible between the intellectual and experiential aspects of life. What we're seeking is light that makes sense of them both and does not deny one or the other.

Does the mystery of life have shape?

Aside from the monumental issue of experience and cognition, I would like nature mystics to see that the spiritual mysteries and "universal laws" of life and this world are not ultimately impersonal or "formless and void." In fact, I believe they intensely point toward a transcendent (beyond) and immanent (present) God who is both infinitely personal and highly engaged. Terms such as *energy* and *light* are very good and right when we think of spiritual realities, but are incomplete because they lack the shape, purpose, and personality we encounter in the universe.

There is a sense in which we see and experience the world as a paradox. On the one hand, there is a deep unity in the universe. Everything is interconnected and has its place. On the other hand there is great diversity built into the fabric of life. This cosmological puzzle has often been called the problem of "the one and the many."

At the risk of putting something on the table prematurely, I want you to indulge me in something. I want you to consider the Christian understanding of God as *Tri-unity* or *Trinity* in view of the problem of "the one and the many." I know that religious dogma may strike you as being inherently limited and limiting, but in this case, I think you might find it fascinating and enormously helpful. Some dogmas, and this one in particular bring further enlightenment and wisdom.

There is more to it than I can begin to unpack here, but here is a brief nugget to consider: Although God can be described as being one spirit, energy, or light, He is not merely that. According to Christianity, God has revealed over many millennia that He is an eternal and infinite community of love existing as three Persons—the One and the Many. Each Person shares the same divine being and is coeternal and coequal with no division or separation. There is no formal analogy to His triune being in the world, and His essence cannot be fully grasped by our rational categories.

Christians are not expressing a contradiction—which would be saying we believe in one God and three Gods. No, we are articulating a paradox—one God existing in three Persons. This is not a contradiction, but only an apparent contradiction that we could spend eternity trying to fathom.

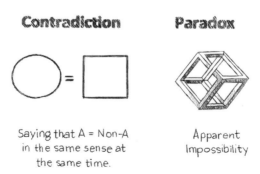

God's divine triune community of eternal love radiates with life-giving shape and power. When Christians confess that God is love, that is not a metaphor or drippy sentimentalism. We are saying that love is an inescapable attribute of God's one-and-many being because He exists as a Trinity. How could God be love if there was not a plurality of Persons eternally existing within Himself? Love, connection, and relationship are at the heart of His very essence. The *Spirit* of God is the source energy that undergirds and sustains all things. The apostle Paul wrote, "From Him, through Him, and to Him are all things" (Rom. 11:36).

One of the key teachings of the Bible is that God wanted to expand His fellowship of love by creating a vast universe that other beings made in His likeness would inhabit and enjoy in mutual love and care. We are made to live in families and community because God lives as a family and a community.

The mystery of God becomes even deeper when we realize that one of the Persons of the Trinity took on human flesh to show us who God is and who we are meant to be. Far from stuffing God in a box, this is the most boundless mystery and paradox of all.

Knowing God in this way doesn't make the world less mysterious, but it throws more light on why many mysteries exist. The infinite expressed in human flesh is both startling and liberating because it starts to bring the disparate threads of the universe together.

Rather than merely connecting to a vague sense of light, faith in the Triune God connects us to a community of love and relationship. This community extends from God to the rest of humanity. I think if nature mystics dug more into this mystery, they would see how much light it sheds on so many aspects of reality.

How should we understand evil, suffering, and death?

The final issue I would respectfully ask nature mystics to consider is the so-called problem of evil. I certainly won't pretend to tackle all the dimensions of that in this brief section; however, I would like to suggest that the various forms of nature mysticism do not account for evil in ways that are particularly helpful or coherent.

Consider the concept of karma that is often prevalent in these systems. It is quite attractive and accurate in one sense because it rightly posits that our actions and thoughts have consequences. If I make an angry comment to my wife, I should probably expect a hurtful outcome to return to me now or in the future. Conversely, if I love and respect my wife. I may experience love and respect in return. Examples such as these are abundant and can be applied to our relationships, our health, and our environment. We all experience this dynamic and should feel encouraged to take greater personal responsibility because of it.

However, when we see a young child dying from the ravages of hunger and malnutrition or an entire village wiped out by a tsunami, should we conclude that this must ultimately be the manifestation of pent-up punishment that these souls justly deserve? If a drunk driver kills my young teenager, how should I process that? Do these circumstances represent the balancing cosmic consequences for past choices that we have made as individuals? Should we be oddly thankful that such experiences serve to purge bad thoughts and actions on the infinite path to enlightenment? Karma goes far beyond the simple truth that we will reap what we sow and posits a universal accounting ledger of debits and credits that will be eternally equalized through infinitely iterative lives.

The life of Adolf Hitler is a convenient modern example of how karmic theory falls short of coherently accounting for evil in the world. As the embodiment of personal wickedness, he stirred up senseless hatred that resulted in the deaths of millions of men, women, and children. According to karmic theory, we must ultimately believe that Hitler was a tragically unenlightened soul who unleashed untold suffering on other unenlightened souls who were mutually reaping karmic consequences. In the nature mystic's karmic system, Hitler becomes the ironic balancing instrument of justice on the path to enlightenment.

While I deeply appreciate the personal responsibility that karmic theory seeks to encourage, it is a severely incomplete way of grappling with the problem of evil, sin, and death. As the example of Hitler demonstrates, evil outcomes become a cosmic offset variable as retribution is meted out to those who deserve it. The concepts of justice and injustice are severely warped by this perspective. Death and suffering become depersonalized and our individual dignity deeply compromised. We become infinite slaves to a universe ruled by this-for-that outcomes.

Quite understandably, nature mystics often respond to the problem of evil by trying to distance their minds and inner selves from physical and emotional suffering and corruption. Evil and death are not to be confronted and ultimately defeated as much as escaped through an individual progression of inward illumination.

As the late British theologian John Stott once observed, some of the iconographic contrasts between Buddhism and Christianity are very striking.[14] Consider many of the depictions of Buddha we see in various works of art. Sitting still in quiet meditation with eyes closed and the hint of a small smile, he shows the way of peace and tranquility. The message of the peaceful Buddha icon is clear—evil can be overcome as we individually achieve enlightenment.

This icon and philosophical paradigm represent a profound contrast to the brutal Christian icon of Jesus tortured and crucified to death. In Judaism and Christianity, evil and human death are not natural parts of the created order, but are corruptions of it. The problem of evil is that it carries an infinite offense against an infinitely holy God and can there-fore only be solved through His direct intervention and participation.

According to Christianity, human evil and death are inextricably linked to one another. Human death is the tragic universal consequence of human corruption and deviation from God's love. This is why the cross of Christ is so central. Defeating evil and suffering also means overcoming the conse-quence of death. Christianity teaches that only God could achieve this feat on our behalf—by not only dying, but also rising to new life.

My intent is not to bash Buddhism as all wrong, but I maintain that its monist cosmology ultimately falls short of the fullness offered by true transcendence.

For all of our talk about light, I want you to consider just how dark the darkness is. As glorious as life and the universe may be, it can also

14 John R.W. Stott, *The Cross of Christ* (Downers Grove: InterVarsity Press, 1986), 326.

be a bitterly cruel and horrific place. The suffering exacted by nature and by human behavior is almost too much for me to write about. I can't bring myself to list the terrors that many people endure in this life. I am sure you can mentally access such a list very easily on your own.

I fear that in a rush to embrace the light, many nature mystics do not seriously account for the problem of evil and the gravity of death. Death is not merely part of the circle of life. Death is a signal to us that the created order is suffering from brokenness. Evil and suffering cannot be merely escaped, but must be confronted.

Again, I sincerely hope that you will press further into these matters with me. There is no pressure to agree with anything I have said. This is meant to be food for thought before we go any further with the discussion.

CHAPTER FOUR

Dueling Dualists

One man's theology is another man's belly laugh.

—Robert A. Heinlein

It is amazing how abruptly the trajectory of our life journeys can change in the face of a simple misunderstanding. I have personally experienced its incredible power at a critical juncture in my life. During high school and college I dated a small handful of girls, and toward my junior year in college one young woman in particular had captured my attention. She seemed to be the whole package and I found myself wondering if she might be "the one."

One summer evening she and I were having a poignant conversation about how much we were enjoying our mutual friendship. It was the sort of talk that made me feel like the relationship was about to take a serious turn from friendship to courtship.

As our date was coming to an end and I drove toward her house I heard her say, "I could marry your cologne." Time froze. My inner monologue went into hyperdrive. *Marry my cologne? Um—what? I guess she likes how I smell?*

Deeply puzzled and not sure if I should be flattered or not, I think I clumsily said, "Oh. Cool." I was too stunned and confused to ask what she meant. A deep silence ensued. Within a few minutes of her awkward comment the date was over and it was the last date we ever had. When I went back to college in the autumn my communication with her came to an end.

Over a year later I was thinking about her and the strange comment about my cologne when all of a sudden I realized that she had not said *cologne*. She said *clone*. Her words flashed through my mind as if spoken for the first time. "I could marry your clone." All of a sudden the sentence took on a radically different meaning. She essentially said, "I would like to marry you or someone like you, Brett." It was her not-so-subtle way of putting her feelings out there—inviting some affirmation from me in return. Oops.

There is no question—simply no question at all—that if I had understood what she had really said, I would probably have responded in kind, and my life might look very different than it does today. For the record, I am personally glad for the confusion, but that is not my point here. If a small misunderstanding can be life-changing, how serious can a big one be?

Jesus was constantly dealing with the misunderstanding of others. People were confused and conflicted about Him throughout His whole ministry. Who was He and what was He doing?

Interestingly, when we carefully study Jesus we see a core strategy emerge in response to the people who sought Him out. When people came to Him seeking answers about his identity, He constantly challenged them to pause in radical self-reflection. He would rarely answer directly, and He usually turned the questions and the focus back on the inquirer. A visit with Jesus often ended up with more probing personal challenges than immediate answers.

Many of us are familiar with people in various public contexts who wear T-shirts and carry signs or other paraphernalia bearing the slogan "John 3:16." This verse reads, "For God so loved the world that He gave His only Son, that whoever believes in Him should not perish, but have eternal life."

People must hope that flashing this Bible reference will remind others of God's love so that they turn to Him. But whenever I see someone displaying John 3:16, I think of something very different—the full story recorded in the third chapter of John's Gospel. It is about Nicodemus, a Jewish leader and teacher who secretly met with Jesus.

The narrative begins with Nicodemus sincerely acknowledging that Jesus is a true prophet because the miracles He is doing prove He is from God. But Jesus doesn't reply by confirming his prophetic status or commending Nicodemus for putting two and two together. Rather, his opening response is enigmatic and unexpected, "Most assuredly, I say to you, unless one is born again, he cannot see the kingdom of God."

I don't know about you, but to me it seems that Jesus was a little off-topic. Nicodemus is equally bewildered, and in confusion he asks, "How can a man be born when he is old? Can he enter a second time into his mother's womb and be born?"

Jesus proceeds to answer using multiple allusions from the Old Testament that Nicodemus would be intimately familiar with as a Jewish teacher. These allusions show how we must be personally and spiritually transformed by God to participate in God's kingdom. Again in confused astonishment, Nicodemus asks, "How can these things be?" *How does such personal transformation happen for us? How does this work, Jesus?*

Before pressing on with the central answer to Nicodemus's question, Jesus challenges him: "Are you the teacher of Israel, and do not know these things?" We could loosely paraphrase the response as, "Nicodemus, this is basic Old Testament teaching about spirituality. You're telling me you don't know about it? No wonder you are confused about me and what I'm doing."

Pause and think about this for a moment. Nicodemus is a highly educated religious leader who is sincerely seeking to know more about Jesus. Where are the hugs and confirming words? Why doesn't Jesus embrace this man and patiently unpack everything for him in plain terms? Where is the meek and mild Jesus we hear about?

Part of the difficulty for us in understanding what was going on in this exchange is that we don't know the Old Testament very well. If we did, we would see that Jesus was referencing issues that were familiar to His Jewish contemporaries. Jesus jumped right into the area of Nicodemus's expertise and began challenging him to consider whether he really knew or believed his own convictions.

As each of us moves toward a greater understanding of the mystery of Christ, we should expect to be confronted in a similar fashion. One of the first orders of business is to assess our own positions with more scrutiny—to become unsettled in what we think we know. This uncomfortable self-examination is critical to our journey.

To My Generically Spiritual Friends

As I indicated in chapter two, my emotional sympathies run strongly in your direction. Embracing ambiguity in philosophical-religious matters and living in that space is very attractive at many levels. It is certainly the path of least resistance because it allows so many divisive issues to remain open-ended.

I am not suggesting that generically spiritual people are intellectually indecisive. Sometimes recognizing ambiguity in religion and life is the intellectually honest position. My life and faith reflect that.

For example, one of my beliefs as a Christian is that Jesus is the King of kings and Lord of lords. There is a political dimension of my religion that is inescapable. Unlike many right-wing Evangelical conservatives, I don't think that the United States is or ever was an explicitly or implicitly Christian nation. Yes, many of its founding principles were derived from a Judeo-Christian framework, but our Constitution never mentions or insinuates fidelity to Jesus Christ anywhere.

Our Founders did not make this omission by some sloppy mistake. They were intentionally crafting a quasi-secular experiment in statecraft. Therefore, while I believe that Jesus is the de facto King (and we will discuss this more in a later chapter), I recognize that I also live as a citizen of a de jure "secular" state. This inherent ambiguity impacts my voting patterns as a Christian in many respects. I don't want to wade into the specifics of that now, but the point is that I understand the need to approach these issues with nuance.

Here are some questions I would like to ask you:

1. Aren't we all exclusive in our own way?
2. Should you revisit your thinking about comparative religion and myth?
3. Do you have a higher calling on your life?
4. Does the hypocrisy of Christians disprove their faith?

Aren't we all exclusive in our own way?

In some respects, the generically spiritual position is very close to agnosticism because you are saying, "We can't know some of these religious matters for certain." While you are not explicitly hostile to the idea of God or certain kinds of religious perspectives, you are very uncomfortable with faith claims that are exclusive.

Here is the difficult thought I would like you to chew on: You may think that taking a generically spiritual view is the epistemologically humble and nonexclusive path, but all of us are on a level playing field when it comes to the issue of making exclusive faith claims. Your generically spiritual belief is as exclusive as my Christian belief.

If a Muslim says that Allah is the only true God, that claim is exclusive to all others. If a Christian says that Jesus is the only true God, that claim is exclusive to all others. If an atheist says there is no such thing as god, that claim is exclusive to all others. And here's the kicker—when a generically spiritual person says that any of these iterations is true for each individual and that all positions are approximations of the same truth, that claim, too, is exclusive to all the other claims just mentioned.

When you dismiss the possibility of one faith being exclusively true, you have made an exclusive faith claim. You have ruled out the possibility that the Muslim faith is exclusively true, even though that is what the Muslim faith claims. You have made a competing counterclaim. It may seem more ambiguous and nuanced on its face, but it is just as sweeping a claim as any particular religion makes.

When I was going through diversity training at student orientation for Indiana University, I remember feeling very confused about the position being touted. On the one hand, the speaker and the panelists were preaching tolerance toward those with different views, and I thought that was legitimate. On the other hand, they were quite clear about their own intolerance of those who believed that their beliefs were exclusively true.

I was bewildered by the diversity training because the panel preaching tolerance would only tolerate people who shared their prescriptively pluralistic faith claim. They seemed to think that anyone who made a faith claim that disagreed with them on a significant matter was necessarily hateful and would inevitably engage in persecuting behavior. On the one hand, they had an absolute belief that all faith claims were equally valid and should be equally tolerated, and on the other hand, they maintained that anyone with a contrary view would not be tolerated.

My point is simply this: If you take a generically spiritual position because you believe it places you above the narrow-mindedness of the religious adherent, you should reconsider whether that is really the case. The generically spiritual position rejects the exclusive possibility of any other position—my Christian faith, for example. You believe I am wrong to be exclusive in the same way that I think you are wrong to profess to be nonexclusive.

Like it or not, we are operating from the same ground. We are all exercising faith in a way that excludes other claims. Once you grasp this concept, I think we can dig deeper into considering the merits and demerits of certain faith claims, rather than simply dismissing all of them as equally valid for each person.

Should you revisit your thinking about myth and comparative religion?

I am sensitive to the objection that we can never fully weigh all the different faith claims against one another. This may be true, but this is where rightly applied ambiguity kicks in, don't you think? Do we really need to know every possible faith claim before exercising faith? Is such an effort even possible? I believe we can recognize different families of belief systems and then can start to sift through the ones that are the most coherent with reality as we experience it. It may not be easy, but it is not impossible.

In comparative religion classes throughout the United States, many undergraduate students are taught that all religions are just conceptual amalgams of similar themes. Stories about incarnation, virgin birth, heroes, dragons, plagues, resurrection, moral codes, and the like are endemic to the vast religious enterprise in its many manifestations. Many people believe that each religion is merely a reworking of these themes in its unique context.

One of the greatest examples of a pervasive religious narrative is that of the universal flood. Here is a sampling of some of the ancient cultures that report the deluge:[15]

- *Greek*: Zeus wiped out the men of the Bronze Age by sending a flood. Deucalion loaded his family and animals on an ark and landed on a mountain peak when the waters abated.[16]

- *Roman*: Jupiter wanted to destroy evil humanity by setting fire to earth, but was worried that it might also consume heaven. With the aid of Neptune, he brought a flood that consumed all but the peak of Parnassus, where Duecalion finally landed.[17]

- *Celtic*: The people of Earth were crushed between two giants, Heaven and Earth, so they cut Heaven to pieces to break up the darkness. The blood that came from Heaven's skull caused a flood that wiped out all humanity except for a pair that was saved in a ship built by a Titan.[18]

- *Lithuanian*: Pramziamas, the chief god, sent two giants, Wandu and Wejas (water and wind) to judge mankind's wickedness. He was eating nuts and one of the shells landed on a mountain. Some people and animals were able to seek refuge in the nutshell. When the water and wind came to an end, Pramzimas gave them a rainbow to comfort them.[19]

- *Sumerian*: Even though the gods decided to wipe out mankind by a flood, the god Enlil warned the priest-king Ziusudra and instructed him to build a boat to harbor animals and birds. After surviving the flood, Ziusudra sacrificed to Enlil in worship.[20]

- *Assyrian*: The gods decided to purge humanity from the earth, but Utnapishtim was warned of the coming calamity in a dream. He built a huge ship for his family and living creatures. Utnapishtim

---

15 For an exhaustive treatment and reference list on the subject by Mark Isaak, see http://talkorigins.org/faqs/flood-myths.html#Revision.

16 Sir James G. Frazer, *The Library* (Cambridge: Harvard University, 1921), Apollodorus - 1.7.2.

17 Ovid, translated by Horace Gregory, *The Metamorphoses* (New York: Viking Press, 1958), Book 1.

18 Barbara C Sproul. *Primal Myths* (New York: HarperCollins Publishers, 1979), 172–173.

19 Theodor H. Gaster, *Myth, Legend, and Custom in the Old Testament* (New York: Harper & Row,1969), 93.

20 Alexander Heidel, The Gilgamesh Epic and Old Testament Parallels (University of Chicago Press, 1949), 102–106.

released a dove, a sparrow, and a raven to discern whether the waters had abated.[21]

- *Tanzanian*: When the rivers began flooding, two men were divinely instructed to board a ship with seeds and animals. The flood was so high it covered the mountains. A dove and a hawk were sent from the ship to see if the waters had receded.[22]

- *Nigerian*: The sun and the moon were married, and their best friend was flood. Sun and moon built a large house and invited flood to come. When the flood came he filled the house so that the sun and moon had to make a new home in the sky.[23]

- *Siberian*: Noj was instructed by God to build a ship, but the devil found out and destroyed it. God had to send an iron boat to save Noj, his family, and the animals they had with them.[24]

- *Chinese*: The goddess Nu Kua beat a tribal chief in a battle. In an act of revenge, the chief beat down the heavenly bamboo, which tore a hole in the sky. The flood that ensued killed everyone except Nu Kua and her army. She plastered the hole in the sky shut with a rainbow.[25]

- *Hawaiian*: The god Kane judged the sin of humanity with a flood. Nu'u and his family were delivered by boarding the great canoe provided by Kane.[26]

- *Eskimo*: In the ancient past the oceans flooded everything on earth except for one mountain peak. Some animals survived on the mountain and a handful of people survived in a boat. Eventually, the people landed on the mountain top.[27]

- *Yakima Indian*: There was great wickedness on the earth and a righteous man had heard that a flood was coming. He dug out

21 N. K. Sandars (transl.). The Epic of Gilgamesh (Harmondsworth, England: Penguin Books, Ltd., 1972), Chapter 5.
22 Gaster, 120–121.
23 Alexander Eliot, *The Universal Myths* (New York: Truman Talley Books/Meridian, 1976), 47–48.
24 Holmberg, Uno. Finno-Ugric, Siberian, in MacCulloch, C. J. A., ed., The Mythology of All Races, v. IV,(Boston: Marshall Jones Co.,1927), 362.
25 E. T. C. Werner, Myths and Legends of China (Singapore: Singapore National Printers Ltd, 1922),225.
26 Dorothy B. Barrère, The Kumuhonua Legends: A Study of Late 19th Century Hawaiian Stories of Creation and Origins (Honolulu: Pacific Anthropological Records number 3, Bishop Museum, 1969), 23–24.
27 Gaster, 120.

a canoe from a large cedar and the good people were preserved during the rains. All the bad people drowned.[28]

- *Michoacan*: A man named Tezpi entered a boat with his family, animals, and seeds when the flood came. He sent out birds to see if the waters had receded. Finally, a hummingbird came back with a green bough.[29]

I could go on. This a small fraction of the available data, but it gives us a strong sense of how common this narrative was across cultures and continents. The obvious question is why such a story would persist if it did not contain at least a kernel of truth.

Our ancestors may have been prescientific, but they were not entirely precritical or disinterested in matters of origin. In fact, a leading Egyptologist, Kenneth Kitchen, has postulated that cultures in the ancient Near East did not generally "historicize myth."[30] In other words, they did not come up with fanciful narratives in order to invent imaginary histories for the sake of storytelling. Rather, they "mythologized history," meaning they amplified true events as part of their faith traditions—and these myths evolved over time.

The Bible's account of the universal flood in Genesis 6–9 is a high account compared to other versions. While the story of Noah's Ark is certainly amazing in its own right, nutshells weren't falling from the table of a god who was snacking during judgment. Betrothed planets were not throwing dinner parties.

When we consider that Genesis was written with true historical referents against a background of competing religious narratives, we see that it should not be read as moral fable or mere allegory. Such an interpretation belies an ignorance of its context. There is no problem referring to such literature as myth as long as we understand that it is rooted in true history. Otherwise, we are leaving too much evidence on the cutting room floor.

Since we're on the subject of myth, I would like to get speculative for a moment. While I believe truth can be stranger than fiction, I'm having some fun with this. My beliefs do not hang on this speculation whatsoever. I'm just thinking out loud.

28 Ella E. Clark, *Indian Legends of the Pacific Northwest* (University of California Press, 1953), 45.
29 Gaster, 122.
30 Kenneth A. Kitchen, *On the Reliability of the Old Testament* (Grand Rapids: Eerdmans, 2003), 262.

According to the biblical story, the flood was not just caused by tor-rential rains from above, but from the opening of the "fountains of the deep" below. In other words, there were massive earthquakes and other geological activity happening at the same time. The biblical flood ac-count doesn't merely suggest unceasing rains; it points to a total trans-formation of the earth. Theologically speaking, it was about the death of the old world and the resurrection of a new world.

Have you ever heard of Pangaea? It is what scholars call the united landmass they believe existed prior to the formation of the continents today. Here is a picture—you can see how the continents fit together like puzzle pieces:

Here's my speculation—I believe there is a good chance that the continental drift that broke up Pangaea may be connected to the flood. Instead of happening over millions of years, the separation may have occurred during a massive upheaval that lasted for almost six months. The flood was so cataclysmic that it literally changed the face of the world, and many of the most dramatic features of the world today are evidence of this catastrophe.

Before you dismiss such a notion as totally crazy, recall the destruc-tion caused by various small-scale catastrophes that we have witnessed in recent decades. The most prominent one in my memory was the eruption of Mount St. Helens in May of 1980. The immediate and dev-astating geological impact was amazing to behold.

The Geological Impact of Mount St Helens

- Mountain lost 1,300 feet of altitude
- The explosion spewed a glowing cloud of gas and rock at supersonic speeds
- Shockwave leveled forest for 19 miles
- Devastation of 230 square miles
- Mushroom cloud 12 miles in the air
- 540 million tons of ash spread over 2,200 square miles
- Hot mud moving at 90 mph

Consider that kind of event happening on a more massive, violent, and worldwide scale over the course of forty days. Not four minutes or four hours, but forty days. The waters didn't recede for the better part of six months, and that is why so many ancient religions throughout the world retained memory of it.

My conjecture about the flood myth corresponding to the breakup of Pangaea is nothing new. In fact, *catastrophism* used to be a more prominent feature of geological theory. Geologists used to look at canyons, mountain ranges, and other features of the world through a lens that emphasized geological cataclysm instead of gradualism.

I'm not dogmatic about my understanding of Pangaea and the flood catastrophe. I'm simply saying that rather than approaching religious literature as if it is all a fantasy, we can surmise that the stories are derived from true events and people. I believe that the biblical narrative is the best preservation of these ancient truths that we have.

This testimony gives us reason to take the Bible more seriously, not less seriously. What if the biblical history is the best-preserved version of the underlying history that has been passed down to us? Comparative religion bolsters the case for further investigation rather than denigrating it.

Do you have a higher calling on your life?

Although many generically spiritual people maintain their position based on philosophically principled reasons, others simply feel no need to pursue spiritual matters. They are quite content with their lives as they are and feel no demand to subscribe to anything beyond their current beliefs. There is often a latent fear that a more definitive spirituality will be a net loss in their life and may threaten relationships or behaviors that are dear to them.

This seductive posture of complacence is very pervasive in wealthy cultures where basic needs are met and mental distractions are plentiful. Who needs religion when life is already pretty good? This may be the hardest question of all to answer. A wise man once said that the only thing worse than hatred is indifference.

I have found that the best response to apathy toward a more definitive faith is an invitation to personal purpose and abiding joy. It is so easy for us to confuse pleasure with joy. The trouble with pleasure is that it is momentary and fleeting. It seems to begin fading the minute we find it.

Sometimes the anticipation of pleasure is more satisfying than the actual realization of desire. In fact, a recent study of the brains of monkeys has proven that their pleasure center is more highly activated by the prospect of receiving an expected reward than when they are actually receiving the reward.[31] The biochemical rush associated with anticipation of fulfilling desire is extremely intense.

This is one of the reasons why addictive substances and behaviors have become so prevalent in our culture. The more we seek certain kinds of stimulation, the more chemically numb our brains become to them. We have to seek increasingly strong stimuli to satisfy the pleasurable feelings we once had. The buzz we used to get from one drink eventually requires two or more drinks for the same effect. Left unchecked, this cycle of addiction can become a death spiral that consumes us.

Philosophers have referred to the problem of pleasure-seeking as the hedonistic paradox. Hedonism was an ancient Greek school of thought that believed the highest good we could live for is to maximize pleasure and minimize pain. The paradox is that if you don't achieve pleasure according to your expectations, you will be frustrated, but if you achieve it, you will quickly become bored. Pleasure seeking ends up backfiring on those who make it the center of their life. When the American magnate John D. Rockefeller was asked how much is enough, he famously responded, "Just a little bit more." He had experienced the hedonistic paradox first hand.

---

31 Charles Duhigg, *The Power of Habit: Why We Do What We Do in Life and Business* (New York: Random House, 2012), 46.

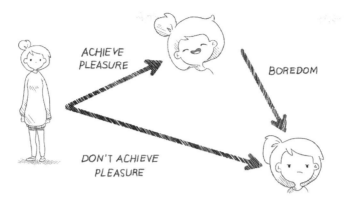

ACHIEVE PLEASURE

BOREDOM

DON'T ACHIEVE PLEASURE

That is not to say that there is anything inherently wrong with pleasure or fleeting moments of happiness. I, for instance, enjoy few things more than a delicious meal. But food doesn't own me or define my life. If it did, I would grow to despise it, and my pleasure would transform into misery.

The highest and best pursuit of life is *lasting* joy that supersedes particular circumstances. This joy comes from knowing and fulfilling your purpose. A life without significant meaning is doomed to depression.

Please consider that life is meant for much more than being filled with distractions and addictions. God is engaged in a universal redemption project and He invites all of His image bearers—all of humanity—to join in. Everyone is called to fulfill their part of the plan, and this is where the greatest pleasure and fulfillment in life are experienced. Don't stop short of living your life to the fullest because you were content with the temporary distractions of this world. Be part of an everlasting legacy of grace.

Does the hypocrisy of Christians disprove their faith?

Even if you agree with me in the abstract, there may be little interest in exploring Christianity because its adherents can be so obnoxious. I get it. There are only two responses I can offer at this juncture. First, on behalf of myself and my fellow Christians, I am sincerely sorry. We have failed in so many different ways over such a long period of time. We are often proud, persecuting, and naive—the very opposite of what we're called to be.

The second response is that *of course* we are. That assumption is built into the Christian faith. We are all a big wreck in a slow process of transformation. In other words, our dysfunction is an ironic validation of the Christian faith's internal consistency. The Christian message is that we are broken people in need of redemption. Our brokenness is one powerful part of the way the claims of Christianity cohere to reality.

Many churches have an announcement sign at the front of the property. Usually they post service times and even the title of the upcoming sermon. One sign that I found particularly poignant read, "This church is not full of hypocrites. There's always room for one more." This is the deeply ironic and true identity of the church. There is no denying it.

As I have said to the atheists and agnostics and to the nature mystics, I don't expect any of this to automatically change your mind. My intent is to get your wheels turning in a stimulating way. I hope as the discussion goes a few levels deeper you will sense where I am coming from. My burden is to wrestle through these issues because I think we are all called to participate in God's plan. We shouldn't be content with superficial answers to the biggest questions of life. If there is any place we should fully apply ourselves, this is it.

To My Non-Christian Religious Friends

Of all four major cosmological groups, this is the one that could most easily become overwhelming and contentious to address, because it is so large and diverse. In some respects it is more emotionally sensitive than any of the others because there are many specific dogmas on the table. Rather than trying to call out each of the major systems individually, I want to address the one question that underlies them all—how do we know who God is?

There are many different ways to approach this question, but the common-denominator answer is that deity makes itself known through some mode of revelation. And that raises the question of which revelation is most credible and worthy of our trust.

My contention is that the more clearly transcendent revelation relates to phenomenal realities, the more trustworthy it is. We live in an orderly world with structure, and it seems reasonable that transcendent realities would mirror this in some significant manner.

Does your religion's revelation strongly correspond to phenomenal reality?

Ironically, this is where the disciplined skepticism of the atheist and agnostic can help us. Like them, we should not be content with faith claims that have little correspondence to our world. If Joe Schmo across the street claimed to be a prophet bearing a unique revelation from God, you would likely look for some phenomenal signs to confirm his authenticity. Without significant verification, you would write off Joe Schmo as a lunatic.

This is also a juncture where nature mysticism sheds light, because we can reasonably expect spiritual realities to share a mysterious relationship to phenomenal realities. Here is the key principle—the transcendent realm may be distinct from the phenomenal realm, but that doesn't mean it is entirely separated from it. For example, our immortal souls (transcendent) are embedded in our mortal bodies (phenomenal). The two are not vastly separated from one another but deeply permeate each other.

In the same way, it makes sense to apply a transcendent-to-phenomenal correspondence test to scriptures that make faith claims. I struggled with this for many years myself, and I think there are several questions that we all need to wrestle with. The first set of questions is more objective and the second set of questions is more subjective.

First, on an objective level, are the contents of the scriptures merely meditative abstractions about deity or about how the deity has been known and experienced by a historic community of people? In short, are there multiple witnesses to the revelation? If the contents are purely a collection of spiritual propositions and practices, then I think it is far less compelling than those derived from the account of a historical people that has encountered deity. Scriptures that lack a communal historical witness make certain faith claims almost totally unverifiable and subjective.

The Hindu scriptures, the Vedas, are a significant example of abstract literature. These scriptures are organized around various hymns, recitations, and spells, but are not rooted in particular historical figures or events. It seems that for whatever merit they may have as a work of poetry or devotional thought, their revelations about the transcendent realm are inherently unverifiable in any objective sense. This lack of witness in the phenomenal realm weakens the Vedas' faith claims about the nature of deity.

The second objective line of questioning is whether the historical claims of certain religious scriptures cohere to historical and archaeological evidence. For example, the enduring scriptural strength of the Jewish, Christian, and Muslim faiths is very much rooted in their shared Abrahamic heritage. While there are differences among these faiths in their understanding of Abraham, they all share a common historical ancestry that is tied to a real people who actually existed. No one would deny that the Jews were an ancient monotheistic people who sojourned throughout the Middle East. The objective historical remnants that testify to the long and enduring existence of that faith community are beyond doubt.

The Book of Mormon serves as an interesting contrast to the strength of the historical claims of the Jewish and Christian Old Testament. In the 1830s, the chief prophet of Mormonism, Joseph Smith, purportedly received revelation from a set of buried gold plates, glasses, and artifacts that only he could interpret with the special help of an angel. And no trace remains of the plates or glasses.

Pressing further in a similar direction, the revelation of Joseph Smith claims that Jesus Christ miraculously revealed Himself to the indigenous peoples of Polynesia and America. Unfortunately, we have no archaeological or anthropological evidence for any of these claims and no other witnesses to them. There is absolutely no confirmation of these things anywhere, leaving Joseph Smith's faith claims with no objective ground other than his standalone prophecy.

Another fascinating feature of Mormonism is that its holy book, the Book or Mormon, is a curiously constructed revision and amplification of the Christian Old and New Testaments. It is unique in many respects, but it curiously imitates the the, thee, thou, thy style of English in the King James Bible which was the dominant English translation of Smith's day. The Book of Mormon bears the marks of an inauthentic conceptual knock-off of the King James version of the Bible, not of a true historical witness.

Islam is similarly interesting because it claims Muhammad received revelations almost six centuries after the life of Jesus Christ. According to Islamic tradition, Muhammad alone received prophecy over the course of twenty-three years. This largely served to correct, reinterpret, and supplement the existing Jewish and Christian Scriptures, which, according to Muhammad's revelation, were corruptions that needed massive adjustment, especially in regard to the supposedly irrational and contradictory doctrine of God's tri-unity.

Of course I realize that certain historical claims of the Jewish Scriptures, which Christians also claim as our Old Testament, are hotly contested, as well. The historicity of Genesis 1, for instance, is largely rejected by non-Christians, and continues to be debated even among Christians. Without dismissing those concerns, I would submit to you that Judaism and Christianity do not rise and fall on a young-earth interpretation of the Creation account. However, on its own testimony, Christianity rises and falls on the historicity of the Resurrection of Jesus Christ. The Apostle Paul went so far as to say that if Jesus did not actually rise from the dead, Christians are to be the most pitied among men for operating under such a delusion (1 Cor. 15:19).

The important point is that we should expect some correlation between historical claims made by various scriptures and the historical evidence we can verify. Some religious scriptures fall particularly short in this regard.

At a subjective level, we should ask whether the faith claims of particular scriptures resonate with our internal experience—individually and collectively. This is a much tougher project in many respects because it requires careful consideration of the faith claims being made and the ability to be honest with ourselves.

The difficulty lies in being willing to see things as they are, not necessarily as we wish them to be. We might wish that everyone were basically good, but is such a statement consistent with the reality of our experience? These are questions we must strive to answer honestly, even at risk of our own pain.

My project is not to exhaustively compare all of the scriptural options on the table. There are abundant resources available for that path of inquiry for those who want to travel it. We will soon take a tour through the Bible so that you can at least understand its claims. If you find it less than persuasive, perhaps it will at least serve to bring certain aspects of your own faith under more scrutiny.

We have done a lot of work together analyzing the philosophical underpinnings of different philosophical-religious positions while trying to assess our own cosmological lens. Even though we have not been exhaustive in our analysis we introduced some critical questions and thinking to further the conversation.

DISCOVERING THE
CHRISTIAN THEOLOGICAL TRADITION

CHAPTER FIVE

Crossing the Cosmological Chasm

God writes the Gospel not in the Bible alone, but also on trees, and in the flowers and clouds and stars.

—Martin Luther

When I turned sixteen, I started my first summer job at SeaWorld of Ohio. (Yes, Ohio used to have a SeaWorld.)

Most workplaces of any size tend to break down into different subcultural ecosystems, but at SeaWorld the divisions were almost like the caste structure in India. Social status and rank were both obvious and hard to escape. Workers rarely fraternized outside of their assigned group.

The animal trainers, waterskiing performers, and Olympic high dive team members filled the very top of the food chain. They were gods among men. Tanned, attractive, svelte, and comparatively well paid, they had a swagger that was unmistakable. They were living the dream, and every other worker in the park envied their position.

Further down the food chain you could identify each segment of the caste by departmental shirt color. Management wore white, retail wore pink, horticulture wore green, operations wore blue, and at the bottom rung of the ladder there was food service wearing a horrifically dull burgundy with blue stripes and a matching hat.

As you might imagine, a high school kid like me was on that lowest rung. But I learned quickly it would be well worth the hard work of avoiding the drudgery of that station in life. Having no special skills with marine life or water sports, I worked my way up the ladder via the management track.

Having made it to the white shirt strata, I became aware of another invisible, but powerful layer in the business culture—the corporate office in St. Louis, Missouri. Dots started to connect as I realized the four-inch-thick operational manuals and pictures of corporate bigwigs in the employee entrance were not coming from our local offices. It was hard to believe, but there were evidently people with even higher rank than the water-skiers.

By my fifth summer, I was promoted to area supervisor. In addition to a white shirt, I had another status symbol: a Motorola walkie-talkie. My radio handle was simply the number 712. Standard protocol was to say your number followed by the number of the person you wished to reach. 701 was the vice president of food service; 601 was the vice president for operations, and so on up to 101, the president of the entire park. My ability to radio, "712 to 701," meant that I had direct access to the true power brokers.

The park was owned by Anheuser-Busch. SeaWorld management had various codes for certain events, but the big daddy of them all was the signal that the CEO, August Busch III, had arrived in his black helicopter to survey his kingdom. These visits were completely unannounced and unknown beforehand—even to 101. The only warning anyone would get was a radio message: "The Eagle has landed."

I have never experienced anything like what happened the day those fateful words came across my Motorola walkie-talkie. Evaluation by the roaming CEO could be career-making or career-breaking. His utterances carried ultimate and unquestionable authority. He was judge, jury, and executioner. The very mention of his presence sent two thousand employees into a completely different state of mind. August Busch III, the incomparable king from St. Louis, had come.

The morning his majesty arrived, we were short-handed in one of the sandwich shops I managed, so I was frantically helping to get things rolling. As I was lifting a huge jar filled with fresh lemonade, the jar cracked, the bottom fell out, and five gallons of sticky lemonade and shards of glass covered the floor and my shoes. As I tried to figure out my next move, I got the radio signal that Mr. Busch was approaching my area. My radio blared, "101 to 701 and 712, what's your twenty? Are you ready?"

Adrenaline is an amazing thing. It can transform mere mortals into superheroes. If you've never felt its effects, I heartily recommend it.

Feeling suspended from my body, time, and space, I heard myself radio back, "712 to 101, I'm at the Sandwich Shop handling a . . . um . . . situation." Seconds later people in every color of shirts were at the back door of the unit. It was all hands on deck. I don't know how, but within the space of seconds, that floor was gleaming. It has probably never been that clean since.

When August Busch III passed by the Sandwich Shop with his train of executive servants in tow, he simply looked our direction and nodded his head. No words, no condemnation or adulation, just a nod in our direction. It was more than enough. When he passed out of sight we all gave each other hugs.

There's a point to my SeaWorld story: The corporate-to-local communication systems within the Anheuser-Busch world are somewhat parallel to the transcendent-to-phenomenal communication in our world.

Imagine SeaWorld of Ohio as the phenomenal realm experienced by workers and park guests. Now think of the corporate headquarters in St. Louis as the transcendent, invisible realm workers and guests never saw. While the average person might never know that SeaWorld headquarters was in St. Louis, or even who was in charge, they knew they were at SeaWorld. There was no mistaking it because the corporate identity had been so well established through various means.

CROSSING THE CHASM

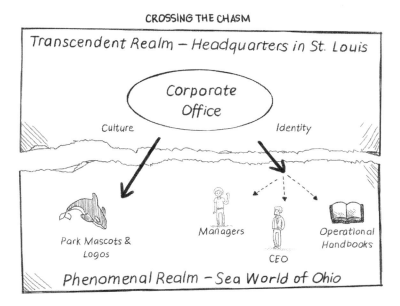

There is a sense in which the business culture itself was dualistic. We had the imperceptible and authoritative corporate offices in St. Louis that were beyond and above SeaWorld of Ohio. However, headquarters' impact was felt in multiple dimensions. Some of the business culture was visually built-in through corporate-designed mascots and logos. Parts of it were passed down through written manuals and memos. Without a doubt, the ultimate effect was felt by the visitation of the owner himself. SeaWorld of Ohio wasn't in St. Louis, but the abiding presence and reality of St. Louis was felt every day.

How Is God Revealed?

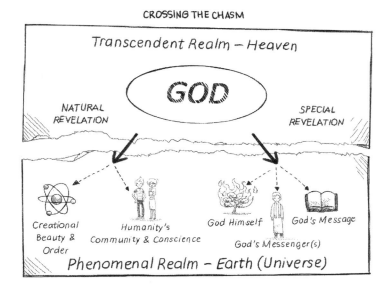

The big idea of the SeaWorld analogy is to help demonstrate the way divine revelation crosses the cosmological chasm between the transcendent and physical realms. Sometimes putting the message of Christ in its revelatory context makes it easier to understand.

For example, many people are concerned that the concept of a Bible puts God in a box. Isn't there something terribly self-limiting about a mere book when it comes to revealing transcendent reality? How can this possibly work? When we see the way revelation functions in Christianity, we may see that we are shadowboxing with issues that are more perceived than real.

The biblical proposal is that transcendent truth is expressed through a handful of modes—not just one. In other words, the Bible does not limit revelation to itself. It is a significant channel of revelation, and it serves as an interpretive lens for other modes of revelation, but it is *not* the only way phenomenal and transcendent truth is revealed.

The modes of revelation can be grouped into two major categories—natural and special. Natural revelation is transcendent information that everyone can immediately access and experience through the design of the phenomenal realm. Special revelation is transcendent information that can only be known by direct contact with God Himself, His messenger(s), or His documented message.

Natural Revelation—Creational Order and Beauty

Natural revelation is very familiar because it comes through the conduits of creation, human community, and human conscience. The meticulously ordered creation as we see and experience it points to the work of a wise, powerful, and eternal Designer. His majestic fingerprints are seen from far away galaxies down to cellular mechanisms. The order and beauty of the world bear a divine watermark. King David wrote in Psalm 19:1–4,

> The heavens declare the glory of God,
>   and the sky above proclaims his handiwork.
> Day to day pours out speech,
>   and night to night reveals knowledge.
> There is no speech, nor are there words,
>   whose voice is not heard.
> Their voice goes out through all the earth,
>   and their words to the end of the world.

The ancient song of King David expresses volumes more than Hallmark card sentimentalism. He was passionate about nature because its beauty testifies to the goodness and greatness of its Maker. A constant and unceasing message without speech is going throughout the whole earth. The chorus of the created order is singing all day and night about the glory of God.

One of the great advantages of living in California is having access to some of the most beautiful topographies in the world. A few years ago I was able to visit Yosemite National Park for the first time. It is one of the most beloved sites in the United States—and it is not hard to understand why.

Although Yosemite covers almost 800 thousand acres, most visitors spend their time in Yosemite Valley. Sheer granite cliffs ascending to heights of 4,700 feet dwarf towering sequoias deep in the valley. Majestic waterfalls, clear streams, and abundant wildlife fill the landscape.

There are several ways to get into the valley. The one I took approaches through a long tunnel from the western edge of the park. When I emerged looked down on the valley from the appropriately named Tunnel View I was stunned. The scale was so much more massive than anything I had ever seen before. For a moment I thought I should sing Handel's "Hallelujah" chorus just to chime in with nature's song. I'm not the kind of guy who cries often, but I have to confess that I felt the sting of a few tears.

I think we've all felt a similar visceral response to something in nature. It might have been when your first child was born or the first time you looked through a telescope and saw Saturn's rings. Maybe it was when you caught your first wave surfing in the Pacific Ocean. Our reactions are not insignificant accidents. They are purposeful and full of meaning. The natural order contains a message revealing an all-wise God.

Natural Revelation—Human Community

As previously mentioned, the Bible doesn't portray nature as the only channel of revelation. The other major conduit of natural revelation is humanity itself. In fact, the Bible says that people are collectively made in the image of God. It is almost like we are created as miniature mirrors that jointly reflect His divine presence and action in the world.

Our ability to form relationships and communities that build civilizations and cultures make us unique. Animals may move in packs or herds and even have quasi-familial configurations and behaviors, but nothing matches the deep relational complexity and interdependence of humanity. Together we emulate the one-and-many social matrix of God's tri-unity.

Humanity's individual and shared brokenness has inhibited the full function of our divine image, but it has not obliterated its fundamental structure. One theologian has referred to humans as glorious ruins. In humanity we encounter the remains and shadow of our full potential.

Natural Revelation—Human Conscience

Perhaps the most compelling dimension of general revelation is the moral agency and conscience that people are endowed with. The concepts of righteousness and wickedness are embedded deep in our psyches. We are not a *tabula rasa*, or blank slate, in an absolute sense. We may acquire social constructs from our environment at some level, but we are hardwired with a foundation of moral precepts.

Some may deny this in the abstract, but affirm it when they are personally violated. Try taking something valuable from an atheist and see whether they think a fixed personal boundary has been transgressed. It won't be a long conversation, I assure you.

The Apostle Paul makes this very clear in his letter to the Romans. He writes, "Therefore you have no excuse, O man, every one of you who judges. For in passing judgment on another you condemn yourself, because you, the judge, practice the very same things" (Rom. 2:1).

In other words, we all pass judgment on others for different reasons. When we do this, we paradoxically judge ourselves, because we are guilty of the same things. This dynamic is built into our being.

While it is very true that consciences can be altered, numbed, and contorted, there is a basic moral and ethical compass that is intrinsic to humanity. Right, wrong, mercy, kindness, and justice are universal concepts woven into the fabric of our psyche. Our conscience distinguishes us from other living creatures and functions as a signpost pointing to God.

One of the reasons some belief systems incorporate karma into their thinking is because we are all thirsty for justice. The very concept of justice presupposes absolute right and wrong. We want to see evildoers being dealt with. We are not easily satisfied with the belief that evil will go unchecked.

I am writing this on the heels of an incredibly disgusting news story about a man in Cleveland, Ohio, who kidnapped three women and kept them as his sex slaves. When they were pregnant he would beat, starve, and poison them to abort the babies. It is so cruel and so revolting that it provokes universal loathing and disdain. When the news came out that he would plead not guilty, the cry from the public and media was deafening. And when he hanged himself in prison, no one mourned his death. There is something deep within us that longs for justice.

None of this can be adequately explained by simple social contract or conditioning. The image of God that we are imprinted with is unavoidable and universal even though we all manage to suppress it in various fashions. We are incredibly efficient at compartmentalizing and adopting double standards and different personas for different contexts.

None of that changes the fact that we are moral agents operating in a deeply personal universe.

Special Revelation—God Himself

For a lot of people, faith in Jesus feels like an exercise in pretending and make-believe. It isn't easy for thinking adults to do. Bill Watterson's comic *Calvin and Hobbes* captured this sentiment perfectly in one particular strip:

> CALVIN: This whole Santa Claus thing just doesn't make sense. Why all the secrecy? Why all the mystery? If the guy exists why doesn't he ever show himself and prove it? And if he doesn't exist what's the meaning of all this?
>
> HOBBES: I dunno. Isn't this a religious holiday?
>
> CALVIN: Yeah, but actually, I've got the same questions about God.

I've observed that natural revelation is something most of us can understand and provisionally agree to without too much resistance. It is so generic and universal that it doesn't immediately offend our sensibilities.

Special revelation, on the other hand, is more complex and pushes our cosmological and psychological boundaries. It is referred to as *special* because it is received by more direct means. The most obvious kind of special revelation is to hear or see a manifestation of God Himself. God spoke audibly to Abraham on numerous occasions and appeared to Moses through a burning bush. He stood before Israel as a cloud of smoke by day and a pillar of fire by night. The prophet Daniel and others had visions and dreams that revealed God's presence and plan.

The ultimate special revelation of God is the incarnation of the second Person of the Trinity, the Son of God, in Jesus Christ. I always teach my Sunday school kids to remember the word *incarnate* by thinking about *carne* asada or chili con *carne*. *Carne* means *meat* or *flesh*. To be *incarnate* means to be *in the flesh*. The incarnation is about God taking on human flesh in order to most fully reveal Himself.

The incarnation is one of the hardest teachings of the Bible for people to swallow. It is one thing to talk about the existence of God. It is another thing to talk about a deposit of truth through a book. But to propose that transcendent deity took on phenomenal human flesh in order to die and rise to new life seems to be pushing it.

This concern is not only a modern one—it was especially significant in the ancient world. The Apostle Paul said that the concept of God incarnate coming to atone for humanity through death was ". . . to the Jews a stumbling block and to the Greeks foolishness, but to those who are called, both Jews and Greeks, Christ the power of God and the wisdom of God" (1 Cor. 1:23, 24).

For ancient Jews and Greeks, the notion of God suffering the humiliation of the incarnation and crucifixion was too much to embrace. It violated the Jewish aspirations for God to be universally vindicated among the heathen in the reestablishment of Israel. It violated Greek philosophy that considered the material world to be inherently corrupt. On its face, this doctrine made no sense to anybody.

I agree. The incarnation *is* pushing it. It challenges everything we might expect. It is very good and right to be astonished and flummoxed—possibly even offended—by the teaching of the incarnation. If you don't have that sort of reaction, you probably don't truly grasp the significance of it.

It helps many people to know that the Bible represents the incarnation as a radical act of humility and service by God. But reducing God to the form of a man still seems to make God too small. There is a sense in which the Bible agrees and disagrees with this.

On the one hand, the Bible teaches that in the incarnation the Son of God "emptied himself" as an act of love (Phil. 2:7). He did not empty Himself of His divine nature, which would be impossible, but He emptied Himself of His rights, privileges, and immediate glory. God was willing to stoop down and suffer as a human in order to serve and have fellowship with humanity.

On the other hand, remember that the Bible presents man as bearing the image of God. Therefore, Christ's taking on human flesh was not an automatic step in the direction of existential corruption or indignity. Humanity has the potential for glory that we have not yet witnessed in its fullness. Jesus came not only to die, but to be resurrected to a glorified life that is beyond our wildest reckonings.

We will be talking more about the *why* of Jesus in a later chapter. For the moment, it is simply important to understand that Jesus Himself is the highest expression and revelation of who God is. When we think about who God is, God wants us to think in terms of Jesus. We should not conceive of God as a blinding light or the vastness of infinite space. God reveals Himself in terms we can most clearly and intimately understand—as a man.

Special Revelation—God's Messengers

Of course Jesus is no longer physically present with us. So how can we know Him? Prior to his ascension, Jesus was quite clear that the world would know Him through two means—His Spirit-empowered people (the church) and His Word (the Bible).

The Bible often refers to the church as the "body of Christ." Christians are likened to living stones being built together as the new Spirit-filled temple of God. The Apostle Paul compared the church to a new man that brought Jews and non-Jews (Gentiles) together in peace.

The church is called to demonstrate a renewed humanity—new image bearers who reflect God's transforming presence in the world. As Christians unite in love to bringing healing and justice, we mirror the love and intention of God to make all things new.

The thought that Christians are a mode of special revelation is almost laughable to many of us. Have you ever seen a more dysfunctional group of knuckleheads? Am I going to tell you the Three Stooges were messengers of God too?

Of all the aspects of special revelation, this is the hardest one to believe and to participate in as a follower. Again, the Apostle Paul offers insight. He wrote,

> For consider your calling, brothers, not of you were wise according to worldly standards, not many were powerful, not many were of noble birth. Buy God chose what is foolish in the world to shame the wise; God chose what is weak in the world to shame the strong; God chose what is low and despised in the world, even things that are not, to bring to nothing things that are, so that no human being might boast in the presence of God. (1 Cor. 1:26–30)

In other words, God assembles some of the most severely broken pieces of humanity to reveal Himself. It is rare to see the most beautiful, powerful, and successful people called to God's purpose. God works this way to prove that it is ultimately His presence and wisdom that deserves praise, not ours.

When I meditate on this dynamic I can't help thinking about *The Bad News Bears*. The movie features the late Walter Matthau as Morris Buttermaker, an alcoholic former minor-league baseball player who is called on to coach a team of misfit children.

The story goes that a California-based competitive league was sued for being too exclusionary in their selection of players and teams. As a concession, they assembled the worst players in the city and assigned them to coach Buttermaker. Among the motley crew of players were an overweight catcher, nearly blind pitcher, and an outfielder with delusions of grandeur. In their first game they didn't get a single out and had to forfeit when the score reached 26 to 0.

By the end of the season the Bears were playing as a functional team and, this being Hollywood, they made it to the championship game. At that big moment, in a moment of self-awareness that his competitiveness had taken over in an exclusionary and destructive way, Coach Buttermaker put the benchwarmers on the field to make sure they had a chance to play.

And the Bears lost. But everyone acknowledged that the team had been transformed. The Bad News Bears had changed the way the league viewed the spirit of competition and dysfunctional people. Even the proud and privileged Yankees embraced them in a spirit of camaraderie.

The church is like the Bad News Bears. We're an extremely imperfect collection of bumbling and broken individuals. It is probably fair to say that we're "losers." We're clearly underdogs. When we're out on the field of play we often embarrass ourselves and deserve the laughs and scorn we receive. But that isn't where the story ends. Over the long course of time we are learning to play as a team, and the world will take note. Things will never be quite the same.

Special Revelation—God's Message

The last significant mode of special revelation is the Bible itself. I won't belabor this too much here since the next chapter is entirely devoted to it. However, there are a couple of things that are important to point out.

First, it is important to recognize that God's normative modes of special revelation have changed with different epochs of human history. The reason that we don't see miracle-working prophets and apostles moving from city to city today is that the era of revelatory foundation laying for the building of the church is over. The church itself is such a miracle that it is now sufficient to promote God's program. The age of miracle-workers has passed.

The Bible even goes so far as to say that the complex law code of the Old Testament, which addressed everything from what clothes to wear and what food to eat to the intricacies of the sacrificial system, functioned like temporary training wheels for God's people. The temple itself operated as a picture book for a child to visualize and experience a holy and sacrificial life in God's presence. The Apostle Paul says that these aspects of the Old Testament worked like a grade school tutor that is no longer necessary with the coming of Christ and his Spirit.

When it comes to God revealing Himself via miracles, we must remember that they are the rare exception, not the rule. If miracles were normative they would cease to be miracles. When people say things like "life is a miracle," they are missing a vital truth. In a specific theological sense, miracles are meant to be spectacular signposts pointing beyond themselves to the veracity of a given messenger or message from God.

I understand the impulse to refer to many wonderful aspects of our lives as miracles. We have lost our wonder and appreciation of basic things that convey profound beauty. But when we call these everyday occurrences and phenomena miracles, I believe we cheapen the nature of true miracle. Even the most spectacular sunset, the most breathtaking scenery, or the cutest baby appear according to the ordinary rules of nature. Miracles, on the other hand, break those rules—they are *super*natural.

Specific messengers validated by their ability to work fantastic signs and wonders are no longer necessary because we live in the age of the Spirit-filled Body of Christ. The days of adding to the Bible ended with the death of the first century apostles who were eyewitnesses to the resurrected Christ. The church of God proclaiming and demonstrating the word of God is the way God communicates at this point in history. The book of Hebrews states,

> Long ago, at many times and in many ways, God spoke to our fathers by the prophets, but in these last days he has spoken to us by his Son, whom he appointed the heir of all things, through whom also he created the world. He is the radiance of the glory of God and the exact imprint of his nature, and he upholds the universe by the word of his power (Heb. 1:1–3a).

If we want to encounter God and hear His voice, we do so now by the power of God's Spirit in close communion with His worshiping people who live according to His Word. The church is Christ's body and the Bible is like its DNA. Encountering God in nature is profound, but incomplete. In our current age, God speaks to us most clearly through these modes of special revelation.

When we come to the Bible, it is critical to understand it as a *performative document*. It is not meant to be merely read and mentally understood. It is supposed to be performed and experienced. It is more like sheet music to be played by musicians than a book full of spiritual abstractions to be pondered. If we read every issue of *Food & Wine* magazine but never make a single recipe, can we really say we have grasped its true significance?

Approaching the Bible as if it were a long Russian novel will completely miss the point. We may glean some important thoughts and ideas, but we will not get more than a glimpse of what it has to offer us. To properly understand the Bible we must pray over it, discuss it, sing and chant from it, pass it on to others, and, most importantly, obey it. Failure to perform it is tantamount to a failure to understand it.

Science and the Scriptures

Many people believe that scientific knowledge makes natural and special revelation superfluous and unnecessary. They think that the appearance of design and orderliness are mental projections onto nature rather than qualities inherent to nature. In a strictly materialist system, no divine existence, intention, or communication is suggested or required.

Without a doubt, the debate over origins and the role of God has been the chief battleground between science and Scripture for more than a century and a half. The big bang and its resultant evolutionary mechanisms are often touted as sufficient evidence to supplant transcendent explanations for the existence and development of life. Some have even promoted its tenets as a quasi-religious grand theory of everything—a fundamental explanatory framework that allows us to interpret all disciplines from cellular biology to human psychology.

Not all scientists adopt such ambitious philosophical extensions of big bang cosmology and evolutionary biology; however, belief in the mechanisms themselves has become a litmus test of intellectual credibility. They have attained the status of axiomatic first principles.

When the big bang and evolution are referred to as *theories*, that does not imply mere speculative hypothesis. *Theory* refers to accepted principles and propositions that guide activity—such as the notation conventions in "music theory." Music theory is not a hypothesis; it is the fundamental understanding of the way music is composed.[32] Failure to adopt big bang and evolutionary theory is therefore worthy of scorn within the scientific community and can even be career ending.

32 Collins, 142.

There is little doubt that multiple scientific and mathematical disciplines appear to substantiate the case for evolution from astronomic to atomic levels. The current evidences for the big bang are particularly persuasive. To the possible dismay of nature mystics, steady state theory of an eternal universe that is in a constant cycle of flux has collapsed. Galaxies in outer space are expanding outward from one another as if they were blown apart from a central blast point. The big bang's shock waves are still reverberating in the form of background microwave radiation.

Current biological research makes an equally compelling case for evolution. The genomic evidence showing commonalities across and between species is overwhelming. Chimpanzee DNA sequences differ from human DNA sequences by a mere 2.7 percent. Even the fruit fly shares 60 percent of its DNA with humans. The genetic record appears to be filling the physical gaps in the fossil record.

Intelligent Design and Creation Science

Some scientists have sought to scientifically justify the need for a governing designer in the study of origins by arguing for irreducible complexity. The aptly named intelligent design movement's reasoning is that some aspects of nature could not possibly have developed gradually. They argue that certain biological apparatuses would fail without the preexisting structure or function of some of its component parts.

While the intelligent design crusade made an initial media splash, it has suffered repeated blows as researchers systematically document mechanisms that explain how exceedingly complex systems and structures can arise over time. Plausible pathways for everything from eyeballs to flagellum have been postulated. Complexity alone does not appear to be sufficient to argue for a designer—whether divine or alien.

Even the concept of redundant design efficiency in the hands of a Creator is bending under the weight of shared chromosomal sequences that are akin to our apparently useless appendixes. The shared sequences seem to be genetic leftovers from a common family tree. They have no apparent function and have been frequently referred to as "junk" or "silent" DNA. It is as if technologically sophisticated automobiles are still being made with an antique style hand-crank on the front of the engine. Can such structures legitimately be signs of divine design efficiency? In the words of one geneticist, such design shows signs of being very "sloppy" and not particular intelligent.

Great swaths of the Christian establishment have assented to and incorporated the physical mechanisms of the big bang and evolution into their theological systems. However, resistance is still very strong in many religious quarters. Recent statistics show that up to 40 percent of the U.S. population still subscribes to a relatively young earth that was directly shaped by God's creative activity. Some Christians have even spawned their own creation science research to contend with aspects of big bang and Darwinian dogmas.

I find that creation science tends to push back on evolutionary orthodoxy in a couple of major ways. First, it continues to question how a strictly independent or random process could produce the kind of universe we find ourselves in. Such complexity requires an incredible amount of fine-tuning to exist. It seems to strain mathematical credulity to suggest that our universe generated under the precisely required cosmological conditions that would prevent matter from collapsing in on itself—not to mention support the emergence of life. The mathematical improbabilities are astronomical.

Some nonreligious astrobiologists have coined the term *Goldilocks zone* to describe the planetary conditions necessary to support a thriving biosphere. As in "Goldilocks and the Three Bears," the conditions cannot be too hot or too cold—they must be "just right." If you're too close, like Venus, the temperatures are too hot. If you're too far, like Mars, you freeze to death. The odds for life—not to mention sentient life—seem too great to be ascribed to so-called random events. Someone once compared the odds of intelligent life in our universe to the works of Shakespeare eventually being written by a room equipped with typewriters and occupied by monkeys for a long period of time. It is absurd.

A recent noncreationist book by Paul Davies, *The Goldilocks Enigma*, attempts to respond to this by outlining options to such life-limiting parameters. He postulates the following handful of possible conclusions:

1. *The absurd universe*—Things are just the way they are.
2. *The unique universe*—Some future theory of everything will explain why things are the way they are.
3. *The multiverse*—There are multiple universes and we happen to live in the one with the right possibility of combinations.
4. *Intelligent design*—A creator set the conditions that would support complexity and intelligence.

5. *The life principle*—A governing principle guides the universe toward life and sentience.
6. *The self-explaining universe*—Only universes capable of spawning consciousness can exist.
7. *The fake universe*—Our minds are part of a virtual reality simulation.

Creation science basically looks at these options and maintains that number 4 is the most reasonable option because there is historical evidence of revelation supporting it. The other possibilities do not have such support and are mere speculation. All of a sudden faith in God doesn't appear to be such a leap, does it?

I recently saw an online video that showed a shallow water octopus that had disappeared into the surrounding algae. And when I say disappear, I am not exaggerating. It looked like something from a Hollywood movie special effects team. The octopus had simultaneously and instantly changed its pattern, color, brightness, and surface texture to perfectly match the algae. It was one of the most astounding things I have ever seen. Creation science loves to find abundant examples like this and basically say, "Really? Random? Really?"

The second strategy of creation science is to point out anomalies and gaps in current scientific orthodoxy. For example, recent studies have shown that so-called "junk" or "silent" DNA may not be silent after all. Rather, the silent DNA appears to be active at different points in the life cycle. Even the analogy of the leftover or vestigial appendix is challenged as biologists find that it does have a function.

The bottom line is that creation science attempts to challenge the hubris of current orthodoxy by saying, "Not so fast, guys. There is so much we don't know; we should be careful about the way we think through this stuff. For goodness' sake, don't leap to massive quasi-religious conclusions based on what you think you know."

Parameters of Genesis 1

I am not a scientist, so it is difficult for me to weigh the merits of the discussion at that level. I certainly realize that even theories like the Goldilocks zone have been hotly debated and challenged.

However, at a theological level I definitely understand the reticence of many Christians to jump on board with some of the underlying assumptions of the scientific community. The very first chapter of the Bible, Genesis 1, is not scientific, but lays out significant parameters regarding origins. These are some of the principles that rise to the top:

1. *Creation was initiated by God*—God initiated and was highly engaged in the creation of the universe. It was not a wholly independent or random process that functioned autonomously.

2. *Creation was providentially guided by God*—God's process was purposeful and directive. The text says God made everything "according to its kind," which suggests that speciation was the result of some governing design.

3. *The phenomenal realm is good and very good*—In contrast to philosophies that denigrate the physical realm as inherently corrupt or existentially inferior, Genesis makes it clear that the material universe is good. It is something to be celebrated, cultivated, and enjoyed.

4. *Humanity was made in the image of God*—Humanity holds a special position and purpose in the created order. We are not merely sentient animals.

These theological and philosophical parameters significantly challenge any attempt to see the big bang or evolution as a grand theory of everything. They may represent mechanisms God used in a means to an end, but are not an end to themselves.

You may notice that I am not mentioning the old universe versus young universe debate tied to the six-day creation narrative of Genesis 1. While that is an issue for many people, I do not believe it is absolutely necessary to interpret these days literally or make them a point of contention. I will get into this more in later chapters, but allow me to briefly explain.

I have a very high view of the Scriptures and trust them very deeply, but I don't think the literary character of Genesis 1 requires belief in six literal days. The literary structure of Genesis comprises three major literary units that are unmistakable and widely accepted:

- Genesis 1 is the exalted prose narrative concerning origins.
- Genesis 2–11 traces the primeval history of mankind.
- Genesis 12–50 begins to record the history of God's redemptive program through Abraham's family.

Once we recognize that Genesis 1 stands as a particular literary segment, it frees us to look at it with special care. I believe that Genesis 1 is works like a literary diamond with multiple facets. When we hold the text in the light one way, we see a flash of brightness. If we turn it another way we see the burning flame in the center. We will be looking at this in much more detail in chapter seven, but let's look at one facet on the diamond of Genesis 1 for the sake of this conversation.

Some people approach Genesis 1 as if it is a straightforward historical and sequential telling of the days of creation. Fair enough—it is understandable how someone could read it that way. However, if we approach Genesis 1 as a hyperliteral historical account, one of the things we would have to conclude is that God created by verbalizing certain commands such as "Let there be light." Such a conclusion comes from a very simple and direct reading of the text.

But let's look at how one of Christ's preeminent apostles dealt with Genesis 1. As theologians would say, "Scripture interprets Scripture." In the first chapter of the Gospel of John, we read a parallel version of the creation account that reads,

> In the beginning was the Word, and the Word was with God, and the Word was God. He was in the beginning with God. All things were made through Him, and without Him nothing was made that was made. In Him was life, and the life was the light of men. And the light shines in the darkness, and the darkness did not comprehend it. (John 1:1–5)

This is fascinating. The Apostle John interprets the creative action of God typologically and symbolically, not hyperliterally. According to John, the verbal commands of God were not literal words that came from God's mouth. Rather, they were the creative agency of the second Person of the Trinity. The Word of God in the Genesis 1 creation narrative isn't a verbal command; it is Jesus, the Son of God.

If the Apostle John interpreted and even rephrased Genesis 1 in this manner, why should we be bound to a woodenly literal approach to the text that requires twenty-four hour days? When we make demands on a text that do not necessarily exist, we create unwarranted stumbling blocks for more important parts of the conversation.

I'm not offended by the interpretation that God created in six twenty-four-hour days. God was certainly capable of doing that, and I don't believe His ability to do so is in question. I don't even think it is a problem to find evidence that might argue for a young universe. I simply don't believe we should apply six-day creation as a litmus test for fidelity to the Bible. That is simply unjustified in the face of the particular text we're dealing with. Holding the conviction of a young earth is fine—making it a standard of orthodoxy or scientific reasoning is not.

History and Science

The larger concern Christians have is actually found in Genesis 2 and 3, concerning the fall of a literal Adam and Eve. Two theological issues are at stake here. The first is *original sin*, the belief that all of humanity inherited a sinful nature from our first father, Adam. The second is Christ's identity as the *second Adam*, a role that allows Him to redeem humanity by giving us a new, righteous nature. Part of the logic provided by the Apostle Paul for salvation is that since all of humanity fell through the disobedience of one man, Adam, it is also possible for many to be saved through the obedience of one man, Jesus. Removing the first Adam severely weakens and undermines the representative or "federal" model of sin and salvation. The threat of this logic unraveling the second Adam's atonement is very real.

A literal Adam is a very significant theological parameter for a coherent Christian worldview. A more symbolic reading of Genesis 1 is justifiable because of the way the Apostle John deals with it, but when the Apostle Paul interprets and uses Genesis 2 as true history, we need to pay close attention.

Different theories attempting to reconcile an evolutionary perspective with a historical Adam have been postulated, but I will not get into that here. Suffice it to say that the Bible does make historical claims that are part of the lifeblood of its system. If the historicity of the Bible is stripped away, its truth is lost.

The Bible is not a merely symbolic treatise on spirituality. Therefore, whatever provisional conclusion one comes to concerning evolutionary mechanisms, the parameter of a literal fall of a historical Adam is an extremely sensitive and important matter that must be carefully taken into account. A nonliteral reading of Genesis 1 does not undermine the Christian faith, but a nonliteral reading of Genesis 2 and 3 does. Hand-waving explanations about symbolic myth seem irresponsible at best.

I realize that scientists are concerned that inserting God into the scientific conversation of origins is inappropriate and tends to short-circuit scientific inquiry. Wherever we encounter ignorance it is easy to use God to fill in the gaps. Such a posture can circumvent, rather than promote research.

However, I believe that the issues at stake are largely philosophical and theological, not scientific. One can rigorously pursue scientific truth concerning origins without the philosophical baggage of a grand theory of everything, randomness, or mechanistic autonomy. Such assumptions are not prerequisites to the acquisition of knowledge. If the Scriptures are properly understood to put forth broad philosophical principles rather than specific mechanisms, that is no existential threat to scientific inquiry. It is a threat to monist materialism, but not to science, per se.

Though the empirical method of science is legitimate and necessary, our pursuit of knowledge—particularly scientific knowledge, is rarely linear or fixed. The process is iterative. In other words, we establish provisional knowledge about something and then it is challenged and further nuanced as time goes on.

The philosopher Georg Hegel described this activity as being *dialectic*. In dialectic process a thesis gives rise to a competing antithesis. The conflict of the thesis and antithesis then result in a synthesis—which becomes the new thesis. The process spirals on and on in our pursuit of knowledge and progress.

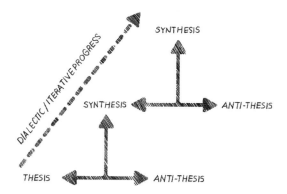

There is no need to interpret this model rigidly in order for it to have value. The point isn't that every position must be precisely negated in order to arrive at some kind of hybrid compromise. The idea is that points of tension in our conceptual paradigms are aids. They help us advance. We should look for them and become more aware of them instead of being resistant. Anomalies, apparent conflicts, and dots off the curve are our friends. They keep us humble and searching. This is especially true for the sciences that thrive on a "culture of doubt."

This iterative model of knowledge acquisition is not unique to the sciences. Every discipline works like this in some respect. You can even find it in the arts. Competing perspectives and internal challenges to the status quo activate creative activity.

I point this out because when we come to the issue of science and Scripture, we need to come with a high degree of self-awareness about our own philosophical biases and an epistemic humility about our provisional conclusions. All sides of the conflict would benefit greatly by taking a step back and reevaluating their working assumptions and interpretive models.

Epistemic Authority

For this reason, the debate over origins is a blessing to Christians. It allows us to point out that the disputes over certain details are outcomes of our underlying beliefs. They are the veritable tip of the iceberg.

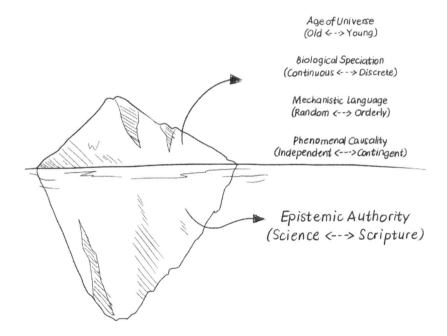

The true conflict isn't primarily about different empirical evidences. The primary conflict is over our sources and relationships of epistemic authority. Is it science *or* Scripture, or science *and* Scripture? If it is both, does one trump the other or are they separate? People don't tend to realize their assumptive framework in this regard, but they tend to fall in one of the following categories:

- *Science Alone*—Science is in no need of a revelatory reference point for its working philosophies or historical frameworks.
- *Scripture Alone*—The Bible is sufficient in and of itself to handle any issues of real significance in matters it speaks directly about.
- *Science Superior*—Where there is conflict between science and the Bible, science wins.
- *Scripture Superior*—Where there is conflict between science and the Bible, the Bible wins.
- *Separate Spheres*—Science and the Bible can never be in true conflict because they inhabit totally different conceptual spheres. Science addresses phenomenal realities and the Bible addresses transcendent and spiritual realities.

COMMON MODELS OF EPISTEMIC AUTHORITY

Science Alone	Scripture Alone	Science Superior	Scripture Superior	Separate Spheres
Science	Scripture	Science	Scripture	Scripture
NOT	NOT	OVER	OVER	Transcendent Spirituality
Scripture	Science	Scripture	Science	Science
				Phenomenal Realm

Thankfully, we don't have to work with the unwarranted assumption that evolution and creation or science and Scripture are mutually exclusive. They can coexist and even complement one another. Many people with deep commitments to the Bible believe that God used evolution as His chief mechanism in creation. If evolution is your scientific hill to die on, there is no need to throw out the concept of natural revelation. It is conceivable that God used evolution as part of His process.

The age-old theological debate in this regard is the tension between the so-called "book of nature" and "book of Scripture." Are they on par with one another, or does one trump the other? Should we see each as having authority in separate domains—science for physical realities and Scripture for spiritual realities?

At the outset I want to push back on an epistemological framework that radically divides physical and spiritual realities in this manner. I cringe when people say that the Bible is only valid when speaking in the spiritual sphere. After all, the Bible does present itself as a true historical witness. It is not just a book filled with spiritual meditations.

I think that we should view science and the Bible as having an integrative, iterative, and dialectical relationship, with each shedding light on the other. Rather than making one superior to the other, we simply recognize them as both reflecting truths that should be mutually complementary. One is more empirically oriented and the other is more historically and philosophically oriented, but these concerns don't operate in completely unrelated orbits.

Science

Empirical Data

Scripture

First Principles

Theory of Everything

Historical Points of Reference

We must be careful to distinguish without dividing. We can see things as distinct without separating them from each other. The Bible may directly address spiritual concerns, but it does not follow that it has no relationship or bearing on physical, historical, or scientific matters. All of these issues interpenetrate each other—the spheres overlap.

Of course, it is critical to recognize that the Bible is not a science textbook. It simply doesn't present itself that way. We must also understand that "all truth is God's truth." The fact that a certain truth is not mentioned or envisioned by the Bible does not mean it is less true. We do not find empirical formulas or techniques in the Bible. The Bible does not directly address the specific composition of the periodic table, how to perform heart surgery, or what flagella are. The Bible does not offer comprehensive knowledge of all things, and we should not expect it to.

String theory or quantum mechanics may be true ways of describing the way the universe works, but they do not explain everything. Science can address some *what* and *how* questions about the material world, but cannot answer the *why* and *what for* questions. They can strain at questions of origins without every totally resolving them. It is like trying to drive a Ferrari through a jungle—it isn't the right vehicle for that terrain.

The scientist must understand that phenomenal realm discovery will always give a proximate and limited perspective on reality. The only ultimate and comprehensive theory of everything is known by and through an ultimate comprehensive perspective. Only God has that perspective.

All of our endeavors, including scientific discovery, are meant to be a means of loving God and loving our neighbor. When scientists stray away from the principle of worship and love in their work, science becomes a false, hollow, and twisted idol. It violates the first commandment, which states that we are to have no other gods before God.

Jailing Copernicus

This all sounds nice in theory, but what happens when a scientific finding seems to be in direct conflict with the Bible? How do we avoid the problem of "jailing Copernicus?"

You may remember that Nicolaus Copernicus (AD 1473–1543) was an astronomer who proposed that the planets in our galaxy revolve around the sun, not the earth. This was in direct conflict with the official teaching and authority of the Roman Catholic Church, so Copernicus was thrown in prison for heresy.

The irony of the story is that the Roman Catholic Church was not anti-science, per se. In fact, they were zealous for science to align with their theology. The complex astronomical system they endorsed had stood for over a thousand years and was actually inherited from the Greeks.

Aristotle (382–322 BC) and Ptolemy (AD 87–150) had proposed a geocentric system that envisioned the planets moving in concentric circles around the earth. There was a very real sense in which the church had adopted scientific findings outside of its immediate tradition in order to validate its system. Philosophers and theologians sometimes refer to this problem as the church's choice between Jerusalem and Athens.

It may sound naive to us now, but we should remember that the geocentric system was an intricate and complex interpretation of observable data. If you observe the path of one of the planets in our solar system against the night sky it will temporarily appear to move backward before resuming its course. To make sense of this "retrograde motion," the ancients proposed that each planet was moving in its own circular path while orbiting earth in a circle. They had elaborate charts to scientifically explain their interpretation of the astronomical information. They weren't operating out of mere superstition and neither was the church.

The proposal of Copernicus upset not only the church, but almost 1,300 years of astronomical science in the West. It was a very big deal. The geocentric view did not arise from bad theology derived from the Bible. It may have been reinforced by bad theology, but it was not a direct result of it.

While there is no question that much of the controversy stemmed from taking earth (and, by inference, man) out of the center of the universe, there is another equally important layer that is often overlooked. The other cause was the Greek scientific commitment to and assumption of circles. Yes, circles. The symmetrical aesthetic and geometrical perfection of the circle was the interpretive lens of the Greek scientist. Even Copernicus was locked into circles—and this caused his theory to fall short of perfect acuracy. It wasn't until Kepler (AD 1571–1630) proposed elliptical orbits that the astronomical data finally aligned.

Neither of the driving assumptions of the Ptolemaic astronomical errors comes from or is supported by the Bible. Neither one. The Bible does not portray the earth as the center of our solar system, and it does not advocate for circles. The problem wasn't that science had been chained to the Bible, but that the institutional church had jumped onto the scientific bandwagon of the day seeking self-legitimacy. Until we understand this, we have not understood what the Copernican revolution represents.

So how do we keep from "jailing Copernicus"? How can science proceed without being chained to bad philosophy and errant theology and vice versa? I believe the answer is that we must stay in engaged in conversation about our working assumptions and interpretations. We must become students of both books—natural and special revelation.

When there is an apparent conflict between a theological position and a scientific finding, we should be excited that we are onto something important about our overall system of thinking. Rather than being dismissive of science on one hand or of the Bible on the other, we can seek out what is causing the tension. This is where we will find true progress in our understanding.

This is nowhere more evident and relevant than in behavioral sciences, such as psychology. I am amazed and dismayed by the divide that often exists between people who study human behavior and people who study theology. The scientists tend to strip the moral and ethical dimension out of human action and thought, while the theologians tend to discount environmental and biological factors. There is no reason for these disciplines to be in contention; they will serve people best when they work holistically and synergistically.

Science and theology can serve each other very well if we let them. If we remain patient with conflict and careful with our intellectual and emotional commitments, we will bear much fruit. There is no reason to fear jailing Copernicus if we approach these issues with greater self-awareness.

Multitalented actor Steve Martin has written a brilliant play entitled *Picasso at the Lapin Agile*. It is a humorous and profound fictional story about a meeting between Picasso and Einstein at a café in Paris. The conversation begins with each talking about the superiority of their approach to life—with Picasso representing art and intuition and Einstein representing science and rationality. By the end of the hilarious and ingenious dialogue, both characters agree that they are better off together than apart.

EINSTEIN: ...theories must be beautiful. You know why the sun doesn't revolve around the earth? Because the idea is not beautiful enough. If you're trying to prove that the sun revolves around the earth, in order to make the theory fit the facts, you have to have the planets moving backwards, and the sun doing loop-the-loops. Too ugly. Way ugly.

PICASSO: So you're saying you bring a beautiful idea into being?

EINSTEIN: Yes. We create a system and see if the facts can fit it.

PICASSO: So you're not just describing the world as it is?

EINSTEIN: No! We are creating a new way of looking at the world!

PICASSO: So you're saying you dream the impossible and put it into effect?

EINSTEIN: Exactly.

PICASSO: Brother!

EINSTEIN: Brother!

Picasso and Einstein hug[33]

I cannot recommend Steve Martin's work highly enough when it comes to these issues. He is able to tease out critical themes—albeit from a non-theological and non-Christian perspective—in ways that I cannot. This discussion can become very heavy, so it is nice to inject some levity into it.

Science and Scripture need not be in conflict. They are meant to be complementary witnesses to one another. Where we find this to be untrue, it is a signal that our understanding of one or the other—or possibly both, is off. Science and Scripture may function like an odd couple, but together they will help us come to more fully understand how *Jesus* is the grand theory of everything.

33 Steve Martin, *Picasso at the Lapin Agile and Other Plays* (New York: Grove Press, 2002), 57–58.

CHAPTER SIX
Demystifying the Dusty Book

Mystery is something that appeals to most everybody.

—Angela Lansbury

Growing up in a suburb outside of Cleveland in the 1970s and '80s was a little like living in an episode of *The Wonder Years*. It wasn't quite as pristine as *Leave it to Beaver*, but it was close. It was a delicious slice of middle-class, middle-income, Middle America. Other than the constant media hype about the threat of nuclear war with the Soviet Union and the token bully that terrorized my daily walk to elementary school, it was a pretty idyllic upbringing.

When I was a young boy my family attended a mainline Presbyterian church that is everything you might expect it to be. The membership was probably around two hundred people, we had a fully robed choir, a quilting club for geriatrics, a Sunday school equipped with flannel boards for Bible stories, and, of course, potluck dinners. What would a Protestant church in the Midwest be without its potluck dinners? I think they may actually have quasi-sacramental status, but I digress.

Like most churches, the pews were stocked with Bibles, hymnals, and scrap paper for doodling—otherwise known as offering envelopes. If there was one thing I found somewhat curious, it was that we did not touch or open the Bibles very much during worship. They more or less stayed in the pews. Most of their spines made a cracking noise when they were opened. I can even remember the unique smell of the pages on the few occasions I actually opened one.

Part of the reason the Bibles weren't opened much is because the sermons were typically semi-topical meditations on loving your neighbor. Not bad stuff, but not particularly focused on the biblical text.

The most memorable sermon I recall was titled "Is It OK to Pray for the Cleveland Browns to Win?" This was a relevant topic in Cleveland at the time and remains so to this very day. It is a live pastoral concern. Perhaps Clevelanders aren't praying hard enough.

As important as that football-themed sermon was, it left me wondering whether the Christian faith had any real relevance to the big questions of life. I remember looking at a pew Bible and thinking that it was a very large and mysterious book beyond my understanding. Some of the more serious-minded Christians I knew actually had thumb tabs sticking out of the sides of their Bibles—almost like it was an old-school dictionary. Was knowing the Bible somehow related to the dictionary or thesaurus? Needless to say, I was intimidated and confused about the character of its contents. Looking back on it, I think I was in good company.

While the precise statistics are hard to nail down, the Bible is recognized as the most widely published book in human history. According to some estimates there have been anywhere from 5 to 6 billion copies printed throughout time. Just to give that some context, Islam's Koran stands at roughly 800 million copies and J. K. Rowling's first Harry Potter book at 107 million copies.[34] In terms of its relative presence in the world of literature, the Bible is the 800-pound gorilla.

With so many copies in circulation and billions of adherents around the world, we might expect the general background, structure, and contents of the Bible to be better understood. Unfortunately, we would be sadly mistaken. The most basic characteristics of the Bible are not well grasped—even among Christians and Jews.

I was watching TV recently and one of the news commentators started pontificating about how the Bible is just an extended allegory that should be read accordingly. He never stopped to define allegory, but it sounded like a legitimate literary term so he went unchallenged.

---

34 PublishingPerspectives. "The Bible vs. Mao: A 'Best Guess' of the Top 25 Bestselling Books of All Time" http://publishingperspectives.com/2010/09/top-25-bestselling-books-of-all-time/.

In the same week a good friend of mine told me she believed the whole Bible is a metaphor. Again, there was no explanation of what the metaphor was, but it sounded like a thoughtful term so she went with it.

Just for the record, allegory is a literary device that uses fictional characters or settings to symbolically represent factual characters or concepts in a one-to-one relationship. For example, in the Chronicles of Narnia, by C. S. Lewis, the Lion, Aslan, symbolizes Jesus Christ. The whole story is an allegory for Christ's work in the world using Aslan and Narnia as the figurative tools. Allegory is a great literary device, but it is not the only literary mode of the Bible. In fact, it is barely present in a strict sense.

Metaphor differs from allegory, because it doesn't use a particular character or setting in a one-to-one symbolic relationship. Rather, metaphor uses a word-picture to describe another reality. For example, if someone says that Bill has the heart of a lion, that means that Bill is strong and brave. It doesn't mean he has a transplanted lion heart in his chest. Metaphor and figures of speech are used throughout the Bible, but saying "the Bible is a metaphor" makes no sense. It is not written as a mere figure of speech.

What Is the Bible?

So what is the Bible, anyway? Before we get into its contents, let's try to demystify it at a few levels. Here are some basic features to keep in mind:

- The Bible is not one long book, but a library of sixty-six books written by forty authors over the course of about 1,500 years.

- One of the reasons the Bible is long and diverse is because it reveals God's progressive work with humanity through history. It is an unfolding and epic drama of God's engagement with a severely broken world.

- The Bible's library collection includes many different types of literature—poetry, prophecy, history, and personal correspondence.

- The books of the Bible are organized by type of literature rather than strict chronology. (An outline of the categories appears on the next page.)

Old Testament	New Testament
Pentateuch – 5 Books The primeval history of the world and the formation of the Nation of Israel.	**Gospels – 4 Books** Four literary witnesses to the life, death, and resurrection of Jesus Christ.
Historical Books – 12 Books The history of the nation of Israel from approximately 1400 BC to 450 BC.	**History Book – 1 Book** The first 40 years of the early church after the ascension of Christ.
Wisdom Literature – 5 Books Worship, wisdom, and devotional literature of the Old Testament.	**Wisdom Letters – 21 Letters** 21 Letters from Christ's Apostles to churches in the 1st century AD.
Prophetic Books – 17 Books Texts that warned Israel about the consequences of its behavior and consoled Israel about its future.	**Prophetic Book – 1 Book** Book affirming the establishment of the new heavens and new earth in the face of persecution.

- The Bible is arguably the best-preserved and most proliferated ancient literature in history. These writings were received, painstakingly copied, and widely distributed by Jewish and Christian communities. Even though the original manuscripts no longer exist, the signs of the unspoiled preservation of their contents are compelling. There are more ancient copies covering a larger span of geographical space and time than any other text. Homer's Iliad boasts 643 early copies while we have over twenty-four thousand early copies of the New Testament. While there are some small differences in the extant reproductions due to scribal errors and editing, they are few and immaterial.

- The recent discovery of the Dead Sea Scrolls is a testament to the amazing preservation of the Old Testament texts. Even though they date to about one hundred years before Christ, books like the prophet Isaiah are more than 95 percent identical to the Hebrew Bible we use today.

- The original Old Testament was written in Hebrew and Aramaic, and the original New Testament was written in Koine (common) Greek. The texts of the Old and New Testament did not have assigned chapter and verse numbers until AD 1551.

- The books that finally "made the cut" as Scripture were organically received and recognized over time, rather than officially adopted by an anointed committee. For example, when the Apostle Paul wrote a letter to the Galatian church, that letter was copied and immediately went into circulation throughout the region. The broader faith community rejected other writings that aren't included in the Bible, such as the Gospel of Thomas, because they contradicted previously received Scripture or did not bear recognizable marks of genuine authority and authenticity.

What About All of the Different Bible Translations?

I often hear people complain that the Bible is unreliable because it has so many different translations. This is a great place to try and clear the air a bit.

Most people cannot read Hebrew or Koine Greek, so the biblical manuscripts have been translated into hundreds of different languages. While there may be many translations in any given language, there are two schools of thought when translating—formal equivalence and functional equivalence.

Formal equivalence attempts to translate word for word—even leaving culture-specific idioms and measurements in place for readers to decipher through further research. The goal is to minimize the role of the translator in implying shades of meaning so that the reader can do that on his own. The flow of thought can feel wooden and foreign at times, but that is a result of translation—not of the underlying text itself.

Functional equivalence attempts to translate more thought for thought and will seek approximate contextual idioms and measurements to make reading easier and more natural. This approach puts a greater burden on the translator not only to translate words, but also to interpret meanings on behalf of the reader. This makes the texts easier to read, but often obscures shades of meaning and nuance that are latent in the original language.

Differences in translations are a fact of life when dealing with any foreign language, but the differences are usually not so material that the basic meanings are lost. If someone wants to get closer to the actual texts themselves without a translator, there are many tools available to help them drill into the Hebrew and Greek. I personally like to have many translations available to me so I can get a sense of the way others are approaching the text.

Consider a section written from the Apostle Paul about his imprisonment in Rome. The following text is from Philippians 1:12–14, translated from Greek to English by the two schools of thought:

Greek Text (SBLGNT)

Γινώσκειν δὲ ὑμᾶς βούλομαι, ἀδελφοί, ὅτι τὰ κατ᾽ ἐμὲ μᾶλλον εἰς προκοπὴν τοῦ εὐαγγελίου ἐλήλυθεν, ὥστε τοὺς δεσμούς μου φανεροὺς ἐν Χριστῷ γενέσθαι ἐν ὅλῳ τῷ πραιτωρίῳ καὶ τοῖς λοιποῖς πᾶσιν, καὶ τοὺς πλείονας τῶν ἀδελφῶν ἐν κυρίῳ πεποιθότας τοῖς δεσμοῖς μου περισσοτέρως τολμᾶν ἀφόβως τὸν λόγον λαλεῖν.

Formal Equivalence Example (NASB)

Now I want you to know, brethren, that my circumstances have turned out for the greater progress of the gospel, so that my imprisonment in the cause of Christ has become well known throughout the whole praetorian guard and to everyone else, and that most of the brethren, trusting in the Lord because of my imprisonment, have far more courage to speak the word of God without fear.

Functional Equivalence Example (The Message)

I want to report to you, friends, that my imprisonment here has had the opposite of its intended effect. Instead of being squelched, the Message has actually prospered. All the soldiers here, and everyone else, too, found out that I'm in jail because of this Messiah. That piqued their curiosity, and now they've learned all about him. Not only that, but most of the followers of Jesus here have become far more sure of themselves in the faith than ever, speaking out fearlessly about God, about the Messiah.

The point of this small example is that while there are differences in translation, they are minor. There is no right or wrong way to translate—only variances depending on your goals.

Should We Read the Bible Literally?

One of my favorite family stories is about an evening my wife reviewed the Ten Commandments with my boys when they were about five and six years old. She asked them what the sixth commandment was and they correctly answered, "You shall not murder." The ensuing dialogue went something like this:

GINA: So what does, "You shall not murder," mean?

BLAKE: It means we can't kill people.

GINA: Well, not all killing is murder. Sometimes it is OK to kill people in self-defense or as a soldier in war. That kind of killing isn't murder. Murder is when we kill people by our own judgment out of anger or hate.

JORDAN: [Astonished] Wait, so we can kill people?

GINA: If someone is trying to hurt you or someone else, and the only way to stop them is to the kill them, then yes you may. You may also kill people if your country sends you to war.

BLAKE: [After a long pause] Can we kill them with a sword?

GINA: I guess you could kill them with a sword, but I don't think you would.

JORDAN: [Excited] So will they teach us to kill people with a sword in Sunday school at church?

I love this story because it is cute, but also because it makes an important point. We all come to the text of the Bible with our own priorities and perspectives. My little boys, under the influence of Power Rangers, couldn't quite interact with some of the nuances of the Ten Commandments without combining swords with Sunday school.

We may not have Power Rangers on the brain, but we struggle with the same dynamic. It is difficult to interpret anything with full objectivity because we see the world through our own biases, assumptions, and training.

This reality makes interpretation of literature—especially the Bible—one of the biggest issues on the table. The one comment I hear most frequently is, "You don't interpret the Bible literally, do you?"

A favorite scholar of mine likes to respond to this by saying that it depends on what *literally* means. It would be wrong to take a metaphor and understand its meaning in a concrete way. For example, when Jesus says, "I am the door," we do not interpret that to mean He is a boarded entryway with a brass handle. That kind of interpretation is literalism gone wrong and represents a form of hyperliteralism.

Without being hyperliteral, interpreting the Bible literally means we approach it *as literature*. If I pick up a work of poetry, I do not read it in the same way that I read a physics textbook. Poetry demands one form of literary engagement and analysis, and a physics textbook demands another.

Since the Bible is composed of various genres of literature, we must be prepared to read different parts of it in different ways. We interpret metaphor as metaphor, propositional teaching as propositional teaching, poetry as poetry, history as history, and so forth. To say that the whole Bible is an extended allegory or metaphor is nonsensical.

Scholars call this interpretive approach the historical-grammatical method of interpretation. Instead of looking for a hidden spiritual meaning behind the text, the primary goal is to discern what the authors originally intended to communicate to their audience. Before we can ask what a particular text means to us as individuals or as a community, we must first seek to know what it meant for its original audience.

Therefore, to properly interpret any literature we begin by trying to understand the history and context of the text—who authored it, who received it, the timing and circumstances of the writing, and so forth. We also give close attention to the genre, grammar, words, idioms, and literary devices that were used by the author.

The Protestant Reformation of the sixteenth century was particularly emphatic about this approach to the Bible. The Roman Catholic Church had promoted the idea that each biblical text had four meanings—literal, moral, allegorical (pointing to Jesus), and anagogical (pointing to eternity). While there is truth to the fact that there are different lenses through which we can approach certain passages of the Bible, this fourfold approach created deep concerns about fanciful interpretations that were not warranted. It tended to shroud the Bible in a cloak of impenetrable mystery that discouraged nonclergy from interacting with it.

Protestant reformers insisted on the perspicuity of the Bible—its "see-through-ableness." One of the largest Protestant councils of the seventeenth century declared that the Bible could be understood by anyone who made "due use of the ordinary means" of literary interpretation.[35]

---

35 Westminster Confession of Faith 1:7.

The intent was to take away unnecessary layers of mystery so that everyone would be encouraged the study it.

Even though we can never fully escape our own mental biases, this interpretive discipline cuts through a lot of the subjective mire and helps us strive toward significant interpretive agreement. There is no doubt that there are differences over many nuances and details, but the central messages are communally comprehensible.

When I was in high school, my family started attending a nondenominational Bible church led by a very gifted Scottish preacher, Alistair Begg. His wry sense of humor, charming Scottish brogue, and keen ability to explain the Bible make him an popular teacher and communicator. In fact, his ministry has expanded to include a nationwide radio program.

Pastor Begg was one of the first people in my life who taught the Bible in a way that made it strikingly relevant. I'll never forget a phrase he liked to use when describing the Bible. Try to imagine hearing this in a winsome Scottish accent: "The main things are the plain things, and the plain things are the main things." I love it. This is such an important truth that I wish more individuals would embrace. People should be encouraged to read the Bible because it is ultimately very accessible.

The only caveat I'd add to the "plain things" slogan and the overall Protestant interpretive ethos is that interpreting the Bible can still take a lot of hard work. Making the "due use of ordinary means" to interpret a text doesn't imply that it is always an easy task. Not all genres or texts are as user-friendly as others, and not all truths are immediately self-evident. In fact, some of the most satisfying understandings are the ones that are puzzled over for many years in concentrated study.

We would be well served to reconsider biblical literature as carefully constructed and intricate works of art. The authors of these books did not simply write whatever they recalled to mind in an everyday way, as if they were newspaper journalists reporting the who, what, where, and when. The authors functioned more like skilled architects or painters who painstakingly organized their content.

Perhaps you have had the experience of walking through a museum with a well-trained docent. Without the docent you can take in artwork at a very basic and immediate level. However, as the docent unpacks the story of the artist—the setting of the work, and the techniques used in the creation—you begin to appreciate the art in a deeper and more satisfying way.

Our encounters with the Bible often function in a similar manner. We can each read through the Bible and achieve a simple and sometimes profound understanding on our own—and we should do that. However, with the help of trained docents, our eyes open to other very important features that we might have unwittingly passed by.

For example, the Genesis story of Noah's Ark is well known to most people. According to the narrative, God decided to start over with a new world and a new humanity because original humanity was destroying itself and the earth—the very opposite of God's intention.

God chose a righteous man, Noah, to survive the coming cataclysm in order to preserve the human race and repopulate the new world. Noah's task was to build a large boat that would house his family and all the animal life he could gather—and he did this in the face of many scoffers and detractors.

When Noah finished his work on building and filling the Ark, torrential rains and massive seismic activity ensued for forty days and forty nights—wiping out all life on earth and radically changing its geological features. The waters did not abate for another one hundred and fifty days.

After living through the epic flood, Noah's family and the animals he had saved exited the Ark to spread out and repopulate the earth. God appointed a rainbow as a sign of peace to affirm the promise that He would never again wipe out the whole world with a flood. These glorious visual phenomena continue to show us a picture of a heavenly bow without an arrow—showing that God is not at war with humanity.

This beloved story is very rich in its details, meaning, and application. There is also a sense in which it is straightforward as stories go. Or is it? Allow me to play museum docent for a moment.

Chiasms in Scripture

One of the literary devices used throughout the Bible is something called a *chiasm*. This literary device can be applied to almost any genre of literature and is frequently used to structure the narratives and poetry of the Bible. Think back to your middle school English class and the way you could diagram a rhyming pattern that might look like:

A — (Roses are red)
B — (Violets are blue)
C — (Sugar is sweet)
B — (And so are you)

Chiasms are not rhymes, but they can be diagrammed using a similar A, B, C enumeration. The word *chiasm* comes from the Greek letter *chi* which looks like an X. The concept can be illustrated like this:

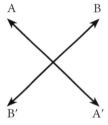

Going from left to right and top to bottom, we read A, B, B', A', and connecting the As and the Bs creates the shape of the X. The prime mark (') distinguishes the repeated letters in the second half of the chiasm.

More typically, a chiastic structure is diagrammed to look like the inside angle of the "x":

A
  B
    C
  B'
A'

The function of a chiasm is to point to the innermost subject (in this case, C). This subject or line is what the author wants us to pay particular attention to in our reading.

Gordon Wenham documents a fascinating example of a chiasm from the Genesis narrative.[36] Look at the following case from the story of Noah's Ark (the numbers to the right are the chapter and verse references from the book of Genesis):

---

36 Gordon J. Wenham, "The Coherence of the Flood Narrative" (*Vetus Testamentum*, Vol. XX-VIII, Fasc. 3), 338.

A   Noah (6:10a)
 B   Shem, Ham and Japheth (6:10b)
  C   Ark to be built (6:14–16)
   D   Flood announced (6:17)
    E   Covenant with Noah (6:18–20)
     F   Food in the Ark(6:21)
      G   Command to enter the Ark(7:1–3)
       H   7 days waiting for flood (7:4–5)
        I   7 days waiting for flood (7:7–10)
         J   Entry to ark (7:11–15)
          K   Yahweh shuts Noah in (7:16)
           L   40 days flood (7:17a)
            M   Waters increase (7:17b–18)
             N   Mountains covered (7:18–20)
              O   150 days waters prevail (7:21–24)
               P   *God Remembers Noah (8:1)*
              O'   150 days waters abate (8:3)
             N'   Mountain tops become visible (8:4–5)
            M'   Waters abate (8:6)
           L'   40 days (end of) (8:6a)
          K'   Noah opens window of ark(8:6b)
         J'   Raven and dove leave ark (8:7–9)
        I'   7 days waiting for waters to subside (8:10–11)
       H'   7 days waiting for waters to subside (8:12–13)
      G'   Command to leave the ark (8:15–17)
     F'   Food outside the ark(9:1–4)
    E'   Covenant with all flesh(9:8–10)
   D'   No flood in future(9:11–17)
  C'   Ark (9:18a)
 B'   Shem, Ham, Japheth (9:18b)
A'   Noah (9:19)

Notice that the center-point of the chiasm is God's remembering Noah. The author carefully structured the story to emphasize God's faithfulness to His promise to preserve Noah. The other details of the story are important, but they have been deliberately ordered to point to this main idea.

The author's intent was not for us to ruminate on God remembering Noah in a one-dimensional sense, but also to see God's mercy coming through at the climax of judgment. Just when all hope for humanity might have been lost—the world destroyed and its last survivors stranded on an ark—God's faithfulness emerges.

This juxtaposition of mercy and judgment is central to understanding God's paradoxical modus operandi and is seen time and again in the Bible. The center of the Noahic chiasm points forward to the ironic extension of mercy that breaks through in the crucifixion of Christ. God's judgment and mercy are intimately intertwined in ways we might never expect.

I am not highlighting chiasms because we must grasp them to decipher the Bible, but because I want people to begin to appreciate that biblical literature is intensely intricate and deliberate. It is more like a complexly woven tapestry worthy of focused awe and attention than a newspaper that is quickly devoured and discarded.

Think of the intentional and painstaking effort any author would have to go through to structure a story using a chiastic structure. It is not easy and it is most certainly not a random accident. Like a painting in a museum, it is a masterpiece to behold. I personally imagine Moses as a literary Michelangelo who labored long at organizing the structure and contents of the Pentateuch.

Of course, the artwork in a museum analogy should not be taken too far. The intent of the biblical authors was not to see the Scriptures enshrined behind glass cases or left on shelves with fine china. These documents were not written to be consumed at a distance, but to consume us down to the very marrow of our bones.

I had a theology professor in college who insisted that the students should never write in their Bibles out of respect for the sacred Scriptures. He was concerned that we might see our own margin notes as on par with the Biblical text.

This was very unfortunate advice, in my opinion. The biblical authors wanted our engagement with the Bible to be a highly active intellectual and emotional endeavor, not a passive scanning of the text. Writing in the margins, circling key words, noticing parallel phrases— these are just the sort of active methods they would approve.

As I reflect on the chiasm we jsut looked at, I am reminded of the award-winning movie *A Beautiful Mind*, featuring Russell Crowe as the ingenious and mentally ill John Nash. Nash was a mathematician who could see patterns in numbers where others could not. In fact, one of his areas of expertise was cryptology, the study of encryption and codes.

In the movie, encoded numbers seem to miraculously pop out of thin air to John Nash. It was almost as if he could magically penetrate streams of data with a quick glance. Unfortunately, because he suffered from schizophrenia he also imagined patterns where no patterns existed and connected events and people in ways that were totally illegitimate. Despite his brilliance, he struggled to discern fact from fiction.

I have wondered at times if a deep understanding of the Bible and seeing literary structures such as chiasms are parallel to the experience of John Nash. Does biblical interpretation require a brilliance that is unachievable to the average person? Should certain truths just pop out of thin air to us? When we think we see a chiasm, how do we know we are not delusional?

I don't believe recognizing a literary device is a pseudo-magical skill restricted to people with high IQs. Rather, it requires an awareness of the literary possibilities, deep textual familiarity, and a rigorous, helicopter-style reading that dives in and out to see details and the greater structure. In short, it takes a lot of time and work.

With that in mind, I believe that the unique genius of the Bible is that we can each interact with it at our own skill level. It is not housed in an austere museum with guards in each room watching your every move. Even children can understand and appreciate the story of Noah's Ark without ever understanding its chiastic structure. The Bible can legitimately engage everyone from the smallest child to the greatest literary scholar.

Scripture interprets Scripture

In fact, sometimes children make significant connections that adults struggle to make. I regularly teach third and fourth grade Sunday school at my church, and I am astounded at what the kids are capable of understanding. Sometimes coming to the text without lots of training works to your advantage.

One Sunday we were studying the life of Jacob recorded in the book of Genesis. That morning we were focused on the story about Jacob wrestling with an angel for a whole night. The strange story ends with Jacob being given a new name, Israel, which may be translated *God's wrestler*. Jacob had wrestled his whole life with God and man and had prevailed. Therefore, he was rewarded with a new name and a nation as his legacy.

Perhaps the strangest part of the story is that Jacob's hip was put out of socket, resulting in a permanent limp. This injury was given to him as a badge of honor. When people asked why he limped he could tell of the night he wrestled with God in order to receive the blessing of God.

I asked the children to think about Jacob's limp. Why would God give Jacob a limp for wrestling with him? Why not something else? What was the symbolism of the limp? I offered three Skittles candies to whoever could hazard a guess.

A little fourth grade boy slowly raised his hand and said, "It reminds us of the seed of the woman in Genesis 3:15 that would bruise his heel when crushing the head of the serpent. Jacob would limp like him." I am not exaggerating—that is what this boy said. Let's look at what he put together.

The third chapter of Genesis records the fall of Adam and Eve into sin. Satan had taken the form of a serpent and led Adam and Eve astray by questioning and undermining their faith God's goodness. This led to Adam losing trust in God and grasping at power on his own terms. When God came to confront Adam, Eve, and Satan, He issued judgments for each one. The judgment for Satan reads as follows:

> Because you have done this, cursed are you above all livestock and above all beasts of the field; On your belly you shall go, And dust you shall eat All the days of your life. I will put enmity between you and the woman, And between your offspring and her offspring; He shall bruise your head, And you shall bruise His heel. (Gen. 3:14, 15)

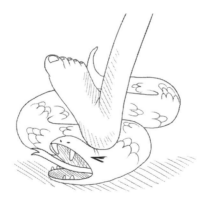

Theologians refer to this amazing passage in Genesis as the *protoeuangelion*, or *first gospel*. Immediately after the fall into sin, God promised to use a miraculously born human (seed of the woman) to destroy Satan and his program of death. It alludes to the fact that Satan would be fatally crushed, but the Savior would merely suffer...and limp away in victory.

Christians believe this points forward to the suffering Savior embodied in Jesus Christ. Jesus had to suffer the cross to defeat Satan. His suffering and death were real, but He prevailed in His resurrection. Jesus is the limping victor prophesied about from the very beginning of Genesis.

This little nine-year-old boy knew the stories well enough to recognize the bruised heel motif. He could not define a motif or a metaphor. He wouldn't know a chiasm from a croissant. But he was able to see how different parts of the Genesis text resonated to one another ... and he could see how it anticipated the suffering Savior to come.

This is one of the great paradoxes of the Bible. Mature interpretation demands a level of familiarity with the text alongside a childlike wonder at the same time. If you lack one or the other you are likely to miss much of what is being offered to you.

Of course, there are some childish errors to avoid. The most common mistake is to approach the Bible as if it is a merely an elaborate version of Aesop's Fables. You probably remember familiar tales such as, "The Boy Who Cried Wolf," "The Tortoise and the Hare," and "The Lion and the Mouse." Aesop wrote these amusing stories to teach moral lessons to children. Each fable carried a clear message about human behaviors and attitudes.

What often happens is that people interpret the narratives of the Bible as if they are nothing more than historicized morality plays. A well-known example of jumping to a moralistic reading can be found in the account of David versus Goliath. In this beloved story, the Israelites are constantly being threatened and terrorized by the neighboring Philistines. Instead of engaging in full-blown battle, warring peoples would occasionally send their respective champions into a one-on-one fight. For this conflict, the Philistines challenge the Israelites to find a champion worthy of contending with their heavily armored giant, Goliath. Unfortunately, no Israelite warrior is willing to step forward in the face of such an opponent. The situation looks hopeless for Israel.

And then something truly amazing happens. A young country boy named David volunteers to fight. He is deeply angered by Goliath's insults of God, and can no longer tolerate Goliath's slanders. As a faithful Israelite and a skilled shepherd who often defended his family's sheep from dangerous predators, he knows he can vindicate Israel with the help of God. Refusing unfamiliar weapons and armor that was too heavy to carry, he steps onto the battlefield with a mere sling. It looks like sure suicide.

As the story goes, David quickly drops Goliath by slinging one smooth stone into his forehead. Before Goliath can even swing his sword, he is dead. David, the country shepherd, steps up to Goliath's body, grabs the giant's sword, and proceeds to chop his head off. As he holds the decapitated head aloft for all to see, the ranks of soldiers stand in awe. God has been vindicated through the faithful and small act of a mere boy. Israel not only wins the battle, they have a new champion who will later become one of their most important kings.

So what should we take away from this story? I cannot tell you how often I hear interpretations that simplistically conclude we should imitate the qualities of David. We are called to be faithful or brave like David. Our faith can slay the giants in our lives, and so forth. The approach is to find a moral quality or lesson in the story and directly apply it to our situation.

Now for the record, I think we *are* encouraged to be faithful and brave like David. Our faith *can* slay giants and move mountains. I don't dispute any of that in principle. However, I don't think that is how we're supposed to approach this text or others like it. As hard as it is for us to do as modern readers, we need to take a step back and see what other themes emerge.

The story of David and Goliath is very rich, so we can only scratch the surface here, but allow me to give three examples of what I'm referring to. We will briefly look at each one and then put them together.

First, we encounter the theme of a shepherd doing battle. This is huge. Abel, the first son of Adam and Eve, was a faithful shepherd. The patriarchs, Abraham and Jacob, were shepherds. Even Moses was a shepherd after fleeing Egypt. Some of the most faithful men recorded in the Bible were assigned the unglamorous job of guarding defenseless sheep.

We know that this occupation has symbolic meaning because of its inherent imagery and because one of the most familiar Psalms, one written, in fact, by David, tells us so. David begins Psalm 23 with, "The Lord is my shepherd...." There is a sense in which we see God shepherding His people, who are like defenseless sheep. He tends and guards them from treacherous predators.

Second, a wound to the head killed Goliath. He could have died a number of ways, but God chose to kill him by a swift strike to the head. Students of the Bible will notice that this is only one of several significant head wounds in the Bible. Remember the one we just reviewed from Genesis 3, which foretells the seed of the woman striking the head of the serpent Satan. Another famous head wound was delivered to Sisera, the commanding officer of a Canaanite army that had tormented Israel. A devout Israelite woman, Jael, lulls Sisera to sleep and drives a tent peg through his temple. A fatal wound to the head vanquishes the enemy leader and his minions.

Finally, God defeated a powerful enemy in a totally unexpected and deeply ironic way. If Hollywood had scripted the story, Israel would have rolled out an even bigger giant riding a tank with awesome flame-throwers. Strength would have been met with greater strength. However, God prefers to do the opposite. He uses the weak to defy the strong. God loves to win battles using unexpected means.

When we put this all together we start to see that the story of David and Goliath tells us more about God than about our own behavior and attitudes. It tells us something about the kind of deliverer God is and the kind of deliverance He provides for His people. He is like a shepherd who comes to battle as the clear underdog. Defeat appears inevitable, but God wins by dispensing a lethal blow to our enemy. As the sheep of His pasture, we can look to Him to deliver us accordingly. The story of David versus Goliath points us to this reality.

Of course this is also where Jesus comes in. He identified Himself as the true shepherd of Israel. He was willing to lay down his life for the sheep. We would never expect such an ostensibly powerless man who was put to death on a cross to vindicate God and save us, but that's just what he did. Jesus is King David's greater Son. He is God's true champion, the seed of the woman, who delivered the head wound to Satan by his death on the cross. The irony is intentional.

This kind of interpretation is called *typology* because it recognizes character types and narrative themes that appear throughout the whole Bible and sees how they resonate with one another. Some people perceive this as a rather fanciful and daunting approach. However, we see that Jesus and his followers interpreted the Old Testament in precisely this way. When Jesus said that no sign of his identity would be given to certain individuals except for the "sign of Jonah," He was saying that He would be dead for three days—like Jonah was in the whale for three days. Jesus interpreted Jonah typologically, not moralistically. Other examples abound.

A helpful reference point for typology in modern literature can be found in J. R. R. Tolkien's *Lord of the Rings* trilogy. Many people thought that this epic should be read as an extended allegory that reflected the world wars of the twentieth century, as if the evil Sauron stood in a one-to-one symbolic relationship for Hitler. Tolkien was very emphatic in his general disdain for allegory as a genre and was clear that he had not written one.

However, there is little doubt that Tolkien used typology. The Christ-types are obvious. Gandalf dies and resurrects to a glorified state of being. Aragorn suffers humiliation as a ranger, but is later exalted to his rightful place as king. Sauron is defeated by a small and seemingly harmless Hobbit. Evil is ironically conquered when Gollum grasps for power one last time. The Christ figures are unmistakable, but none of them has an allegorical one-to-one correspondence. Each of them resonates to Christ in a unique way.

Bottom line: if people read the Bible as if it is just a book of rules or a morality play, they are missing the big picture. The Bible does contain rules and an ethical code, but that is not its main subject. God's deliverance of a broken world is the central point and everything pivots around that center of gravity. When we lose sight of this, we simply miss the point.

I have to chuckle when people are dismissive of the explicit ethical code of the Bible as if it were oppressive. After all, the first command found in Genesis 1 is for humanity to "be fruitful and multiply." In other words, get married, have a lot of sex, and make babies. That is literally God's first command. Pretty oppressive stuff, right?

Another common misstep is to interpret the Bible in an individualistic vacuum. The books of the Bible were mostly written for communities of people. That means that we should not interpret exclusively in isolation from others, but in community. Sometimes this is very challenging, but it brings a depth of understanding that cannot be achieved on one's own.

Interpreting the Bible literally—or as literature—is one of the most stimulating endeavors we can engage in. Instead of approaching the text with cynicism or intimidation, we should be encouraged to roll up our sleeves and get to work.

Doesn't the Bible Contradict Itself Since It Is Man-Made?

Perhaps the chief concern people have about the Bible is its claim to be of divine origin and authority. There are two lines of related reasoning: First, shouldn't we expect the Bible to be flawed since flawed humans wrote it? Second, if there are contradictions within the text of Scripture, how can it be relied upon as a divine guide?

It is very true and worth noting that the Bible does not present itself as a tome that fell out of the heavens one day. An angelic host did not drop the Bible off while CNN covered it on live television. As we previously noted, that is not how revelation works in the Judeo-Christian system.

While humans are deeply flawed individually and collectively, remember that the Bible presents humans as being made in God's image. Therefore, it is possible and even logical to use humans as God's messengers.

Can't humans achieve amazing things with incredible accuracy? Can't we draw perfect circles using tools of our own making? Haven't we built pyramids, sent people to the moon, and plumbed the depths of the human genome? Humans are flawed, yes, but to assume they cannot be used to communicate some aspects of transcendent truth is unwarranted.

One of the beauties of the Bible is that it reflects human diversity over a long period of time. It is not an exercise in word-by-word divine dictation. There are portions that are a direct transcription of God's words, but most of it is a providentially guided product of the minds of the people who were writing. God uniquely and purposefully shaped their lives in ways that prepared them to compose words that convey His truth.

I have quoted the Apostle Paul quite a bit so perhaps we should consider him for a moment. Before converting to Christianity, Paul's name was Saul. He was a high-ranking Jewish religious leader who led vicious persecutions against Christians because he thought they were blasphemous and dangerous. His violent response did not come from pure ignorance, because he was a very well regarded Jewish teacher and theologian of his day. He knew his Old Testament Scriptures very well.

One day Christ miraculously confronted Saul on his way to Damascus. In an astonishing turn of events, Saul converted to Christianity and went on to become one of the most important Christians of all time. He wrote a good portion of the New Testament Scriptures and planted churches throughout the Mediterranean. He is widely recognized as one of the most prominent figures of theological and philosophical thought.

His extensive theological background and cultural networks combined with his repentance for persecuting Christ to prepare him specially to be used by God. When we read Paul's letters we are not reading divine dictation. However, we are reading someone who was rightfully given authority to explain the death and resurrection of Christ in light of the Jewish Scriptures of the Old Testament.

The wide diversity of the people who were used to write the Bible actually speaks to its veracity. It is no small thing to have such literary coherence from forty authors over a period of 1,500 years. In fact, it is its own kind of miracle and why the Bible has stood the test of time.

But doesn't the Bible contradict itself, nevertheless? Isn't the Bible internally inconsistent with itself even if we grant that humans are a possible vehicle for passing on God's truth? Don't these problems prove that the Bible is merely manufactured?

Narrative Discrepancies

When I was a freshman at Indiana University, one of my classes was an introduction to the New Testament. My professor had us start in the synoptic Gospels—Matthew, Mark, and Luke. They are called *synoptic* because they are *seen together* (syn = together + optic = seen). They are so-called because they cover substantially the same material about the life of Jesus Christ. In fact, some of them tell the same stories in almost the same way. And that is the key—*almost* the same way.

For example, some of Christ's famous teachings are recorded with variations in the details. Here is a particularly poignant parable from Jesus for us to chew on:

Matthew 13:18–23
Hear then the parable of the sower: When anyone hears the word of the kingdom and does not understand it, the evil one comes and snatches away what has been sown in his heart. This is what was sown along the path. As for what was sown on rocky ground, this is the one who hears the word and immediately receives it with joy, yet he has no root in himself, but endures for a while, and when tribulation or persecution arises on account of the word, immediately he falls away. As for what was sown among thorns, this is the one who hears the word, but the cares of the world and the deceitfulness of riches choke the word, and it proves unfruitful. As for what was sown on good soil, this is the one who hears the word and understands it. He indeed bears fruit and yields, in one case a hundredfold, in another sixty, and in another thirty.

Mark 4:13–20
And he said to them, "Do you not understand this parable? How then will you understand all the parables? The sower sows the word. And these are the ones along the path, where the word is sown: when they hear, Satan immediately comes and takes away the word that is sown in them. And these are the ones sown on rocky ground: the ones who, when they hear

the word, immediately receive it with joy. And they have no root in them-selves, but endure for a while; then, when tribulation or persecution arises on account of the word, immediately they fall away. And others are the ones sown among thorns. They are those who hear the word, but the cares of the world and the deceitfulness of riches and the desires for other things enter in and choke the word, and it proves unfruitful. But those that were sown on the good soil are the ones who hear the word and accept it and bear fruit, thirtyfold and sixtyfold and a hundredfold.

Luke 8:11–15
Now the parable is this: The seed is the word of God. The ones along the path are those who have heard; then the devil comes and takes away the word from their hearts, so that they may not believe and be saved. And the ones on the rock are those who, when they hear the word, receive it with joy. But these have no root; they believe for a while, and in time of testing fall away. And as for what fell among the thorns, they are those who hear, but as they go on their way they are choked by the cares and riches and pleasures of life, and their fruit does not mature. As for that in the good soil, they are those who, hearing the word, hold it fast in an honest and good heart, and bear fruit with patience.

You can easily see that each version of this parable is different. No difference is particularly material to the message, but the versions are not precisely the same. Doesn't this negate any possibility that they are divinely inspired words worthy of our trust?

There is more here than we can cover exhaustively, but let's try to hit a few important issues. First, for all of their differences, they are strikingly similar. Most modern scholarship has been focused on how these documents could be so similar. Some scholars even theorize that the authors of the synoptic Gospels were copying either each other or another source that is no longer extant.

Whatever conclusion one draws about the author's source materials or documents, I think we need to start by recognizing the amazing *consistency* of these testimonies. That is actually what I believe ancient cultures would have noticed, and the purpose would have been clearer to them. Namely, according to the Jewish Scriptures a matter had to be established by two or three witnesses. Deuteronomy 19:15 says, "Only on the evidence of two witnesses or of three witnesses shall a charge be established."

We are given multiple Gospel accounts because they function as multiple witnesses to establish evidence. They are not needlessly redundant, but are a collective argument for the true history of Jesus Christ.

This is why the early church recognized them as bearing the marks of Scripture. Do we think people in the first and second centuries were oblivious to the differences in each record?

It is helpful to remember that Jesus was an itinerant teacher of sorts. He was almost like a Jewish Johnny Appleseed, throwing the seed of his teaching up and down the nation of Israel. It only makes sense that he told the same parables over and over again to different audiences. I'm sure he varied some of the language from time to time as any circuit speaker does.

Therefore, the authors are not passing on a corrupted and anti-historical record of the teachings of Jesus. Each author is bringing forward a legitimate version or amalgamated version of Christ's teaching. This doesn't constitute a contradiction or an inconsistency, just an important perspective that gives us more to shades of meaning to interact with.

Of course this is one of the easier kinds of so-called Bible problems to handle. There are tougher ones, such as how many angels were at the empty tomb after Jesus was resurrected. Matthew 28:5 mentions one and John 20:12 mentions two. How can both be true?

In most examples like this we have to make a distinction between an omission and a formal contradiction. In this case and others like it, the text doesn't necessarily commit a formal fallacy. It is not as if Matthew said there was *only* one angel. He simply chose to focus on the angel who spoke. We should not be overly concerned that a simple omission by one narrative version constitutes an irresolvable conflict with another.

Transcription Errors

We must acknowledge that there have been some transcription errors in the copying of the Bible that leave us with gaps in our knowledge of the original writing. For example, Jehoiachin is said to be coronated at age eighteen in 2 Kings 24:8, but at age eight in 2 Chronicles 36:9. This reveals flaws in scribal transmission, but does not necessarily imply that the original texts were untrustworthy. It simply means that there are minor issues with the preserved manuscripts that we have in our possession.

Historical Correspondence

Some people are very concerned that there is a lack of historical correspondence between particular historical claims of the Bible and other historical records. For example, there is an apparent conflict between

Luke and the extrabiblical historian Josephus concerning the census that was taken around the time of Jesus' birth. Luke's Gospel suggests that Quirinius was governor around 7 BC, while Josephus suggests that Quirinius was governor around AD 6. Is the Bible incorrect?

In this case and others like it, there is some evidence that vindicates the Scriptural record, and there are some cases where the extrabiblical record and the Bible simply differ. At that point we are left with two different historical testimonies. Should we assume that the Bible is the invalid witness? I don't see why that should be the case in light of the incredibly accurate testimony the Bible consistently presents.

Thematic Inconsistencies

Perhaps the biggest area of concern beyond these technical challenges is where the Bible seems to contradict itself more broadly and thematically. Should we still stone adulterers as the Old Testament law suggests, or should we have mercy as Christ had on the adulterous woman?

These kinds of issues need to be approached as theological questions rather than textual problems. The Bible is a long book that covers many different eras of God's engagement with humanity. Diversity is inherent to the Biblical enterprise. This doesn't reflect explicit incoherence unless we are unwilling to wrestle with the possible meanings of such variety.

Since we will begin the next chapter by looking at Genesis 1, I want to briefly address a concern I often hear: Don't Genesis 1 and Genesis 2 constitute two differing and competing narratives of creation? Doesn't this back-to-back conflict right from the outset of the Bible show that this book is fundamentally flawed?

This particular line of questioning belies a superficial approach to the biblical literature itself. Genesis 1 is clearly constructed in a very different way than Genesis 2. We will explore its structure more in the next chapter, but for the moment we only need to recognize that the difference between Genesis 1 and 2 is a literary signal, not a textual problem.

Think of it this way. Genesis 1 functions almost like an overture to a Broadway musical. Before the curtain is raised and any actors come out on the stage, the orchestra plays a musical preview of all the themes you will hear throughout the play. We get a sense of the kind of play we're going to watch before the first scene is even started. The overture helps us anticipate what lies ahead and what kind of musical we have come to see.

From a literary perspective, that is the relationship between Genesis 1 and Genesis 2. Genesis 1 is the overture, and in Genesis 2:4 the curtain is raised. Scene 1 of Act 1 begins in Genesis 2:4. There is no conflict at all—only literature that begs to be interpreted.

Isn't the Bible Culturally Antiquated and Irrelevant?

I hope that after working through these questions that you have a greater appreciation for why the Bible has stood the test of time. Even if the Christian faith is not compelling for you, I trust that you will look at the Bible with different eyes.

That being said, I know many people think the Bible is a culturally antiquated, ethically backward, and completely esoteric book that is irrelevant to modern life. Isn't it an inherently patriarchal, chauvinistic, and naive view of life and culture?

The only way to really answer this is to wade into the Bible itself. However, I would like to ask—is teaching about private property and communal responsibility irrelevant? Are sexual ethics and the ordering of the family irrelevant? What about the limits and function of government? The list goes on and on—penal justice, economics, educational pedagogy, loving the poor, principles for marriage, etc. The Bible may be very ancient, but to say it is irrelevant is highly irresponsible.

Is the real problem that the Bible is irrelevant or that we don't like what it has to say? Or maybe we don't know what it has to say?

Whenever I have the opportunity to teach the Bible I am reminded of one of my favorite quotes. A great preacher, Charles Spurgeon, was once asked how he defended the Bible. He answered, "Very easy. I defend the Bible the same way I defend a lion. I simply let it out of its cage."

CHAPTER SEVEN

The Bible's Big Idea(s)

Heaven is under our feet as well as over our heads.
                                        —*Henry David Thoreau*

Every high school in America has one or two notorious classes that rep-resent a kind of rite of passage. When I attended Solon High School outside of Cleveland, those classes were AP calculus with the veteran Mr. Thompson and AP English literature taught by the infamous Mrs. Reed. Since I have generally been more verbally inclined I opted out of AP Cal-culus and decided to wade into Mrs. Reed's class. It was a game-changer.

Until the time I took Mrs. Reed's class I had a very narrow understand-ing of literature. Literature was just an elitist and snobbish form of enter-tainment—kind of like ballet or something. Shakespeare and the like were about as appealing as tea and crumpets to a hillbilly. If you're looking for a good story, try Star Wars (preferably Episode V), for goodness' sake.

True to my Midwest roots I felt that if people wanted to articulate an issue of principle they should be up-front about it. Don't beat around the bush. Skip the fancy talk. Say what you mean and mean what you say. Give me the bottom line. I wanted to take the straight-talk express, all the way.

In that straightforward spirit, I have an important theory: Some teach-ers teach because they enjoy watching the positive transformative process that happens in the lives of students as they become more educated. They find satisfaction in watching another person's understanding grow. Oth-er teachers seem to be motivated by watching certain students writhe in agony as their mental frameworks are slowly destroyed and ground into

149

dust. With all due respect and begrudging affection to Mrs. Reed, I think she was driven by the latter motivation. She loved and lived for the chance to get her claws into naive students like me. We were her natural prey, and she relished every tasty morsel of our psychological anguish.

Since we're thinking about high school AP literature, please solve this analogy:

Kryptonite is to Superman as _____ was to teenage Brett Bonecutter.

A. Pizza
B. *Wonder Woman*, starring Lynda Carter
C. Cheeseburgers
D. *The Love Song of J. Alfred Prufrock*, by T. S. Eliot

If you chose D, T. S. Eliot, you have passed this part of the exam with flying colors; please read on. If you didn't pass, please read on, anyway.

I'm not sure why, but something snapped in my soul on the day Mrs. Reed introduced the poetry of Eliot. I had clearly met my personal nemesis and it was obvious that Eliot and Mrs. Reed would win the battle. All was lost.

Eliot was an American-British writer, playwright, and literary critic who became famous in the early twentieth century for helping to usher in the modern age of poetry. He was even awarded the 1948 Nobel Prize in Literature for his accomplishments. On the lighter side of Eliot's work, his collection *Old Possum's Book of Practical Cats* is the basis of Andrew Lloyd Webber's Broadway musical *Cats*.

But *The Love Song of J. Alfred Prufrock* was not on the lighter side. If you have never read the poem, don't worry. I am not going to an extended foray into it here; I just want to dwell on it for a moment. Here is an excerpt from the beginning of the poem:

> *S'io credesse che mia risposta fosse*
> *A Persona che mai tornasse al mondo,*
> *Questa fiamma staria sense piu scosse.*
> *Ma pericicche giammi di questo fondo*
> *Non torno vivo alcun, s'Todo il vero,*
> *Senza tema d'infamia ti rispondo*

Let us go then, you and I,
When the evening is spread out against the sky

Like a patient etherized upon a table;
Let us go, through certain half-deserted streets,
The muttering retreats
Of restless night in one-night cheap hotels
And sawdust restaurants with oyster-shell:
Streets that follow like a tedious argument
Of insidious intent
To lead you to an overwhelming question . . .
Oh, do not ask, "What is it?"
Let us go and make our visit.

In the room the women come and go
Talking of Michelangelo . . .

As I began to read the poem I became aware of a critically serious problem. The first stanza was incomprehensible gibberish. What language was it, anyway? Who had time to read this kind of stuff? Do I get a secret decoder ring with the poem to figure this out? Is this a word-scramble from the back of a cereal box? Why describe an evening on a date to an anesthetized patient awaiting surgery? Why, Mrs. Reed and Mr. Eliot, why? My internal alert status was at DEFCON 1.

But then something changed.

Specific memory of the way my resistance transformed from understanding to passion is a little hazy because of my emotional state. Only fragments of the incident remain. As we discussed the initial allusion to Dante's *Inferno* and the meaning of the achingly exquisite lines I felt something strange stirring in me. T. S. Eliot had managed to communicate deep frustration and angst without saying, "J. Alfred Prufrock was a sexually frustrated man who felt isolated and futile in his superficial and drab urban environment. Don't you feel like that too?"

Mrs. Reed had successfully cracked the ice. She showed me that literature isn't just about propositional truth—it is about the beauty of truth. Sometimes the beauty can be felt before we totally understand it. Barren propositions rarely move us because they are not interesting. They have no heart.

As we wade into the first text of the Bible, Genesis 1, I sense that many people will feel the same kind of resistance I did to Mrs. Reed and Eliot. Our patience for wrestling with certain literary forms of communication may not be particularly high. It may be tempting to emotionally opt out or become frustrated with the process of discovering what is set before us, but we need to hang tough.

Think back to some of your English classes in high school and college. The opening sentence of any great literary work is vitally important. Remember these great words?

Call me Ishmael. (*Moby-Dick*, Herman Melville)

It was the best of times, it was the worst of times. (*A Tale of Two Cities*, Charles Dickens)

Mother died today. (*The Stranger*, Albert Camus)

He was an old man who fished alone in a skiff in the Gulf Stream and he had gone eighty-four days now without taking a fish. (*The Old Man and the Sea*, Ernest Hemingway)

It was a pleasure to burn. (*Fahrenheit 451*, Ray Bradbury)

Perhaps the most famous first literary words of all time are found in Genesis 1:1.

In the beginning, God created the heavens and the earth.

These words may be very familiar to us, and that can create a problem because we read them far too quickly and miss the intended meaning. I want to suggest an alternate, albeit nonliteral reading of Genesis 1:1. Consider understanding it like this:

This is the story about God, heaven, and earth.

It is important to suggest this because as modern readers in a digital age we don't easily recognize literary motifs. Sure, in our high school literature class, we heard the word *motif* mentioned, and a scant few of us went on to become literature majors, but the bottom line is that we rarely encounter or think about sustained themes and concepts that span thousands of pages over hundreds of years. But when we come to the subjects of heaven and earth in the Bible, this is precisely what we have come to.

The Governing Motif

A motif can be defined as *a distinctive feature or dominant idea in an artistic or literary composition*. The Bible has many important literary structures and motifs, among them Sabbath, temple, covenant, blood, and even the tree of life. But the overwhelmingly dominant ideas that frame the Bible from beginning to end are heaven and earth.

One of the ways we can confirm this theme is to see the way heaven and earth are used in the rest of the Bible. Here are a handful of examples of this central motif:

"O Lord God, you have only begun to show your servant your greatness and your mighty hand. For what god is there in heaven or on earth who can do such works and mighty acts as yours." (Deut. 3:24)

"And as soon as we heard it, our hearts melted, and there was no spirit left in any man because of you, for the Lord your God, he is God in the heavens above and on the earth beneath." (Josh. 2:11)

Then the earth reeled and rocked; the foundations of the heavens trembled and quaked, because he was angry. (2 Sam. 22:8)

"O Lord, God of Israel, there is no God like you, in heaven above or on earth beneath, keeping covenant and showing steadfast love to your servants who walk before you with all their heart." (1 Kings 8:23)

"Yours, O Lord, is the greatness and the power and the glory and the victory and the majesty, for all that is in the heavens and in the earth is yours. Yours is the kingdom, O Lord, and you are exalted as head above all." (1 Chron. 29:11)

Whom have I in heaven but you? And there is nothing on earth that I desire besides you. (Ps. 73:25)

Of old you laid the foundation of the earth, and the heavens are the work of your hands. (Ps. 102:25)

"For as the heavens are higher than the earth, so are my ways higher than your ways and my thoughts than your thoughts." (Isa. 55:9)

"For behold, I create new heavens and a new earth, and the former things shall not be remembered or come into mind." (Isa. 65:17)

"Heaven and earth will pass away, but my words will not pass away." (Matt. 24:35)

And Jesus came and said to them, "All authority in heaven and on earth has been given to me." (Matt. 28:18)

"If I have told you earthly things and you do not believe, how can you believe if I tell you heavenly things?" (John 3:12)

As if these examples weren't enough to make the point, consider a verse from one of the last chapters of the last book of the Bible—Revelation:

Then I saw a new heaven and a new earth, for the first earth had passed away. (Rev. 21:1)

What is most interesting about the particular Greek word for *new* in Revelation 21:1 is that it doesn't mean brand-new or new in origin. That would have required the Greek word *neos*. Instead, the Apostle John used the word *kainos*, which means *renewed* or *refreshed*. The ultimate future reality that the Bible holds out is not a totally foreign world for which we have no context. The Bible doesn't teach that this world will be destroyed and replaced by something else. Not at all. In fact, we are to look forward to the recovery and rejuvenation of the very earth we now stand on.

I grew up watching a lot of the cartoon *Tom and Jerry*. Truth be told, I still like to watch it. Part of the theology of *Tom and Jerry* is that when one of them dies, his soul is issued a harp, a halo, and a cloud to sit on. I think most of us share this cartoon theology. We have the idea that disembodied spirits float around in the sky somewhere, strumming praise songs to God.

But the Bible doesn't envision such a future. The biblical future isn't about disembodied spirits in heaven—it is about the new heavens and new earth. It is about people being resurrected to new life, in new bodies, and inhabiting an earth that has been revamped, remodeled, and reset.

The end of the biblical story isn't about heaven alone; it is about the full renewal of heaven and earth. Or, as I like to say, it is about the *heavenization* of earth. But we are getting ahead of ourselves. To fully grasp what this all means, we have to go back to Genesis.

Genesis 1 functions as a thesis statement for the rest of the Pentateuch and certainly the Scriptures themselves. As we saw in chapter five, it lays out the first principles about the way God stands in relationship to His creation. In chapter six we showed how it is like the overture to a musical. Let's dig in even further.

The opening words of the Bible could have been written as a list of facts—God exists, God created the world, God made man in His image, etc. However, it isn't a list of propositional statements or dry syllogisms. It is an *exalted prose narrative*, meaning that it reads like history and has the structural elements of a poem. It may look like God's daily diary entries on the surface, but there is much more to consider.

The first six days of creation are symmetrically ordered as two pairs of triplets and three pairs of couplets. The triplets break up God's action into three days of dividing and three days of filling. The couplets segment God's action into three different arenas—two days for the heavens, two days for heaven and earth, and two days for earth. Picture it this way:

	Triplet 1 *God's Action - Divides*	Triplet 2 *God's Action - Fills*
Couplet 1 Action Arena: Heavens	<u>Day 1</u> DIVIDES Light from Darkness	<u>Day 4</u> FILLS WITH Sun, Moon, Stars
Couplet 2 Action Arena: Heaven & Earth	<u>Day 2</u> DIVIDES Heaven from Earth	<u>Day 5</u> FILLS WITH Birds, Fish
Couplet 3 Action Arena: Earth	<u>Day 3</u> DIVIDES Earth from Sea	<u>Day 6</u> FILLS WITH Animals, Man
	Day 7 — RESTS	

This kind of literary structure is neither arbitrary nor academic. It is there to help us burrow more deeply into what it has to tell us. One of the amazing features we notice as we do this is that there is a songlike refrain from day to day: "And God saw that it was good," "And God saw that it was good," "And God saw that it was good." These lyrical benedictions crescendo through day seven when "God saw all that he had made, and it was *very* good."

The repeated refrain about the goodness of the phenomenal realm is incredibly important because it flies in the face of philosophies and religions that denigrate the material world and our bodies. Genesis 1 virtually shouts that the physical world is something we should highly value. We should embrace it as a glorious gift rather than view it as something we need to spiritually escape or rise above.

One of the most common mistakes I see from virtually every Sunday school teacher, pastor, and theologian is that they read Genesis 1 too quickly. They commonly teach that the daily benediction is repeated on every day of creation. It isn't. At the end of one of the days there is silence. There is no benediction at all.[37] Consider the following:

---

37 James Jordan, *Through New Eyes: Developing a Biblical View of the World* (Eugene: Wipf & Stock Publishers, 1999), 45.

	Triplet 1 God's Action - Divides	Triplet 2 God's Action - Fills
Couplet 1 Action Arena: Heavens	"GOOD"	"GOOD"
Couplet 2 Action Arena: Heaven & Earth		"GOOD"
Couplet 3 Action Arena: Earth	"GOOD"	"GOOD"
	Day 7 – "VERY GOOD"	

I know the matrix is a little distracting for some people. If you're one of them, I will put this in a list form without all of the triplet and couplet conventions:

DAY	ACTION	ANALYSIS
One	God divides light from dark.	Good
Two	God divides heaven from earth	_____
Three	God divides earth from sea	Good
Four	God fills with heavenly lights	Good
Five	God fills with sky/sea creatures	Good
Six	God fills with animals/mankind	Good
Seven	God enjoys His creation	Very Good

On day two there is no benediction. If you doubt me, take the time to look it up and confirm it. This is important.

Silence is very powerful—especially in an intricate structure like this. Sometimes it speaks much louder than words ever could. I submit to you that the lack of a benediction on day two is supposed to stop us in our tracks. This is a clear literary signal that something is amiss. Why leave it out unless there is a reason for it?

It is not very hard to arrive at an answer: The division of heaven and earth was always meant to be temporary. Dividing the light from the darkness and filling the heavens with celestial orbs is good. Dividing the earth from the sea and filling them with creatures is good. That is how God wants those features of creation to remain. But dividing heaven from earth—that was only provisional. Heaven and earth are ultimately meant to be together, not separate.

Theologians often say that Genesis 1 lays out *protology* (protos = first), or *first things*, and *teleology* (telos = purpose) to set a trajectory. Genesis 1 isn't just about the past; it points toward the future. The silent day of dividing heaven and earth tells us that there is more to the story. God didn't create a steady-state world with an unchanging equilibrium that infinitely cycles toward no end. From the beginning, God's intention was to eventually merge heaven and earth together.

This obviously suggests that even though the initial creation was good and very good, there was something raw and unfinished about it. Something incomplete. People often look back on these narratives of the early world and presume that things were perfect. I don't believe that is quite the way the story reads. If it were perfect, humans could not have thrown it back into chaos as Adam did when he sinned. The ironic message of early Genesis is that God's project for merging heaven and earth was both contingent on humanity and vulnerable to humanity.

Before we launch headlong into the way this all works, let's reflect on a couple of things and define terms. First, let's acknowledge that Genesis 1 teaches a dualistic cosmology as the first order of business. Instead of using philosophical terms like *transcendent* and *phenomenal*, it uses *heaven* and *earth*. While there is a sense in which heaven visually corresponds to outer space with stars and planets, it represents much more than that. One of the most significant creeds of the early church understands this and confesses that "We believe in one God, the Father Almighty, Maker of heaven and earth, and of all things visible and invisible."

Hebrew thought and language patterns were much more concrete than the abstractions of ancient Greeks. It is easy to forget that we stand more in the tradition of Athens (Greek philosophy) than Jerusalem (Hebrew philosophy). This is an example of the way we need to slow down and understand the philosophical information that is deeply embedded in the distinct messaging of Genesis 1.

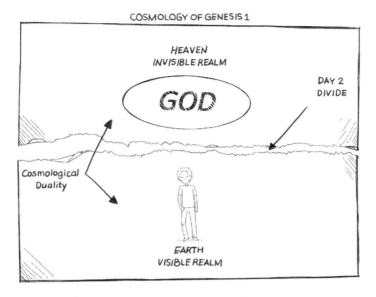

This raises at least two big questions—*What is heaven?* and *What is the nature of the divide between heaven and earth?* Once we have those answers we can go further into the story.

The Nature of the Day Two Divide

It may be counterintuitive, but let's begin with the second question: What is the nature of the divide between heaven and earth? Over and over again the Bible uses visual language to describe the division. For example, near the end of the New Testament, we read this from the Apostle John:

> Beloved, we are God's children now, and what we will be has not yet appeared; but we know that when he appears we shall be like him, because we shall see him as he is. (1 John 3:2)

The Apostle Paul wrote,

> For now we see in a mirror dimly, but then face to face. Now I know in part; then I shall know fully, even as I have been fully known. (1 Cor. 13:12)

The writer to the Hebrews pointed out,

> Now faith is the assurance of things hoped for, the conviction of things not seen. (Heb. 11:1)

And again we read helpful words from Paul:

> Since we have such a hope, we are very bold, not like Moses, who would put a veil over his face so that the Israelites might not gaze at the outcome of

what was being brought to an end. But their minds were hardened. For to this day, when they read the old covenant, that same veil remains unlifted, because only through Christ is it taken away. (2 Cor. 3:12–14)

There is some sense in which heaven and heavenly realities are hidden from our immediate sight. They are knowable in a limited way by faith because Christ lifts up the veil. Nevertheless, we still see "dimly." We have not yet seen God face to face.

The language of these texts leads me to believe that the division between heaven and earth is more visual than spatial or physical. We should be careful about thinking of heaven as being in another location or in different universe. Think of it almost like a fourth dimension that will ultimately become visible and in full alignment with earth (the phenomenal realm). In God's time, the veil will be taken away.

One of the most startling places this nearby dimensional dynamic is affirmed is in the New Testament book of Hebrews, chapter twelve. It follows a section often referred to as the "Hall of Faith," which enumerates some of the great Old Testament heroes of Judaism. After remembering the lives of people such as Abraham, Isaac, Jacob, Moses, and David, the writer says,

Therefore, since we are surrounded by so great a cloud of witnesses, let us also lay aside every weight, and sin which clings so closely, and let us run with endurance the race that is set before us, looking to Jesus, the founder and perfecter of our faith ....(Heb. 12:1)

A little later in the same chapter, the writer says that when Christians come together as the worshiping church they ...

...have come to Mount Zion and to the city of the living God, the heavenly Jerusalem, and to innumerable angels in festal gathering, and to the assembly of the firstborn who are enrolled in heaven, and to God, the judge of all, and to the spirits of the righteous made perfect, and to Jesus, the mediator of a new covenant ....(Heb. 12:22–23)

Let's recap. Heroes of the faith who have gone before us are watching us as a "cloud of witnesses." There is some sense in which we have arrived at Mount Zion, the heavenly Jerusalem. We're in the presence of innumerable angels who are celebrating. And finally, we stand in an assembly with the spirits of dead people who have been made perfect. It all sounds pretty creepy.

As crazy as this sounds, let's take it a step further. In the Old Testament we find a story about the witch of Endor. The king of Israel at the time was Saul. Samuel, the judge who had appointed and guided him, had died. The Philistines were preparing to go to war with Israel, and King Saul was very afraid. Even though Jewish law expressly forbade it, Saul asked a medium to summon Samuel's spirit for advice. Sure enough, the witch of Endor called Samuel forward from that invisible dimension and the first words out of Samuel's mouth were, "Why have you disturbed me by bringing me up?" (1 Sam. 28:15).

This almost starts to feel like the movie *The Sixth Sense*. Bruce Willis plays a child psychologist who meets with a little boy who claims he can see and speak to dead people. The poor boy is terrorized by his ability to see what others cannot, and he needs help. The psychologist takes a deep interest in trying to help the boy overcome this troubled state of affairs, but by the end of the movie there is a stunning twist. It turns out that the psychologist himself is dead—and has been for some time. But he only learns of his own death through interacting with the boy. I still get chills thinking about it.

However you want to slice it or dice it, the Bible makes it clear that some incredible invisible realities are right at our doorstep. They're not beyond the Milky Way somewhere in space; they're right here. We're not seeing them, but that doesn't make them less real. I can't see radio waves, but they're still there. I just don't have a natural ability or apparatus to tap into them.

Already and Not Yet

Does that mean that heaven is already here, but we just can't see it? That would sure be disappointing to many of us. After all, the Bible does portray the new heavens and new earth as a place where "He will wipe away every tear from their eyes, and death shall be no more, neither shall there be mourning, nor crying, nor pain anymore, for the former things have passed away" (Rev. 21:4).

Theologians throughout the centuries have recognized that there is an *already-and-not-yet* dynamic to the way heaven relates to earth. There is a sense in which heaven is already present, but not in its fullness. The fullness of heaven is still invisible to us and the phenomenal realm is still not operating in complete alignment with God's intention. Nevertheless, heaven is not entirely removed from us. We truly stand between the times.

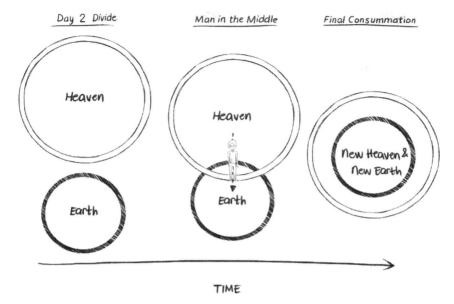

At some point in the future we will fully experience the merger of the new heaven and new earth. Right now we only get small glimpses and tastes of it. It is not entirely foreign to us, but we are a long way from knowing it in an intimate and complete way. That experience lies ahead.

But if heaven isn't a specific place, then what is heaven? What is it like and what's the point? Before I take a crack at this I want to issue a very broad and sweeping disclaimer by reflecting on something the venerable C. S. Lewis observed. There is a sense in which describing heaven is like trying to describe the joys of sexual intimacy to a young child. They have the physiology that will grow to understand and appreciate it, but they're not mature enough to grasp it yet. It lies just out of their reach and given a choice, they would prefer to stick with chocolate, thank you very much. In the same fashion, we're all made for heaven, but we're not able to totally comprehend it yet.

It is important to come to the topic of heaven with that level of humility. We're not given a comprehensive and detailed picture of what lies ahead. We have some snapshots and can come to some provisional understanding, but that's all. A few postcard pictures of the Golden Gate Bridge may introduce me to some of the central imagery of San Francisco, but it will not give me a full sense of what it means to be in San Francisco. I won't know the joys of eating a fresh loaf of sourdough bread with butter on a cool and cloudy day while overlooking the bay until I visit there. Our attempts to describe heaven work somewhat the same way.

What Heaven Is Like

With that in mind, I think the best thing to do is to look at several of the most explicit glimpses of heaven that the Bible gives to us. They are interesting because even though they come from different authors at different times, they see many of the same features and work almost like parallel accounts. There is a fair amount of text, so be patient with it. I think these visions are worth reproducing because they are not usually given the attention they deserve:

Isaiah 6: 1–4

I saw the Lord sitting upon a throne, high and lifted up; and the train of his robe filled the temple. Above him stood the seraphim. Each had six wings: with two he covered his face, and with two he covered his feet, and with two he flew. And one called to another and said:

> "Holy, holy, holy is the LORD OF HOSTS;
> the whole earth is full of his glory!"

And the foundations of the thresholds shook at the voice of him who called, and the house was filled with smoke....

Ezekiel 1:22–28

Over the heads of the living creatures there was the likeness of an expanse, shining like awe-inspiring crystal, spread out above their heads. And under the expanse their wings were stretched out straight, one toward another. And each creature had two wings covering its body. And when they went, I heard the sound of their wings like the sound of many waters, like the sound of the Almighty, a sound of tumult like the sound of an army. When they stood still, they let down their wings. And there came a voice from above the expanse over their heads. When they stood still, they let down their wings.

And above the expanse over their heads there was the likeness of a throne, in appearance like sapphire; and seated above the likeness of a throne was a likeness with a human appearance. And upward from what had the appearance of his waist I saw as it were gleaming metal, like the appearance of fire enclosed all around. And downward from what had the appearance of his waist I saw as it were the appearance of fire, and there was brightness around him. Like the appearance of the bow that is in the cloud on the day of rain, so was the appearance of the brightness all around.

Such was the appearance of the likeness of the glory of the LORD.

Revelation 4:1–11

After this I looked, and behold, a door standing open in heaven! And the first voice, which I had heard speaking to me like a trumpet, said, "Come up here, and I will show you what must take place after this." At once I was in the Spirit, and behold, a throne stood in heaven, with one seated on the throne. And he who sat there had the appearance of jasper and carnelian, and around the throne was a rainbow that had the appearance of an emerald. Around the throne were twenty-four thrones, and seated on the thrones were twenty-four elders, clothed in white garments, with golden crowns on their heads. From the throne came flashes of lightning, and rumblings and peals of thunder, and before the throne were burning seven torches of fire, which are the seven spirits of God, and before the throne there was as it were a sea of glass, like crystal.

And around the throne, on each side of the throne, are four living creatures, full of eyes in front and behind: the first living creature like a lion, the second living creature like an ox, the third living creature with the face of a man, and the fourth living creature like an eagle in flight. And the four living creatures, each of them with six wings, are full of eyes all around and within, and day and night they never cease to say,

"Holy, holy, holy, is the Lord God Almighty,
who was and is and is to come!"

And whenever the living creatures give glory and honor and thanks to him who is seated on the throne, who lives forever and ever, the twenty-four elders fall down before him who is seated on the throne and worship him who lives forever and ever. They cast their crowns before the throne, saying,

"Worthy are you, our Lord and God,
to receive glory and honor and power,
or you created all things,
and by your will they existed and were created."

So much could be said here, but some things rise quickly to the surface. First and foremost, God's presence on the throne is the central feature of heaven. London has Big Ben and Paris has the Eiffel Tower, but heaven has God's throne. Think Mount Olympus, but with a lot more color. Instead of stone columns, there are hues and brightness surrounding the throne that can only be described as being like jewels. The throne room scene is filled with thunder and lightning. Voices of the worshiping attendants chant about God's holiness day and night. Heaven is primarily characterized by the pervasive presence of God's royal splendor and holiness.

A throne is a symbol of monarchy—of kingship and kingdom. God is not a politically elected official or an executive chairman of the board. God is King, and all authority in heaven and earth is His. His benevolent reign over all things is absolute and inalterable.

If you want to try to visualize heaven, take whatever mental images you may have of earthly royalty and magnify them by as many times as you can. Perhaps the closest comparison we have in our day to this kind of majesty is the monarchy of the United Kingdom. Whenever there is a royal wedding or coronation people flock to see the incredible pomp and circumstance that surrounds the event. I will never forget seeing the twenty-five foot long train of Princess Diana's wedding dress. The whole affair seemed to be a real-world attempt to enact a fantasy world. It was amazing to behold.

Christ's frequent teaching about the arrival of God's kingdom pivoted around God's royal splendor and majestic priorities being enacted and reflected on earth. In the Lord's Prayer we ask, "Your kingdom come, your will be done, on earth as it is in heaven." Jesus defined the kingdom as God's presence, priorities, and glory being revealed and accomplished on earth. The heavenly kingdom Jesus spoke of was not an ethereal principle or a far away galaxy; it is the progressive realization of God's will being done on earth as it is in heaven.

I find it interesting that ostensibly freedom-loving Americans resist monarchy as a political system, but go to great lengths every four years clamoring for a quasi-monarch. Despite our supposed commitment to the division and balance of powers, the truth is that many people desperately want someone to be in charge and ultimately responsible for fixing problems. We may say that we want a president and not a king, but that claim is becoming increasingly hard to believe from Americans. I have a suspicion that this impulse is not an accident—it is built in. The truly wise and good monarch we long for has always been there, seated on His heavenly throne.

The worship and work of heaven

The other feature of heaven that is clearly evident in these Scriptures is the intense and constant worship of God. God is not in an empty throne room by Himself. Every creature in His presence is worshiping in some fashion. The winged seraphs are covering their faces—shielding their eyes from the brightness of His glory. The twenty-four elders are casting down their crowns and prostrating themselves before God. The throne room is a busy place.

Holiness is the principal theme of worship in God's presence. One theologian pointed out that the chants don't say, "Love, love, love," or "Mercy, mercy, mercy." Holy is not another word for "good." Holiness speaks to the sum total of who God is in all of His magnificence. God is incomparable in His wisdom, power, love, justice, righteousness, and mercy. The bounds of His greatness have no end—He alone is God. He alone is holy and worthy of glory and honor.

At this point we might start to wonder if heaven will be an infinitely long church service. Are we going to be assigned a seat in a pew (with kneelers) and our own personal hymnal? Is heaven just a really long liturgy? If so, I'm not sure how excited I am about that. I like to worship, but I get tired of sitting pretty quickly.

The answer is yes and no. Yes, heaven is about constant and unceasing worship. It is about a devotion and love for God that never takes a break. Heaven is consumed with the acknowledgment that God is God and that He is holy. But that doesn't mean that heaven is just a long worship service. It won't be about sitting through an eternally exhausting liturgy. What these Biblical glimpses into heaven tell us is that every aspect of our lives—all of our future work and play in the new heavens and new earth will be expressions of our unbroken love and communion with God.

In our already-but-not-yet state, we tend to worship God occasionally, if at all. Sometimes our work and leisure are in alignment with God's authority and holiness, but much of the time they are not. Our lives are usually spent serving ourselves and our own interests. When the fullness of time comes, the realities of heaven will sweep all of this away. The consummation of heaven will consume our hearts and minds.

Some people envision heaven as a place of eternal retirement and recreation with no work to do. Perhaps there will be some incredible golf courses with thousands of holes to play. Maybe there will be white sandy beaches with comfortable chairs and umbrella drinks for everyone. We think of it as an awesome, all-inclusive resort.

It would not surprise me to see those kinds of activities in the new heavens and earth, but there is no evidence that there will be an elimination of work. Work is a significant part of what it means to be made in God's image. God is a worker, and because we are like Him, we are called to work. Work and enjoyment of work have always been an original and integral part of what it means to be fully human.

One of the most interesting facets on the diamond of Genesis 1 is the paradigmatic pattern of God's work. The rhythm of God's action in creation reveals something about the way we're supposed to work as well. His working pattern was as follows:

1. Take hold (And God said...)
2. Restructure and transform (Let there be...)
3. Evaluate (And He saw...)
4. Give thanks, rest and enjoy (That it was good...He rested)[38]

When we work, we are meant to follow the same outline that ends in thankful rest and enjoyment. Unfortunately, in our corruption we tend to mess up steps two, three, and four. Nevertheless, we can't help but stumble through them in some fashion or another. In the new heavens and new earth we will resume a righteous design for work.

Work itself is good and gives humanity its special dignity and purpose. Unfortunately, people often confuse the post-fall curse on work with work being a curse. After Adam sinned, one of the consequences was that work would become difficult. Instead of progressively expanding Eden's paradisical garden into the four corners of the earth, we were thrust out and thrown into an untamed environment of thorns (trouble) and sweat (fatigue). Work suddenly became a necessary and difficult way to sustain life rather than a meaningful and transformative activity.

Some people who are well trained in theology might object that the Bible teaches that the heavenlike imagery of the Promised Land is of "cisterns you did not dig, and vineyards and olive trees that you did not plant" (Deut. 6:11). In other words, it appears that the new heavens and new earth are a place where all the work is already done for us. To this I ask, have you ever been to the wine country of Napa Valley in California? I have not planted those vineyards or olive trees. I have not tapped their springs for water. But I would *love* to work there in those vineyards. Give me pruning shears to tend the trees and a basket for harvesting. Give me a job. Sign me up. When can I start?

---

38 Ibid., 120.

One of my favorite movies and guilty pleasures is the cult classic *Office Space*, starring Ron Livingston and Jennifer Anniston. I don't think there is a more insightful and humorous exposé of the modern workplace. The setting is a mid-sized 1990s technology company called Initech. Peter, the main character, is a thirty-something staffer who is stuck in an isolated and miserable cubicle under fluorescent lights all day. Adding insult to injury, his annoying and wildly overpaid boss, Bill Lumbergh, hounds him daily for meaningless TPS reports.

Peter's life is an achingly accurate portrait of the unexciting and monotonous work life of so many people in today's economy. He actually enters hypnotic counseling at the behest of his girlfriend because of his mounting despondency and depression. During the initial session with the hypnotist, Peter describes his plight:

PETER: So I was sitting in my cubicle today, and I realized, ever since I started working, every single day of my life has been worse than the day before it. So that means that every single day that you see me, that's on the worst day of my life.

DR. SWANSON: What about today? Is today the worst day of your life?

PETER: Yeah.

DR. SWANSON: Wow, that's messed up.

Dr. Swanson then proceeds to put Peter in a trance so that he can offer suggestions to his subconscious mind about life and work. The hypnosis takes hold with such great force that Peter enters into a state of mindless bliss and begins operating according to his most basic impulses—which is to say he essentially stops working.

Soon after, Peter goes to lunch at a nearby restaurant and meets a waitress, Joanna. Their first conversation goes as follows:

JOANNA: So, where do you work, Peter?

PETER: Initech.

JOANNA: In...yeah, what do you do there?

PETER: I sit in a cubicle and I update bank software for the 2000 switch.

PETER: What's that?

PETER: Well see, they wrote all this bank software, and, uh, to save space, they used two digits for the date instead of four. So, like, 98 instead of 1998? Uh, so I go through these thousands of lines of code and, uh …it doesn't really matter. I uh, I don't like my job, and, uh, I don't think I'm gonna go anymore.

JOANNA: You're just not gonna go?

PETER: Yeah.

JOANNA: Won't you get fired?

PETER: I don't know, but I really don't like it, and, uh, I'm not gonna go.

JOANNA: So you're gonna quit?

PETER: Nuh-uh. Not really. Uh …I'm just gonna stop going.

JOANNA: When did you decide all that?

PETER: About an hour ago.

JOANNA: Oh, really? About an hour ago …so you're gonna get another job?

PETER: I don't think I'd like another job.

JOANNA: Well, what are you going to do about money and bills and . . .

PETER: You know, I've never really liked paying bills. I don't think I'm gonna do that, either.

JOANNA: Well, so what do you wanna do?

PETER: I wanna take you out to dinner, and then I wanna go back to my apartment and watch kung fu. Do you ever watch kung fu?

JOANNA: I love kung fu.

PETER: Channel 39.

JOANNA: Totally.

PETER: You should come over and watch kung fu tonight.

JOANNA: OK.

Peter: [Nods.]

JOANNA: OK. Can we order lunch first?

Peter: [Nods again.]

JOANNA: OK.

How many of us have wished we could follow in Peter's hypnosis-induced footsteps? How great would it be to stop going to a work at a job we don't like to pay bills we don't want to pay? Wouldn't it be nice to just sit in front of a TV instead? For many people, work is not a source of fulfillment; it is a source of boredom and stress. It can even be borderline dehumanizing.

Work in a Promised Land context is satisfying labor that results in an abundant and continual feast in God's presence. Labor in the vineyards and olive tree groves of the new heavens and new earth will not leave us feeling empty. We will be massively fruitful and will regularly celebrate at God's banquet table.

In fact, if I had to pick out my favorite motif in the Bible, it would actually be the motif of food and drink. From beginning to end, food is a very big deal in the Scriptures. It is not merely a means of sustenance; it is a primary vehicle of communion and happiness. There is a very good reason why Jesus' first miracle was turning water to wine at a wedding in Cana. He was symbolically underscoring the message that He came to get a party started. His ultimate project was to initiate a feast, not a fast.

C. S. Lewis once wrote that "Joy is the serious business of heaven." I don't know what the precise nature of our work and feasting will be, but I can imagine. Maybe we will transform planets on other galaxies into habitable environments. Maybe we will all become culinary experts and sommeliers. I don't know. Remember the forces that have shaped my imagination. As one of my favorite professors in college used to say, "Imagination is the correlative of hope."

Whatever the case may be, the new heavens and new earth is a place where we will be most fully human again. We will no longer be at war with the deterioration of our bodies, the selfishness of our egos, or the ravages of nature. Our humanity will not be diminished, but radically established and intensified. One of the early church fathers, Irenaeus, wrote, "The glory of God is a human being fully alive." That is well said and begins to capture the essence of what we have to look forward to in the consummation of time.

But where is heaven?

The issue of heaven as a location rather than a relatively close dimension is a lingering question. Don't people "go to heaven"? What about the descriptions of heaven we see in Revelation 21?

Let's roll up our sleeves and do some major Bible interpretation. I am going to reproduce the whole chapter of Revelation 21 here so that we can try to deal with it:

> Then I saw a new heaven and a new earth, for the first heaven and the first earth had passed away, and the sea was no more. And I saw the holy city, new Jerusalem, coming down out of heaven from God, prepared as a bride

adorned for her husband. And I heard a loud voice from the throne saying, "Behold, the dwelling place of God is with man. He will dwell with them, and they will be his people, and God himself will be with them as their God. He will wipe away every tear from their eyes, and death shall be no more, neither shall there be mourning, nor crying, nor pain anymore, for the former things have passed away."

And he who was seated on the throne said, "Behold, I am making all things new." Also he said, "Write this down, for these words are trustworthy and true." And he said to me, "It is done! I am the Alpha and the Omega, the beginning and the end. To the thirsty I will give from the spring of the water of life without payment. The one who conquers will have this heritage, and I will be his God and he will be my son. But as for the cowardly, the faithless, the detestable, as for murderers, the sexually immoral, sorcerers, idolaters, and all liars, their portion will be in the lake that burns with fire and sulfur, which is the second death."

Then came one of the seven angels who had the seven bowls full of the seven last plagues and spoke to me, saying, "Come, I will show you the Bride, the wife of the Lamb." And he carried me away in the Spirit to a great, high mountain, and showed me the holy city Jerusalem coming down out of heaven from God, having the glory of God, its radiance like a most rare jewel, like a jasper, clear as crystal. It had a great, high wall, with twelve gates, and at the gates twelve angels, and on the gates the names of the twelve tribes of the sons of Israel were inscribed—on the east three gates, on the north three gates, on the south three gates, and on the west three gates. And the wall of the city had twelve foundations, and on them were the twelve names of the twelve apostles of the Lamb.

And the one who spoke with me had a measuring rod of gold to measure the city and its gates and walls. The city lies foursquare, its length the same as its width. And he measured the city with his rod, 12,000 stadia. Its length and width and height are equal. He also measured its wall, 144 cubits by human measurement, which is also an angel's measurement. The wall was built of jasper, while the city was pure gold, like clear glass. The foundations of the wall of the city were adorned with every kind of jewel. The first was jasper, the second sapphire, the third agate, the fourth emerald, the fifth onyx, the sixth carnelian, the seventh chrysolite, the eighth beryl, the ninth topaz, the tenth chrysoprase, the eleventh jacinth, the twelfth amethyst. And the twelve gates were twelve pearls, each of the gates made of a single pearl, and the street of the city was pure gold, like transparent glass.

And I saw no temple in the city, for its temple is the Lord God the Almighty and the Lamb. And the city has no need of sun or moon to shine on it, for the glory of God gives it light, and its lamp is the Lamb. By its light will the nations walk, and the kings of the earth will bring their glory into it, and its gates will never be shut by day—and there will be no night there. They will bring into it the glory and the honor of the nations. But nothing unclean will ever enter it, nor anyone who does what is detestable or false, but only those who are written in the Lamb's book of life.

Before we go too far, I want to make note of something. Namely, some scholars and Bibles translate the part concerning the city's measurements as follows:

The one who spoke with me had a gold measuring rod to measure the city, and its gates and its wall. The city is laid out as a square, and its length is as great as the width; and he measured the city with the rod, fifteen hundred miles; its length and width and height are equal. And he measured its wall, seventy-two yards, according to human measurements, which are also angelic measurements. (vv. 15–17, NIV)

Note the contrast: The first translation leaves the Greek units as they are—twelve thousand stadia and 144 cubits. The second tries to convert the number of stadia and cubits into our units of measurement—fifteen hundred miles and seventy-two yards.

The differences reveal two very different readings and approaches to the text. The first one retains the Greek units in order to preserve the obvious interplay of the numbers—twelve gates, twelve angels, twelve tribes, twelve kinds of jewels, twelve pearls, twelve apostles ... twelve thousand stadia ($12 \times 1000 = 12{,}000$). Even one hundred and forty-four cubits represent the product of twelve by twelve ($12 \times 12 = 144$). There is clearly some kind of symbolism around twelve and its exponents that is very important.

The other translation neglects the compounding symbolism of twelve and favors the calculated equivalents of fifteen hundred miles and seventy-two yards. The symbolic string of twelve is abandoned in favor of a hyperliteral measurement of the new city. This leads many people to believe that the new heavenly Jerusalem will literally be in the shape of a square with four sides that are each fifteen hundred miles long and walls that are seventy-two yards thick.

As you might guess, I find the second translation unfortunate and misleading. The book of Revelation itself is built on a repetitious raft of symbolic numbers and allusions to the Old Testament. Despite the way many people approach the book, it should not be read as science fiction or fantasy.

Remember that reading the Bible *literally* means we read it as *literature*. One of the first rules of literature is recognizing what genre we are dealing with. The book of Revelation is what scholars refer to as apocalyptic literature. The Greek word, apokaluptikos, means to *uncover* or *reveal*. It typically uses fantastic and cosmic end-of-the-world types of language and imagery to radically underscore its point. It does so not only to anticipate the actual end of the world, but also to vividly communicate that its message is fundamentally world-altering.

A great scriptural example of this can be found in the way the Apostle Peter quotes a passage from the Old Testament prophet Joel. Hundreds of years before Peter lived, Joel gave an apocalyptic prophecy that reads,

> And it shall come to pass afterward, that I will pour out my Spirit on all flesh; your sons and your daughters shall prophesy, your old men shall dream dreams, and your young men shall see visions. Even on the male and female servants in those days I will pour out my Spirit. And I will show wonders in the heavens and on the earth, blood and fire and columns of smoke. The sun shall be turned to darkness, and the moon to blood, before the great and awesome day of the LORD comes. (Joel 2:28–31)

It would be easy and natural to assume that Joel was referring to the end of the world, when God comes in judgment. When God comes, the sun will go dark and the moon will turn blood red. But actually, we would be wrong.

Peter quoted this verse many centuries later to explain what happened after Jesus ascended to heaven and sent His Spirit upon the disciples. On Pentecost, a rushing wind blew through their midst, tongues of fire appeared over their heads, and they started miraculously speaking different languages. While everyone was still trying to understand what was going on, Peter basically said, "I'll tell you what's going on—Joel's prophecy is coming true right now!" The sun didn't literally go dark, and there were no wonders in the heavens, but Peter maintained that the Pentecost event in Acts 2 was the realization of the apocalyptic prophecy in Joel 2.

The cosmic and apocalyptic imagery of the sun and moon isn't about science fiction; it is about a change so dramatic that it is as if the whole cosmos has shifted. Imagine the moon turning blood red—that's how significant the impact of this message will be. We're not supposed to read these descriptions in an overly literal way; we're supposed to see them as signals to pay close attention.

Rather than getting out our calculators to understand Revelation 21, we actually have to keep our noses in our Bibles. When we do that, we notice that the chapter is piling biblical symbol upon biblical symbol. Think of it as a massive symbolic symphony. Layer after layer of allusions are intertwined together into an image of the new heavens and earth.

I'm a great fan of Beethoven, and my favorite composition may be his last complete symphony, the Ninth. In the final movement, the various musical themes he has used throughout the piece come together in a great crescendo with every instrument playing and every chorus member singing the words of the "Ode to Joy" in loud unison. What started as a mere whisper ends as a deafening and frenzied chorus that almost carries a physical impact. Beethoven throws everything he has to give in the final bars of the piece. Many consider it the most important orchestral and choral music ever written.

Revelation 21 is a lot like the final moments of Beethoven's Ninth. All of the prior themes of the Bible come together in a frenzied fashion. If a conductor could direct the reading of the chapter, you would see his arms wildly flailing and his frazzled hair waving with intensity and sweat. Literary elements from Genesis to the prophet Isaiah to the letters of Paul are thrown into the composition. In the last bars of the last movement, everything comes together as loudly as the orchestra and chorus can possibly perform. It is meant to be completely overwhelming in its force.

Symbolic Symphony of Revelation 21

New Jerusalem

Bride of Christ

Dwelling Place

12 Tribes

12 Apostles

12 Jewels

No Temple

No Sun / No Moon

The literary layering begins with the New Jerusalem, described as a bride adorned for her husband. This would be easy to pass by as sentimental imagery, but it is much more than that. Throughout the Bible, God refers to His people of Israel—and then the church—as His beloved bride. In fact, Jesus is explicitly said to be married to the church. Look at this from Ephesians 5:27–32:

> Husbands, love your wives, as Christ loved the church and gave himself up for her, that he might sanctify her, having cleansed her by the washing of water with the word, so that he might present the church to himself in splendor, without spot or wrinkle or any such thing, that she might be holy and without blemish. In the same way husbands should love their wives as their own bodies. He who loves his wife loves himself. For no one ever hated his own flesh, but nourishes and cherishes it, just as Christ does the church, because we are members of his body. "Therefore a man shall leave his father and mother and hold fast to his wife, and the two shall become one flesh." This mystery is profound, and I am saying that it refers to Christ and the church.

The church is identified as the bride of Christ. The heavenly Jerusalem is not supposed to be understood as an alien city that descends from the clouds and replaces earth. Rather, it should be seen as the arrival of a holy people that God is in intimate communion with.

Then look at the next layer of this symbolic symphony, which proclaims, "the dwelling place of God is with man. He will dwell with them, and they will be his people...." Throughout the Bible, this *dwelling place* language refers to the tabernacle and the temple of the Lord. When God gave designs for the initial tabernacle in the Old Testament, they were clearly blueprints for His heaven-on-earth house. We read this in Leviticus 26:11–12, "I will make my dwelling among you, and my soul shall not abhor you. And I will walk among you and will be your God, and you shall be my people."

The tabernacle (and later the more permanent temple building) was the central feature that showed that God had come to dwell in the midst of Israel. In so doing, He would teach them what it meant to live as a holy people and as a light to the nations. This would seem to suggest that perhaps the New Jerusalem has a temple in it, but we are told in Revelation 21 that the New Jerusalem would not have a temple. God Almighty and the Lamb, Jesus, are said to be its temple. What is going on here?

Stick with this exercise because we're about to get into one of the thickest and most complex symbolic parts of the whole Bible. Jesus claimed that the Old Testament dwelling place of the Temple actually pointed symbolically to Him. The sacrifices and offerings pointed to His sacrifice. The servant priests pointed to Him as the High Priest. The glory presence of God in the Holy of Holies anticipated His human presence on earth. He said that His mission was to not to abolish the law and the prophets, but to fulfill them. This is why Jesus was given the title *Immanuel*, which means *God with us*. God took on flesh in order to "tabernacle" among us.

In fact, one of the reasons Jesus was killed was that He called the temple his Father's house. He acted like He owned the place and even threw out the money-changing profiteers who exploited it as a place to run an illegitimate business. He said that if they tore down the temple, subversively referring to his body, He would raise it again in three days. This incensed the religious leaders of his day.

Here is the twist—the apostles pressed the radical symbolic identification of Jesus as God's presence even further and said that his followers were being knit together as His body on earth. In Romans 12:4 and 5, the Apostle Paul wrote, "For as in one body we have many members, and the members do not all have the same function, so we, though many, are one body in Christ, and individually members one of another."

Christ's presence on earth is now physically realized through the presence of His followers. Over and over again, the New Testament refers to Christians as being the body of Christ. But the apostles again pressed further. They said that as the body of Christ, Christians are also being built into the new Spirit-filled dwelling place. Peter writes, "As you come to him, a living stone rejected by men but in the sight of God chosen and precious, you yourselves like living stones are being built up as a spiritual house, to be a holy priesthood, to offer spiritual sacrifices acceptable to God through Jesus Christ" (1 Pet. 2:4–5).

Limb by limb and brick by brick, the people of God are being built into a new temple—each person a living stone connected to Jesus, the cornerstone. The new temple of God is not a literal fifteen hundred mile-wide building that will drop from the sky; it is the people of God, the church. God has made us into new His dwelling place.

Symbolic Symphony of Revelation 21

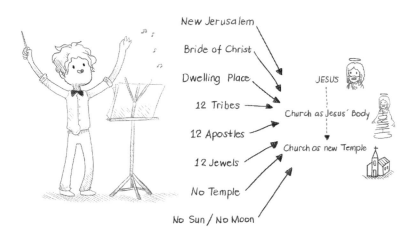

As the symbolic symphony continues we are told that the city has twelve entrances, each bearing the name of one of the twelve tribes of Israel: three on each sides of the city—north, south, east, and west. The four walls of the city are built on twelve foundations named after the twelve apostles.

Again, imagery from one of the Apostle Paul's letters shines through. In Ephesians, when Paul is describing the way Gentiles have become included with Jews as God's people, he writes,

> So then you are no longer strangers and aliens, but you are fellow citizens with the saints and members of the household of God, built on the foundation of the apostles and prophets, Christ Jesus himself being the cornerstone, in whom the whole structure, being joined together, grows into a holy temple in the Lord. In him you also are being built together into a dwelling place for God by the Spirit." (Eph. 2:19–22)

The city of God—made up of the people of God—is built on the foundation of Israel's family of prophets in addition to the New Testament apostles. In other words, the twelve entrances and twelve foundations of the New Jerusalem are symbolic constructions that point to the sum of God's renewed humanity. The point isn't that each fifteen-hundred-mile-long side of the city square has three entrances with plaques naming each Old Testament tribe. Not at all. The point is that the city of God brings Jew and Gentile from Old and New Testaments together as a new people on earth.

I have no problem envisioning the new heavens and new earth as a kind of Emerald City, made of jewels. However, interpreting the gemstones in this passage merely as God's building materials misses the mark. What we're supposed to be struck by is that this new city of God, made of the people of God, is unspeakably and unimaginably precious, beautiful, and diverse. As the church is knit together and forged by the Holy Spirit, we will become an awe-inspiring city of incredible riches and abundance. The only way to even conceive of its value and wonder is to think in terms of jewels.

This interpretation of Revelation 21 might be somewhat unsettling to many readers. We were looking forward to gold streets and now we're left with a bunch of people? What a huge letdown. Pearl gates sound so much better.

My intent is not to rob anyone of the hope of heaven by explaining away the imagery that is used in Revelation 21. Rather, I want to radically realign our understanding of heaven with the actual teaching of the Bible. The "not yet" aspect of the new heavens and new earth that awaits final fulfillment is inextricably linked to the utter transformation of God's people into God's new holy city.

Have you ever had a teacher say something like, "If you learn one thing from me this semester, it's _____"? This is that moment. Get out your highlighters—feel free to underline this: The fundamental reality of heaven is less about a particular place that is out there somewhere and more about the transformative presence of a people fully functioning as God's image bearers. Heaven is less about *where* and more about *who*.

This is precisely why Jesus taught His disciples to pray by saying,

Our Father in heaven, hallowed be your name,
Your kingdom come,
Your will be done,
On earth as it is in heaven. (Matt. 6:9, 10)

Let that sink in. When we understand the motifs and the cosmological relationship between heaven and earth, the central prayer of Jesus takes on radically new meaning. His words carry massive theological freight. Jesus is asking that the separation of heaven and earth on day 2 of creation would be undone. He wants us to pray for heaven and earth to merge into the new heavens and new earth so that the benediction that was skipped can finally be uttered: It is good.

The priority of Jesus isn't necessarily to pray for people to "go to heaven." The primary request is for the heavenization of earth—God's kingly authority and righteous will wholly enacted in the phenomenal realm. This is what it means to live according to God's kingdom. The full glory, worship, and work of heaven may not be fully manifest yet on earth, but they will be.

Don't misunderstand me. The new heavens and new earth have not been finally consummated in our time—not even close. Even though I don't read Revelation 21 in a hyperliteral fashion, I believe the day will come when Jesus will return to bring everything to completion. Nevertheless, the principle and provisional presence of God's heavenly kingdom are here in seed form. The promise of an unbroken communion with God and neighbor in all of aspects of life is here in the manifestation of God's people, the church.

Those who have died in communion with God are with Him in a way that I cannot begin to describe. They are not gone in any final sense, and their consciousness and spirit live on while they await the reunion to their resurrected bodies. But even they are waiting for the fullness of time to come so that all things can be made new. They are at peace in God's presence, but they have not yet experienced the fullness of heaven because the new heavens and new earth haven't been completed. Like us, they wait.

The famous twentieth-century existentialist Jean Paul Sartre wrote a fascinating short play about life and the afterlife entitled *No Exit*. The storyline revolves around three people sentenced to hell. Instead of being tortured by some medieval pain-inflicting devices, they are punished by being trapped in a room together for eternity. As they begin to seriously annoy each other one of the characters poignantly realizes that "hell is other people." At the end of the play they sardonically laugh at the utter absurdity of their existence and damnation.

Certainly, Sartre was not hypothesizing about the future afterlife; he was offering a commentary on our lives in the present. While I am not an existentialist by any stretch of the imagination, I think Sartre almost hit the nail on the head. Hell can, indeed, be other people, but God's plan has always been for *heaven* to be other people. When we live according to God's design we will experience the joys of heaven.

We could linger on issues revolving around the afterlife, but that would distract us from the main aim of this chapter. My heart's desire is for people to know what the big story of the Bible is—and that is suggested to us from the very first words of Genesis: God created the heavens and earth so that in time they might fully come together. While God created a world that was good, it was not finished or perfected on arrival. There was work to be done in bringing His heavenly will to earth.

The key thing to recognize is that from the very beginning, God had a strategy for making this merger happen. His approach was to engage humans—His image bearers—in the high and holy work of heavenizing earth. If you will, He put man in the middle. And that, my friends, is where the story gets truly interesting.

CHAPTER EIGHT
Man in the Middle

Clothes make the man. Naked people have little or no influence on society.

—Mark Twain

The slow journey from childhood to adulthood is marked with many milestones, but one of the biggest is the first day of kindergarten. Toys that used to be the centerpiece of activity slowly start to fade into cabinets. Letters, numbers, and days of the week replace nursery rhymes. Graham crackers are phased out for lunch boxes. The shifts are subtle at first, but every kindergartner can feel that their world is starting to change. It is time to start the process of growing up.

I was very excited to begin kindergarten with Miss Bell at Roxbury Elementary School. Nothing intrigued me more than jumping in the middle of this repository of hidden knowledge. I felt more than ready to tackle whatever they could throw at me.

Unlike most of my young compatriots I was a kindergartner with well-defined purpose. My educational goal was crystal clear—I was going to study science so that I could be an astronaut...or possibly a Jedi Knight like Luke Skywalker. The details were irrelevant as long as the trajectory of our studies had to do with space, lasers, and spaceships with lasers.

I was so devoted to this singular focus that I insisted on a special outfit for the first day of school. If I was going to be trained for outer space I needed to be dressed for the occasion. With great pride I donned my cherished pair of space pants. Yes, space pants—jeans with printed planets, stars, and UFOs. They were the coolest pants I have ever owned. Even for the flamboyant 1970s, these pants made a lasting impression.

For all of my enthusiasm, there was one small bump in the road on my journey toward astrophysics. Namely, I didn't know my prepositions. I'm not talking about fine nuances of grammar rules; I'm talking about basic concepts of spatial orientation—over, under, through, around. Somehow these terms had escaped my attention and I tended to use them interchangeably. When Miss Bell told us to put our lunch boxes in the cubbies, I thought the correct placement had more to do with vicinity than precise coordinates. Maybe the concepts of over and under were transposable in the vacuum of space. There's no gravity there, right?

After a note came home from Miss Bell regarding the state of my educational readiness, my mother suddenly became engaged at a different level in my schooling. We started going to the library to check out books with various shapes and figures. Our conversations turned increasingly to matters of three-dimensional positioning. In a short period of time I was nailing my prepositions with authority.

Predictably, my dreams of becoming a spaceman slowly faded under the weight of multiplication tables and miserable attempts to write legible cursive. I was a decent student, but when it became apparent that spaceship laser technology was not part of the curriculum, some of the fuel leaked out of my mental rocket. I eventually assimilated into the masses and my space pants were forever lost to the bottom of a clothes drawer. I turned into a run-of-the-mill nerd instead of a geek on steroids.

As strange as it sounds, aspirations of scientific mastery, kindergarten, and funky clothing and aren't just elements of my childhood; they are also central themes of humanity's childhood in Genesis 2 and 3. The story begins there with an uneducated naked man in a garden. God's plan may have been for humans to heavenize earth and rule as kings and queens of creation, but they had a long way to go.

For most of my life I thought that the story of Genesis 2 and 3 was rather silly. Could God really be so capricious that He condemned humanity to death for one guy eating a piece of forbidden fruit? How can this be taken seriously? It seemed terribly naive.

But over the years I came to realize that we first encounter some of the intricate narratives of the Bible in these chapters. Jesus, the apostles, and the prophets repeatedly refer back to the framework that is set here.

Every detail from gardening, to food, to nakedness is a profound conceptual pillar for the rest of what follows. The seemingly small features of the Genesis narrative establish critically important theological foundations.

Anytime we encounter a compressed and somewhat obscure biblical text like this we are on sacred ground. Every inch of textual territory is important and nothing can be taken for granted. This is a place for interpretive maximalism, not interpretive minimalism.

This should not surprise us because the God of the Bible is a God of symbols, monuments, and memorials. He created a world that is full of icons with momentous associations. Humans are symbolic of God, animals are symbolic of humanity, stars are symbolic of God's people, rainbows are symbolic of peace, wine is symbolic of blood and life. The universe is bursting with communication to reinforce His identity and plan. Everything matters.

God's heavenization program outlined in Genesis 1 continues to be developed in Genesis 2 and 3. Merging heaven and earth isn't a grand idea without corresponding structure and implications. Heavenization is an earthly goal with divinely designed principles, relationships, and strategies. If we speed-read these texts as a mere sequence of events—this happened, and then this happened, and then this happened—we will substantially miss the intended meaning.

The first set of realities that the Bible deeply develops has to do with humanity itself, or *anthropology*, as theologians label it. Since God's plan was to heavenize earth through His image bearers, it makes sense that we would need to know something about them first.

The Bible goes to great lengths to advance an understanding of humanity and the world before it fully introduces Jesus. The Old Testament covers a narrative span of thousands of years before the birth of Christ. We take so many basic elements of life for granted, but the Bible does not. It is extremely intentional in addressing nitty-gritty topics that are universally relevant.

I was discussing the reason for this dynamic with a friend who did some missionary work in Africa. He noticed that when missionaries introduced the story of Jesus to native tribes, many of the Africans simply interpreted him as being a supreme witch doctor among witch doctors. In other words, they saw Jesus through their own interpretive grid rather than a biblical one.

Our objective is to avoid this contextualization error by exploring some of the fundamental thematic threads that emerge in Genesis 2 and 3. Before we go deeper into making sense of the mystery of Christ, we must be careful not to conceive of Jesus in a vacuum or a conceptual filter of our own making. If we fail to see Him from a biblical perspective, we will fail to see Him as He is. If our understanding of the world is warped and truncated, our understanding of Christ will also be warped and truncated.

The first step is to understand what the Bible claims about the anthropological framework for God's program. What is God's purpose and structure for human work, feasting, marriage, love, sex, children, sin, sacrifice, and so on? Genesis 2 and 3 lay a foundation for all of these subjects and more. Of course, everyone will decide for themselves whether they believe the biblical claims to be true, but we must first clearly understand them before we can intelligently assess them.

Keeping this in mind, we will briefly explore various elements of the story in Genesis 2 and 3 that contribute to three major philosophical and theological themes. This chapter is very dense, so I am going to outline it here to help you digest it:

God's Garden Model for Human Maturity and Civilization
    Work at the core of humanity's identity
    Masters of art and science
    The two teaching trees
    Food and faith
The Communal Building Blocks of Humanity
    The reason for marriage
    The representational principle
    The glory of women
    Biblical leadership and headship
Sex, Nudity, and Human Destiny
    Sex and the city
    The dehumanizing potential of sexual power
    The nature and gravity of sin
    Humanity's new clothes

God's Garden Model for Human Maturity and Civilization

Being naked in a verdant paradise sounds like a pretty good arrangement—and it was. Nevertheless, the story of Genesis 2 clearly signals that the garden was only a beginning phase for humanity. It was an educational sanctuary where humanity would begin learning how to enact God's primary command to "Be fruitful and multiply and fill the earth and subdue it, and have dominion over the fish of the sea and over the birds of the heavens and over every living thing that moves on the earth" (Gen. 1:28).

We know this in part because the Garden of Eden did not fill the whole earth. The Hebrew word for *garden* can be translated as *paradise*, and Genesis 2 specifically says that God "planted a garden in Eden, in the east." In other words, the paradise in the east part of Eden was a very unique and special place on earth. The rest of the earth had not been cultivated to the same degree.

In fact, Genesis 2 makes it clear that there were at least three other nongardenized lands beyond the region of Eden—Havilah, Cush, and Assyria. The text even describes Havilah as a land of gold and other stones, suggesting that it was to be mined for its precious metals. However we interpret some of these things, it is clear that the paradisical Garden of Eden occupied a limited area of the world. If humanity were going to fulfill the command to have dominion over the earth, we would have to push beyond Eden's borders.

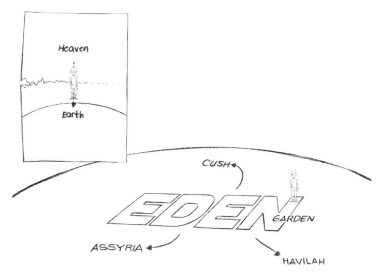

It is worth pausing to consider the significance of putting Adam in a distinct garden. God could have placed him in a utilitarian farm, untamed jungle, or barren desert. He could have placed him outside of Paradise and told him to earn his way in through moral achievement.

Instead, God graciously located Adam in a highly structured context where "every tree is pleasant to the sight and good for food."

This twofold description of the garden is a fascinating feature of enormous consequence. The garden was a place filled with stunning beauty and abundant feasting—of high aesthetics and delicious nourishment. It offered a total immersion in functional beauty that was satisfying at every level of the human senses—sight, touch, smell, taste, and hearing.

DUAL PRIORITIES

"Pleasant to the Sight"
AESTHETICS

"Good for Food"
FEASTING

THANKSGIVING

The dual priorities of the garden framed the fundamental model for humanity's heavenization project. Humanity was placed there so that we could learn how to cultivate civilizations that highlighted aesthetics and feasting—resulting in communal thanksgiving. The earth was not given to humanity for eternal retirement or selfish exploitation, but for comprehensive development and intense enjoyment.

Work at the core of humanity's identity

I think a lot of us read this narrative and assume that the resortlike setting in Eden meant that Adam could lounge around all day, doing nothing but munching on fruit. But if we read Genesis 2 carefully, we see that Adam was given work to do. His first job was to tend and keep the garden. The vocational pathway to worldwide dominion started with humble cultivation and defense of a garden. Adam had to learn how to effectively use a gardener's shovel before holding a ruler's scepter.

Learning the basics of any discipline takes time and effort. One of the great privileges of my childhood was learning to play the piano. I started when I was in first grade and continued to take lessons through college. While I had aspirations of being a performer or a conductor, my gifts were somewhat limited. I was able to play some killer Rachmaninoff preludes by the time I was in my twenties, but being a professional performing artist was never truly within my reach.

Playing classical piano at an advanced level is difficult because it requires an incredible amount of patience and immersion in basic forms. Simple scales and chords must be slowly and carefully practiced over and over again with the correct method and technique. The "Finger Fun" books filled with monotonous exercises were anything but fun, yet entirely necessary. My poor family suffered long hearing me play the same patterns ad infinitum.

After years of practice the forms that had been so foreign became second nature. Muscle memory replaced deliberate forethought. Eventually I internalized note configurations to the degree that I could sight-read many pieces on demand. What used to take months to learn took no time at all.

If my teacher had put a Rachmaninoff prelude in front of me as a first grader I couldn't have begun to tackle it. I might have appreciated it for its dramatic sound and flashy technique, but I could not have executed it. The elementary song "Riding on a Mule" was not as glamorous as Rachmaninoff, but it incorporated the basic patterns that I needed to master and build upon so that I could slowly work my way to more sophisticated music.

In like manner, the garden was a simple context for humanity to learn elementary forms and principles of life so that we could have dominion over the earth. Humanity needed to mature. Fulfilling God's creation mandate to be fruitful and multiply wasn't just about making babies; it was—and is—about extending God's glorious dominion and communion throughout earth. Achieving human civilization requires great wisdom and knowledge. It was never simply a matter of procreation.

As we saw in Genesis 1, humanity was particularly designed to mirror and image God's creational work pattern of taking hold, transforming, evaluating, and enjoying. What better place to learn this form than a well-groomed garden? Adam was placed in an immersive environment that would reinforce humanity's calling.

Imitating God's pattern of work is the very essence of what it means to be made in God's image. Moral agency and sentience are only a small fraction of what it means to be uniquely human. Our capacity to be self-reflective, rational, and morally volitional is not unique to humanity at all. Angels and animals have self-awareness and exhibit forms of sophisticated communication. We are told that angels even have the ability to make moral choices. Nevertheless, animals and angels are not made in God's image.

Being made in God's image is expressly tied to our communal work of glorifying earth. Angels and animals are not tasked with this work; only humans are. Until we understand work together as our defining role, we cannot understand what it means to be fully human. This is one of the reasons why work is so central to human dignity. If we are not engaged in meaningful and fruitful labor, the very essence of our humanity is radically diminished.

One of the reasons the rehabilitative efforts of our prison system fail so miserably is because they don't grasp this fundamental aspect of our nature. When a person is robbed of the ability and responsibility to do meaningful and rewarding work, the potential for true participation in community is all but destroyed. There is a temporary place for menial and even punitive labor, to be sure, but if the goal is rehabilitation to society, then a goal toward truly fruitful work must be part of the program. At our very core, we are made to be fruitful workers.

Masters of art and science

The Garden of Eden, lush with trees that were "pleasant to the sight and good for food," embodied God's educational strategy. In fact, the subtle message of Genesis 2 is that humanity needed to master art and science in order to rule God's creation.[39] We had to learn the working principles of beautiful design and technical knowledge to go about the work of worldwide transformation.

Adam was engaged in scientific discovery as one of his first tasks. Observing the different animals was the initial step in becoming a zoological and biological steward over creation. But he didn't just observe passively; he named the species as an act of authority and parentage. As their caretaker he had to take inventory of his future kingdom.

---

39 James Jordan, *Primeval Saints: Studies in the Patriarchs of Genesis* (Moscow: Canon Press, 2001), 14.

Isn't it interesting that we teach the differences between animals to toddlers? Cows go *moo*, and ducks say *quack, quack*. We consider these distinctions as fundamental knowledge for children, not advanced learning for adults. Our instinct to teach children about our environment and the beings we are supposed to be stewards of can be traced straight back to Adam in Genesis 2. We intuitively train for worldly dominion because it is who we are.

Apple Computer has become one of the most valuable companies on planet Earth. Why? Because the visionary Steve Jobs knew that humans resonated deeply to beautiful tools that were employed in beautiful work. In a PBS interview he described how Apple applied this vision:

> Picasso had a saying. He said, "Good artists copy, great artists steal." And we have always been shameless about stealing great ideas and I think part of what made the Macintosh great was that the people working on it were musicians and poets and artists and zoologists and historians who also happened to be the best computer scientists in the world.[40]

Jobs intuitively understood that the intimate marriage of art with the utility of science is one of the highest expressions of our humanity. A blunt instrument can accomplish a task, and a piece of fine art may move us emotionally, but we experience joy when they are combined. This is by God's design—it is not an accident of nature.

When we realize that the Garden of Eden was an educational sanctuary and blueprint for humans to learn the art and science of culture building, we see a different trajectory in the story of Genesis 2 and 3. The story of humanity doesn't begin with a finished state of affairs. It begins with an immature man who needed to progressively learn and acquire the wisdom necessary for proper dominion over God's creation. Humanity was not immediately prepared to begin the project of heavenization. First they needed to go to kindergarten—literally, a "children's garden."

The two teaching trees

The two special trees in the middle of the garden—the tree of life and the tree of the knowledge of good and evil—further underscore this reading. We read in Genesis 2,

> The tree of life was in the midst of the garden, and the tree of the knowledge of good and evil . . . . The LORD God took the man and put him in the

---

40 *The Triumph of the Nerds: The Rise of Accidental Empires*, PBS, 1996.

garden of Eden to work it and keep it. And the Lᴏʀᴅ God commanded the man, saying, "You may surely eat of every tree of the garden, but of the tree of the knowledge of good and evil you shall not eat, for in the day that you eat of it you shall surely die." (vv 9b, 15–17)

It is tempting to read this and think that these two trees had magical apples on them—one resulting in life and the other in death. However, it is better to see them as teaching trees. Their presence in the garden was meant to train humanity about their relationship to God and the world. They were living landmarks and symbolic monuments to God's program.

I recently took my family on a trip to the nation's capital so I could introduce my boys to our form of government. Even though I had visited Washington, D.C., as a teenager, I was awestruck by the magnificence of the national monuments. At the center of the National Mall is the Washington Monument—a massive obelisk patterned after Egyptian columns. It dominates the city as a symbol of freedom. Anchoring the mall opposite the Capitol Building is the Lincoln Memorial. It is clearly reminiscent of the temple of Zeus in Olympia, Greece—glorifying a man who fought for the unity of our country.

Various government buildings are organized around the perimeter of these monuments along with museums featuring our national heritage. This is no accident—our institutional leaders are supposed to be reminded of our national principles and identity as they work in the shadow of these memorials. The foundations of our republic are enshrined in these central features of the city.

When we recognize the two trees as memorials and monuments of God's program for humanity, it helps us understand their significance. Let's think about it for a moment. Why would there need to be a tree of life in a garden that already provided abundant food on every tree?

God wanted humanity to know and trust that our life source is not merely derived from biological fuel. There were many trees to gain sustenance from, but only one could impart ongoing life. Humanity's existence was ultimately contingent on God's special provision and power expressed through the tree of life. God wanted us to arrange our lives around that reality.

A phrase that is repeated many times throughout the Bible is "the righteous shall live by faith." The word *righteous* essentially means to be in a right relationship with God. Being right with God always begins with trust and faith in Him and His good plans. God is most delighted when we trust in Him because He is God and we are not. This was true for Adam in the beginning and it is true for us today.

This shouldn't be too difficult to grasp, because our close loving relationships work in an analogous way. They are rooted in trust that the other person is worth loving and being faithful to. In order to sustain a right relationship with my wife, we must trust one another and render faithfulness to each other. When we betray that relationship of trust and faithfulness, our connectedness is broken. So it is with God.

The critical issue in the garden is not that the tree of life had magic apples. No, it stood as a monument to our need to be faithfully dependent upon God for life. As the Washington Monument is a symbol of freedom, so the tree of life stood for faith in God. Life with God is a life of faith.

What about the tree of knowledge—what did it stand for, and why did God prohibit eating from it? Some theologians have erroneously interpreted the singular prohibition as a positive command—as if Adam had something to perform as a moral wage earner. However, Adam had nothing to earn, per se, but he had everything to learn. He lacked the wisdom and knowledge to fulfill his role.

People sometimes think that the tree of knowledge was evil in and of itself. It wasn't. The tree was a teaching instrument about the nature of good and evil. God placed it in the garden as a primary means of bringing infant humanity to the wisdom of adulthood. Adam and humanity needed to know the difference between right and wrong in order to sustain their relationship to God and have proper dominion over the world. How could we possibly build culture and civilization without such knowledge?

In fact, humanity would have come to the knowledge of good and evil whether or not Adam had partaken of the tree of knowledge. If Adam hadn't eaten the fruit, he would have come to a *righteous* knowledge of good and evil—knowing what it meant to persevere in faithfulness to God. He would have known evil not experientially, but by conceptual negation. He would have known what it meant *not* to engage in evil.

In contrast, by eating of the tree while under God's prohibition, he came to a fallen knowledge of good and evil—experientially knowing what it meant to break faith with God in disobedience.

If that's unclear, consider an illustration from marriage: A husband and wife can learn the difference between faithfulness and unfaithfulness in two ways. They can either stay faithful to one another, enjoying a loving and unbroken relationship, or they can commit adultery, experiencing the devastation of betrayal. Adam's sin was like adultery—he learned the value of fidelity only by destroying it.

Many theologians believe that God's prohibition against the tree of knowledge was temporary and that Adam could have eaten from it once he was confirmed in righteousness. Whether or not Adam ever ate of the tree of knowledge, it would have taught him what trust and obedience to God were—and that is the essence of good and evil.

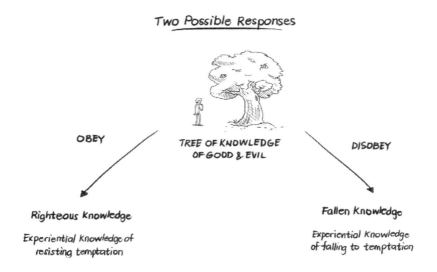

Two Possible Responses

OBEY

TREE OF KNOWLEDGE
OF GOOD & EVIL

DISOBEY

Righteous knowledge

Experiential knowledge of
resisting temptation

Fallen Knowledge

Experiential knowledge
of falling to temptation

Good and evil are not distant abstractions that are hard to grasp. Morality is not made of random rules that God wants to oppress humanity with. The difference between right and wrong can simply be understood as conformity or nonconformity to God's character and His good program for heaven and earth. The Bible sometimes refers to God's program as His *law*.

The adherence or lack thereof to God's law is fundamentally characterized by what we believe about God and His plan. If we trust in His goodness and path for our destiny we will do *good*. If we do not place our trust in God and pursue other paths, we will do *evil*. The standard for good and evil is God Himself, not a poison apple.

King Solomon, one of the wisest men in the history of the world, said, "The fear of the LORD is the beginning of knowledge" (Prov. 1:7). This is not cute sentimentality; this is the way true knowledge works. It begins with a healthy sense of who God is and what His agenda is about. When we lack faith and obedience to God, our knowledge becomes wildly distorted and dangerously misapplied.

The two trees in the middle of the Eden thus held forth faith and obedience as the pillars of human civilization's right relationship with God. There could be no mistake that life was dependent upon God and that fidelity to His program was necessary for the wisdom to rule. Breaking away from the tree of life and the prohibition against the tree of knowledge would be both fatal and destructive.

Garden of Eden
TWO TEACHING TREES

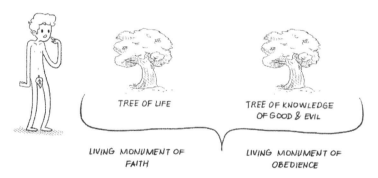

TREE OF LIFE   TREE OF KNOWLEDGE OF GOOD & EVIL

LIVING MONUMENT OF FAITH   LIVING MONUMENT OF OBEDIENCE

The New Testament epistle of James declares that "faith apart from works is dead" (2:26b). In other words, belief without corresponding behavior is proved to be illegitimate and false. People who claim to have faith in God without works demonstrate that their faith is empty and lifeless. True faith produces true obedience, and true obedience springs from faith.

This clearly means that if Adam had kept the faith, he would also have kept God's law. Law-keeping and acting in alignment with God's agenda is not robotic or mechanistic performance of certain deeds. Our works—whether good or evil, flow from the focus of our hearts. Faith has always been the prerequisite for working in accordance with God's program. It was true for Adam and it is true for us as well.

If there is any doubt that faith was at stake for Adam, simply read forward in Genesis 3. There you will see Satan's strategy of attack on humanity. It was to erode trust in God's program and character. Once Adam's faith was sufficiently undermined, he would be vulnerable to taking matters into his own hands. Faith is the foundation of obedience.

Food and faith

We would be seriously remiss if we ignored the link between food and faith in Genesis 2. In fact, there are several food tests throughout the Bible to make the fundamental connection abundantly clear.

Jacob tested his older brother, Esau, who gave away his Abrahamic inheritance for a mere bowl of stew. Israel was tested in the wilderness to trust in God's miraculous provision of manna from heaven. When Jesus was fasting in preparation for his public ministry, Satan tempted him to break the fast by turning stones to bread. Jesus even responded to Satan by quoting from the Old Testament, "Man shall not live by bread alone, but by every word that comes from the mouth of God" (Matt. 4:4, Deut. 8:3).

By making food good and necessary for life, God showed that He wanted humanity to look to Him for life. From the beginning, this required a posture of faith. While it might be natural to assume that our bodies are ultimately sustained by physical means, God designed us to be solely reliant upon Him. This dependence wasn't just a matter of physical proximity or participation to a tree—it was a relationship of faith and trust to God.

Feasting at common tables is symbolic of our communion with God and our neighbors. We acknowledge and cement our relationships by sharing meals together. Food actually becomes the organizing framework and celebratory vehicle of our fellowship with other people. This is by God's design.

You may have already put this together, but I believe the Bible is a very strange book in many respects. It is hard to approach it without realizing that it requires a deeply weird reading at times. We will miss a lot of its message if we try to sanitize it and make it fit a modern notion of rational sophistication.

I'll give you a relevant example. Some scholars have noted that of all the dietary laws in the Bible, only one remains in force. The one food law that still exists is the law about eating an animal with its lifeblood still in it (Gen. 9:4, Acts 15:20, 29). We may enjoy pork and shellfish, but we may not eat animals that are still alive. Why?

This may sound gross—and it is—but throughout history, vampirism has been a prominent feature in certain religions. People have always recognized the close relationship between life and blood. The Bible itself requires sacrificial death to fulfill ultimate justice because "the life is in the blood." However, God does not want us to feast on the blood of other beings as way to derive life. He doesn't want us to be vampires.

There is one startling exception to this law against eating living things: Those who believe in Christ are commanded to drink His blood and eat His flesh. The tree of life we now have access to is Jesus, and we must participate in His resurrection life in order to live eternally. This participation is connected to eating because eating is the biological means of fueling our bodies. We must feast on God Himself and His resurrection life in order to have life.

The Communal Building Blocks of Humanity

We have seen that the garden was a place that highlighted the principles of beauty and feasting, art and science, faith and obedience. But there was still more that had to be learned and addressed. Namely, that it is not good for man to be alone.

In Genesis 1 we noted that there was no benediction after the second day of creation. In Genesis 2 we read the first malediction—or negative declaration regarding the created order: "It is not good that the man should be alone; I will make him a helper fit for him" (Gen. 2:18).

Notice that it was not only "not good" for Adam to be lacking a human mate, it was "not good" for him to be permanently left alone with God, either. From the very beginning of the Bible, individualism—whether ascetic or rugged—is denounced. Humanity was made for intimate fellowship and communion, not individual isolation.

God could, in theory, have solved this situation by introducing any number of relationships for Adam. He could have created a different person from the dust to be Adam's friend or sibling. He could have created a child for him to raise. Or He could even have created a whole group of other people. Instead, God gave him a female wife from his own rib, and, in so doing, established marriage and family as the primary vehicles for extending human civilization throughout the earth.

The reason for marriage

Marriage is not a separate biblical line item that floats around in its own conceptual bubble. It exists in the central context of God's program for heavenizing earth. In order to engage in the creation mandate to be fruitful and multiply and extend human civilization, God first established and employed marriages and families.

Some years ago, First Lady Hillary Clinton made waves with her book *It Takes a Village*. Her thesis echoed proverbs from various African cultures, the gist of which mean, "It takes a village to raise a child." Clinton borrowed the saying to make the point that parents and families do not and should not live in a communal vacuum, and, therefore, we should all take a greater interest in the children of others and how we can participate in helping shape the next generation.

I substantially and enthusiastically agree with the heart of Clinton's thesis. Marriages and family units are discrete communities of people, but they are designed to be culturally integrative. We are directly responsible for our own families and children, but that does not mean that other children and families are of no concern to us. We are called to participate in the lives of others through our example, sacrificial giving, and relationships.

Clinton is correct in positing that there are many things we can better accomplish as groups of families and people—or villages—than as individual families. For example, while I happen to believe that homeschooling is a legitimate and necessary option for many families, I tend to believe that many aspects of education are better accomplished with the resources available from a wider community. This does not necessarily mean that I am a strong advocate for government-run schools. It simply means that villages are better equipped than individual families at serving some initiatives and priorities.

The concern I have with Clinton's thesis is that it tends to take the marital and familial foundations of village for granted in an age when they are deeply misunderstood and disregarded. Villages are not made up of random groups of individuals. Villages are collections of *families*, which are built on marriages made of pairs of men and women. If these basic components of a village are eroded, the power and meaning of village itself unravels. I believe Clinton's vision for effective villages is absolutely correct, but almost entirely unachievable until we recover the more basic units of marriage and family.

Humanity's tragic departure from God's program has naturally resulted in attacks on the essential building blocks of human civilization. The divinely instituted constructs of marriage and family are often derided as mere social or religious conventions that can be defined on an almost ad hoc basis. Instead of being honored as foundational aspects of God's heavenization campaign, they are scoffed at as unenlightened relics of a past age.

The most efficient way to dismantle and escape God's agenda is to eliminate each plank of humanity's core identity piece by piece. The more we attempt to suppress the way we are made to work and to relate in God's image, the more we flee from the feeling that we may be out of accord with His will. It is the ultimate form of self-deception and self-delusion.

In many respects, this breakdown has occurred because of an essential failure to revel in and enjoy the unique identities of manhood and womanhood. How can marriage and family make sense when men and women do not understand their irreplaceable characteristics and purpose in God's plan?

Men have often used their physical strength and intellectual energy for domineering chauvinism and self-serving tyranny rather than gentle service and sacrificial giving. Women have often used their beauty and God-given relational intuition to manipulate and wound rather than to nurture and heal. We have collectively failed to live up to our intended callings.

By no means is it accurate to portray women as weak or men as non-relational. Sweeping generalizations that eliminate women's strength or men's need to emotionally connect are completely flawed. However, there is an opposite error in ignoring some of the distinct physiological and psychological traits that characterize men and women. The ways that we are different are just as important as the ways we are the same.

The early chapters of Genesis trace out some of these features for our consideration. God could have created and commissioned Adam and Eve simultaneously and equally, but that is not the way the story reads. It is no narrative accident that Adam was first tasked with tending and keeping the garden and that Eve was subsequently tasked with being a helper for him. This sequence exists so that we will pause and carefully contemplate the differences between Adam and Eve specifically, and men and women in general.

The representational principle

One of the profound theological dimensions of the creational order of Adam and Eve is that God constructed humanity on a representational or *federal* model. Even though each human being is a unique and individually responsible participant in the world, God created us so that other people can physically and spiritually represent us. We do not stand completely alone before God.

By God's design, we are all naturally born into the human family represented by Adam. The ultimate consequences of Adam's choices were passed on to Eve and his progeny. This is the reason why Eve was taken from Adam's rib, not of the dust of the ground. This has nothing to do with Adam's superiority and everything to do with organic and spiritual connectedness of Eve to Adam. We don't come into this world as blank slates or discrete units; we are biological and spiritual descendants of Adam.

Many people are uncomfortable with this representative or federal principle; nevertheless, it is the explicit and consistent teaching of the Bible. It suggests that we would all have done what Adam did and even that we mysteriously acted in accord with him. He was the perfectly accurate representative in the garden for each one of us.

Before we reject such a notion out of hand, we should consider our own cultural biases. In many parts of the world, a more collectivist and ancestral orientation regarding human identity is widely accepted. What may seem naturally offensive to us is readily assumed by other cultures. We need to be self-aware of our own individualistic and modern prejudices against such a system before dismissing it.

According to the Bible, when we conceive of our core identity in isolation from our origins, we have a distorted vision of ourselves. While we are unique individuals, we exist in close connection to our communal associations. We are all born into the human family—Adam's family. All of us are on equal ground by virtue of our common lineage.

This representational structure for humanity is also how the second Adam, Jesus Christ, provides salvation to all of His family as their federal representative. Without the representational principle, none of this would make any sense at all.

The good news is that while we are naturally connected to the old Adam and his tragic departure from God, faith can graft us into the family of the new Adam—the human tree of life, Jesus Christ. As the Apostle Paul said,

For if, because of one man's trespass, death reigned through that one man, much more will those who receive the abundance of grace and the free gift of righteousness reign in life through the one man Jesus Christ. Therefore, as one trespass led to condemnation for all men, so one act of righteousness leads to justification and life for all men. For as by the one man's disobedience the many were made sinners, so by the one man's obedience the many will be made righteous. (Rom. 5:17–19)

This one-to-one representational correspondence between the first Adam and the second Adam is a critical foundation to God's plan and program. Without understanding Adam's federal disobedience, the very concept of federal obedience becomes unintelligible. God can only accept the sacrifice of a substitute as a means of satisfying justice because representation is a reality.

The glory of women

The other theological implication of the creational order is that women were given a particular emphasis in their earthly work. Women are not only created to colabor in the heavenization project, they also have a special focus—to cultivate and nurture humanity itself. This is one of the reasons they bear children instead of men. Adam didn't need only a cogardener, he needed someone to be bone of his bone and flesh of his flesh—a soulmate.

That doesn't mean that men get to run the office while women function as their servile and doting secretaries. Not even close. The ordering of the story in Genesis 2 says more about men's acute inadequacy in God's program than it does about women's aptitudes. Men's propensity to be lost in their tasks and easily disconnected from communal relationships falls short of the goal for the new heavens and new earth. A vibrant and energetic culture of celebration cannot occur if the foundations of loving relationship are not in focus. Men need all the help they can get in this regard.

May women be scientists, government officials, and entrepreneurs? Absolutely—that is not in question. Women are not exclusively limited to working in the home by any stretch of the imagination. However, their work inside and outside of home should be done with enthusiasm and special attention to the communal dimension of those efforts. Their privilege and high calling is to ensure that the human relationships that result in the new heavens and new earth are fully in focus.

One of the many symptoms of our drift from God's plan is the way we demean and diminish what it means to focus on family life as a home-maker. In Proverbs 31, the Bible portrays an excellent wife as someone who works *for* the home, not exclusively *in* or *from* the home. She is an active entrepreneur and real estate developer who creates wealth and security for the family. This wealth provides a platform for philanthropic giving and the family's involvement in civil leadership and politics. Her children don't rebel—they celebrate her as a powerful matriarch. The city itself recognizes her as a key civic leader.

Humanity's collective perversity has warped this vision of women working alongside men and diminished their calling to being line cooks in the kitchen and maids doing laundry. We have diminished the significance of raising children and facilitating a nurturing home. Tyrannical and vain men have not supported the full scope of women's glorious calling. Women have understandably rebelled in an effort to prove their worth. We have ignored God's design and followed the devices of our own selfish imaginations and human civilization is poorer for it.

Far from being inferior to men in any way, women are actually supposed to receive higher honor. In fact, the Bible clearly and explicitly says that, "Woman is the glory of man" (1 Cor. 11:7). The crowning jewel and highest expression of our humanity isn't expressed through the male sex, but through the female sex. This is not true only in terms of raw beauty—women are clearly more glorious than men in that regard—but also in terms of their penultimate role in God's program.

Who is more glorious in a wedding, the bride or the groom? No one would say the bride is superior to the groom, but everyone understands that the bride is the focal point. When the Bible describes the church as the bride of Christ, that is no accident. Even God exalts His bride as His most glorious love. God celebrates His bride as His most cherished possession. Our individual marriages and families are supposed to be small microcosms of this. Sorry, fellas—women get the highest honor in the created order.

My family loves to watch the Food Network. We literally salivate over all the different culinary masterpieces that are produced on some of the shows. But my favorite program is from the less elegant end of the spectrum: *Diners, Drive-Ins, and Dives*, hosted by Guy Fieri. He visits hole-in-the-wall restaurants from coast to coast in his convertible Chevy

Camaro, sampling some of the best grub available. Every time I watch it I wish I could be Guy Fieri. Surely he has the best job in the world.

Here is the analogy. Someone had to build the restaurants, design the ovens, harvest the crops, and slaughter the livestock before the chef can make the herb-crusted sirloin burger with crispy onions and chipotle mayonnaise on a toasted English muffin slathered with garlic butter. A massive amount of resources and an extensive infrastructure must be provided before the cook ever does his magic. But who gets the glory when the sirloin burger is finally made and eaten? The truck driver who delivered the meat? The farmer who grew the herbs? Never in a million years. The glory goes to the chef who pulls it all together.

To the extent that men are primarily tasked with providing the broader context and resources for communal feasting and celebration, women are primarily tasked with actually developing and cementing the relationships that make the celebration happen. Figuratively speaking, men labor to provide the resources of the house, but women labor to make it a celebratory home.

This is what is going on in the distinct roles of men and women. Women are said to have the glory because they tie it all together and facilitate the deep relationships that make life so wonderful. There is no subservience in view whatsoever. The real joy happens when Martha Stewart lays hold of the dining room as the hostess of the party, not when Tim "the Toolman" Taylor comes to build the dining room table. There is glory in both, but the woman enjoys the greater glory.

It has become common to assume that role distinctions between men and women imply gender superiority or inferiority. This is unfortunate and nonsensical. There are role distinctions within the Godhead itself, and yet none of the Persons of the Trinity are subordinate or inferior to the other. The Son uniquely accomplishes the work of redemption and the Spirit uniquely applies it to humanity. The Father does neither of these things, but directs them as He wills. However, this does not make the Son or Spirit inferior to the Father. They are coequals, yet have different roles in their relationships. Role distinctions do not necessarily imply superior being or status.

It deeply saddens and confounds me when women conclude that role distinctions somehow suggest that women are unequal to men in any respect. In fact, I believe it is quite the opposite. If men have to master beauty and feasting, art and science, faith and obedience, then women have to master all of those *in addition to* an intimate understanding of humanity itself. If anything, men are arguably equipped to master less than women.

There is a very curious portion of one the Apostle Paul's first century letters to the church in Corinth about what men and women should wear on their heads in public worship. He writes,

> Every man who prays or prophesies with his head covered dishonors his head, but every wife who prays or prophesies with her head uncovered dishonors her head, since it is the same as if her head were shaven. For if a wife will not cover her head, then she should cut her hair short. But since it is disgraceful for a wife to cut off her hair or shave her head, let her cover her head. For a man ought not to cover his head, since he is the image and glory of God, but woman is the glory of man. For man was not made from woman, but woman from man. Neither was man created for woman, but woman for man. That is why a wife ought to have a symbol of authority on her head, because of the angels. Nevertheless, in the Lord woman is not independent of man nor man of woman; for as woman was made from man, so man is now born of woman. And all things are from God. Judge for yourselves: is it proper for a wife to pray to God with her head uncovered? Does not nature itself teach you that if a man wears long hair it is a disgrace for him, but if a woman has long hair, it is her glory? For her hair is given to her for a covering. (1 Cor. 11:4–15)

Here we have a classic example of how texts need context to be properly understood. The ancient city of Corinth was known for many things, but one of them was that it featured the temple of Aphrodite, the Greek god of beauty, love, and procreation. The word for something that enhances sexual desire, *aphrodisiac*, is derived from her name.

Aphrodite's temple in Corinth employed hundreds of ritual prostitutes—female slaves who served the male worshipers who came to pay spiritual homage. Worship and sex were highly integrated concepts in the ancient pagan world. Intimate relations with a temple prostitute were not merely an act for personal pleasure; it was an offering to a goddess. Sex cults were common, and Corinth was a center for hypersexualized conceptions of life and worship.

By contrast, one of the unique cultural features of the nascent Christian movement in the first century was that it held women and monogamous marriage in high regard. In fact, women were the first witnesses to the resurrection of Christ—they gave testimony that would have been unallowable in the Jewish judicial courts of the day.[41] The Apostle Paul even wrote that in Christ, "there is neither Jew nor Greek, there is neither slave nor free, there is no male and female" (Gal. 3:28). Ancient boundary lines of sex, cultural station, and familial lineage were no longer status markers in the presence of the true and living God.

Of course, this raised very thorny practical questions for the church in Corinth and around the Mediterranean. If men and women were equal in God's presence, should all gender distinctions—including outward symbolic distinctions of dress and propriety—be eliminated? When Christians worship, should they be appear to be unisex as a symbol of their ultimate equality and solidarity?

Paul's answer was a complex *no*. If you start from the end of the passage, you can clearly see that Paul is straining hard to make the point that women and men are complementary equals. When he writes, "woman is not independent of man nor man of woman; for as woman was made from man, so man is now born of woman," he is making it clear that we are created and born as equals. God may have initially taken Eve from Adam's rib, but now men are born of women. One sex is not superior to the other because "all things are from God."

However, despite our creational equality, Paul maintained that men and women are still functionally distinct and that their differing roles should be acknowledged and maintained. In Corinth's particular cultural context the distinction between men and women was expressed through their various hairstyles or other head coverings. Paul taught that the particular hairstyle traditions of the Corinthian church distinguishing men from women should be kept. Men were supposed to have short hair or shaved heads and women were supposed to keep long hair.

This passage is much easier for me to understand as a bald man. Hair is a symbol of splendor and glory. Oh, how I wish I had a head of hair. I've recently grown a beard to try to offset the lack of coverage on my skull. As my wife likes to say, I need more facial furniture to fill the high-ceilinged room.

Saturday Night Live comedian Chris Rock produced an intriguing documentary called *Good Hair*. It spotlights the obsession many African American women have with straightening and styling their hair

---

41 One of the central texts of Rabbinic Judaism, the Talmud, explains who is eligible and ineligible for testimony in the third chapter of "Sandhedrin."

204 Man in the Middle

in order to meet a societal perception of beauty. They spend thousands of dollars each year on everything from chemical straighteners to hair extensions and wigs. National conventions are devoted to the products and stylists who specialize in providing "good hair." It is a multi-billion-dollar industry devoted exclusively to African American women.

Even though Chris Rock specifically addresses the predicament of African American women striving for beauty, the reality is that good hair is a major priority across races, creeds, and cultures. But why? Why are multiple aisles at retail stores devoted to hair products—especially for women? Is it merely because we're vain?

The Bible offers an answer. Women are designed to be distinctly beautiful and glorious in ways that distinguish them from men. Women should be markedly feminine, not unisex or masculine. Having their heads shaved would be disgraceful and rob them of their female identity. Women should be feminine and men should be masculine.

Further complicating matters is Paul's use of the word *authority*. What does it mean when Paul writes, "That is why a wife should have a symbol of authority on her head, because of the angels"? That seems to imply that wives are supposed to be subservient to the dominance of their husbands. In fact, the sentences just prior to our quoted excerpt seem to suggest a descending chain of command. Paul wrote, "But I want you to understand that the head of every man is Christ, the head of a wife is her husband, and the head of Christ is God" (1 Cor. 11:3).

Does this series of relationships—God is the head of Christ, Christ is the head of every man, a husband is the head of his wife, and the wife wears a sign of authority on her head—relegate her to the proverbial bottom of the totem pole?

That interpretation would be conceivable except that it completely misses the way Paul is nuancing his answer to the Corinthian problem concerning gender distinctions in the Christian community. The Greek word Paul uses for *authority* is *exousia (ἐξουσία)*, which is derived from the Greek word, *exesti (ἔξεστι)*. This word means *it is lawful* and connotes the privilege or rights someone has.[42]

In fact, several paragraphs earlier in the same letter to the Corinthians, Paul uses the word *exousia* a total of six times in a very short space to emphatically reference his rights as an apostle. For instance, "Do we

---

42 BibleHub. "Strong's Greek: 1849. ἐξουσία (exousia). http://biblehub.com/greek/1849.htm.

not have the right (*exousia*) to eat and drink? Do we not have the right (*exousia*) to take along a believing wife, as do the other apostles and the brothers of the Lord and Cephas? Or is it only Barnabas and I who have no right (*exousia*) to refrain from working for a living?" (1 Cor. 9:4–6).

Does this sound a little like a preacher to you, repeating the same word over and over again? You can almost hear Paul sarcastically emphasizing the word *exousia* with each use. The thrust of Paul's use of the word has more to do with lawful permission than with control over someone else. *Exousia* in the sense he is using it has more to do with privilege than power.

So when we read, "That is why a wife should have a symbol of privilege (*exousia*) on her head, because of angels," we should not assume it is to reinforce the diminished status of women. In fact, the supplemental phrase "because of angels" throws us back to some of the glimpses into heaven we considered in the last chapter. Women are privileged with glory in the same way that the angels in God's immediate presence are. Women share in the glory of angels.

So why do so many Bibles interpret the word *exousia* as *authority*? I think this has to do with a critical misunderstanding of headship. When we speak of headship we tend to think of the person in charge and in command. The head honcho. The head man. The boss. When we hear that the husband is the head of the wife and that the wife should be submissive, we assume it means husbands are called to be dominant decision-makers.

Biblical leadership and headship

Biblical headship doesn't quite work like that. It absolutely does speak to a kind of leadership and initiative, but in a very special way. In what way is Christ the head of every man? Paul tells us:

> Wives, submit to your own husbands, as to the Lord. For the husband is the head of the wife even as Christ is the head of the church, his body, and is himself its Savior. Now as the church submits to Christ, so also wives should submit in everything to their husbands. Husbands, love your wives, as Christ loved the church and gave himself up for her, that he might sanctify her, having cleansed her by the washing of water with the word, so that he might present the church to himself in splendor, without spot or wrinkle or any such thing, that she might be holy and without blemish. In the same way husbands should love their wives as their own bodies. He who loves his wife loves himself. For no one ever hated his own flesh, but nourishes and cherishes it, just as Christ does the church, because we are members of his body. (Eph. 5:22–30)

Headship is not primarily explained in terms of commands to be obeyed or superiority to be acknowledged, but in terms of sacrificial giving and leadership that should be received and imitated. Being positioned as the head brings responsibility to sacrificially serve, not to dominate. Headship is about service, not being served.

I recently heard a story about a journalist who had interviewed Afghan women in Kabul several years ago during the reign of the Taliban. She was fascinated by their dress and by the fact that they walked five paces behind their husbands in public. Years later, the journalist returned after the overthrow of the Taliban and was shocked to find that the women were happily keeping the tradition of walking well behind their husbands on the city streets. When the journalist asked an Afghan woman why she continued to submit herself to such repression in the absence of the Taliban, the woman looked at her and said, "Land mines."

In the same way Christ gave his life for the church, husbands should give their lives away for their wives. Paul could have said, "Husbands, take charge of your wives like Christ takes charge of you." He doesn't. He says, "Husbands, love your wives, as Christ loved the church and gave himself up for her, that he might sanctify her...." We must interpret the meaning of headship in the way Paul defines it.

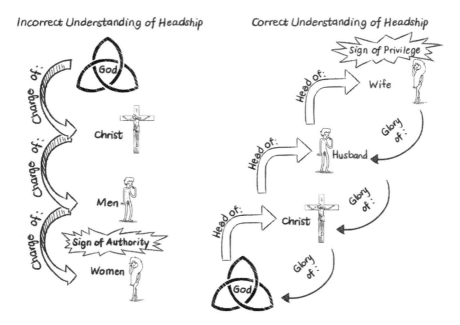

Incorrect Understanding of Headship

Correct Understanding of Headship

The implication is that when a husband gives his life to his wife, she should humbly receive it and enthusiastically reciprocate. Biblical submission isn't primarily about obeying a superior commander; it is about a willingness to be served and sanctified by someone taking sacrificial initiative. This is the paradox of Paul's teaching that so many people miss.

During the earthly ministry of Jesus, a mother of two of his disciples asked if her sons could be seated to the right and left hand of his throne when his kingdom arrived. A dispute arose among the disciples over who should be given such exalted positions of authority. Jesus said,

> You know that the rulers of the Gentiles lord it over them, and their great ones exercise authority over them. It shall not be so among you. But whoever would be great among you must be your servant, and whoever would be first among you must be your slave, even as the Son of Man came not to be served but to serve, and to give his life as a ransom for many. (Matt. 20:25–28)

This arrangement flies in the face of our pride at so many levels, doesn't it? We want to be able to claim that we are self-made people who have attained glory on our own terms and energy. We resist the notion that our glorification is contingent upon receiving the sacrifice of another. But that is how God has set up His world.

Biblical submission is ultimately a mutual and reciprocal affair. It is bilateral, not unilateral. Husbands and wives are supposed to reflect and model the relationship of Christ to his redeemed people. The relationship is not rooted in authoritarian mandates, but in mutual service for the purpose of glorifying and enjoying one another.

Perhaps the more accessible term to describe this dynamic is *love*. Love is more than a romantic or warm, fuzzy feeling. Love is sacrificially serving someone from the heart. Love puts the needs of someone else before our own. It doesn't mean we don't have needs or shouldn't want them to be reciprocally met. However, love is not strictly transactional. It does not function on a quid pro quo basis. Love is giving for the sake of another, not for our own sake.

Patrick Stewart as Jean-Luc Picard was my favorite captain in the various *Star Trek* series. He was a spaceship captain that I could take seriously. What would I give for his voice. I have felt increasingly solidarity with him the balder I have become. He is pretty much the bald man's standard for being a stud.

One of the episodes I really enjoyed was about a planet that bred women specifically to become soulmates to their future husbands. They were trained to fall in love with and completely serve the first man they were introduced to. Their whole life was spent learning the various ways to please a man so that when they finally met him they could become a student of his interests and transform into his dream partner.

By some accident of fate, Jean-Luc stumbled into one of these women on a journey and she bonded with him immediately. Of course he was stunned by the way she perfectly anticipated his desires and preferences. She swept him off his feet. She was everything he could have wanted.

I can't quite remember, but I think he may have broken the relationship off because it violated the prime directive, or something like that. While this story is obviously extreme and slightly silly, it illustrates an interesting point. There is a sense in which spouses have to become students of one another to love each other. We must know them intimately in order to truly delight them. In a highly functional marriage, both spouses are consistently committed to serving the other person in individually appropriate ways. Love serves the other person so that they can better fulfill their special calling in God's plan.

Divorce is serious and grievous to God because it reveals a refusal of two people to live out their human calling to love and mutual service. Divorce is the very opposite of the way we're supposed to behave as God's image-bearers. Sometimes a marital breakdown is one-sided, and the injured spouse is an innocent party. However, it often takes two to tango…or to tangle. In a divorce or a miserable marriage, there is usually failure on both sides—both husband and wife have failed to understand and enact God's self-sacrificial design for their relationship.

Marriage is not a mere civil contract that should be entered into or broken on a whim. It is the primary building block of human culture because it mirrors the interpersonal love God has as Father, Son, and Spirit, and the way He relates to His people. God has set up this system to promote love as His personal program.

I have labored over this point at great length because the fundamental nature of our relationships lies at the very apex of God's heavenization agenda. What good is beauty if it cannot be shared and celebrated together? For what purpose do we employ science except to elevate our common humanity? All of our work exists in a relational matrix that exists for mutual service.

It is not good for man to be alone. When we begin to recapture what it means to be identified as men and women—and to what purpose we have children and raise families—we will know the power of the village. God's city will be assembled from every tribe and tongue, and we will feast together in God's good world.

Sex, Nudity, and Human Destiny

We have compared Genesis 1 to the overture of a musical that introduces the great themes before the curtain is raised and compared Genesis 2 to Scene 1, Act 1, of the play. At the beginning of the scene we saw Adam created and located in the Garden of Eden. He was there to enjoy learning beauty and feasting, art and science, and faith and obedience. By the end of the first scene we hear Adam delighting in his new wife and life partner, Eve. Adam sings praise and the narrator speaks as the scene comes to an end:

"This at last is bone of my bones and flesh of my flesh; she shall be called Woman, because she was taken out of Man."
Therefore a man shall leave his father and his mother and hold fast to his wife, and they shall become one flesh. And the man and his wife were both naked and were not ashamed. (Gen. 2:23–25)

It is easy to imagine the newlyweds, Adam and Eve, embracing in a passionate kiss as the curtain falls and the lights dim. The two became one flesh. They were naked and not ashamed. They could be completely transparent and vulnerable to one another in the most profound way. The special union between husband and wife was physically realized through sex.

Sex and the city

Genesis 2 is incredibly rich in what it teaches about humanity, so it is only fitting that it would include something that is so central to our identities and lives. You cannot come to the subject of human relationships and the building of culture and civilization without addressing sex. It is a big deal and the Bible gives it a lot of attention from the beginning.

The first thing to notice is that sex is purposefully linked to marriage and the one-flesh merger of husband and wife. It is not an indiscriminate recreational activity that exists in a relational vacuum. It is an intense expression of relational bonding that has a unique purpose within human civilization.

Our sexuality was never meant to be arbitrary or haphazard. It is a central and integral part of God's program for heavenization. Marriages and families are of fundamental importance to God's project, so He used sex as the human super-glue and rocket fuel that would ensure its enduring execution. The most powerful way to promote humanity's multiplying activity was to power it with something as incredible and enjoyable as sex. It was a masterstroke of pure design genius.

The multidimensional significance of sex is profound. It is the means for procreation and establishing of families, an act of relational "one-flesh" bonding between spouses, and a means of renewal and enjoyment within marriage. When sex is unfettered by our departure from God's program, it can be experienced as one of His best gifts to humanity. It is a truly wonderful part of being human.

It would be tempting to skip over the procreational aspect of sex because it is so obvious. However, in this day, the priority of bearing children is not well understood or eagerly welcomed.

In extreme cases, some governments suppress childbearing through policies that forcing parents to abort babies that are beyond their designated quota. But for many of us, the pressure against procreation is not so draconian. We face more subtle societal resistance that is ostensibly concerned with the economic and social burden that children are perceived to create. The logic of many abortion advocates raises concerns about whether certain parents or cultures are truly fit or able to take responsibility of the children they conceive. Why populate earth with more problems than we can handle? And for some of us, the resistance to having children comes mainly from within ourselves. We just don't want to make the personal sacrifices parenthood will demand of us.

There is little doubt, and I am speaking from personal experience, that children are an enormous responsibility. They require incredible amounts of resources to love and to raise into adults. Frankly, they take more than they give. Parenting is a very resource-intense endeavor.

Our resistance to having children is one of the best examples of how inside-out we have turned God's program. The brilliant irony of God's plan is that childbearing requires enormous self-sacrifice and self-giving—which is the very heart of God's relational agenda. Childrearing is the built-in mechanism for training us how to give ourselves away.

Jesus said, "whoever wants to find his life will lose it." We don't come to the most profound levels of self-enlightenment by turning inward in meditation or hoarding resources to ourselves, but in giving ourselves away. The more we give of ourselves, the more we experience God's goodness. Having children is one of the most significant ways this model is demonstrated and internalized. Parenthood is extremely costly, but entirely worth it because it is a path of giving your life away in imitation of God's giving of Himself to us.

As someone who has an interest in economics, I find the studies concerning national birthrates and replacement rates to be very interesting. One of the primary reasons Japan is forecasting continued economic weakness is because their death rate is slightly higher than their birth rate. Their population is shrinking and with it the human capital to draw on for innovation and growth. Japan will be a nation in decline until more people begin procreating. The government has awoken to this fact and is even offering incentives for people to get pregnant.

In countries where birth rates are high, economic growth is forecasted to be very strong. Look no farther than India. Its projected growth curve is in the double-digits as far as the eye can see. Why? Because groups of humans find a way to survive and adapt. India will grow and increasingly prosper out of simple creative necessity.

I can personally say that the more responsibility I have had as a husband and father, the deeper I have to dig personally to provide for each hungry mouth and hungry heart. There is nothing like a little pressure and healthy anxiety to provide the motivation for smarter and harder work. If my life were easier, I would be far less productive and have far less to offer others. I discover more about my real capacities and gifts the more I am motivated to sacrifice for others.

Dehumanizing potential of sexual power

Sex is a form of power like money is power and governmental coercion. And for that reason the Bible spends a fair amount of time delineating its boundaries. It can create and destroy. Life can be given and souls can be forever marred. When sex is misused, it can break marital trust, bring children forth into chaos, and create deep confusion for victims of abuse.

Unfortunately, our corruption tends to take God's gifts and systematically disconnect them from His purposes and design. Procreation and children are seen as a burden, not a blessing. The marital and mo-nogamous relational context for sex is ignored or denied. We use sex as a means of selfish fulfillment rather than an act of self-giving and mutual service to our life partner. Some people even use it as a means of exploitation, control, profiteering, and violence.

This is why departures from God's agenda for sex get so much con-demnatory ink in the Bible. It isn't because God is a cosmic killjoy or doesn't heartily endorse good sex. God's program is intensely pro-sex through and through. God wants us to be sexually active people within the context of His design. He doesn't want to suppress or deny us of our innate desire to be sexual.

In fact, His boundaries are meant to protect and prosper our sex lives. Sex is incredibly healthy and satisfying when it is in alignment with His program, but massively destructive when it is not.

Many critics of the Bible portray its sexual ethics as prudish rules that emanated from some uptight, Victorian-era matron. But the sexu-al ethics of Judaism and Christianity have always been radically count-er-cultural. Pederasty, or man-boy sex, was normalized and celebrated in ancient Greece. Sadly, it is still rampant in parts of the world today. Women in certain regions of India are routinely raped as objects of grat-ification for the lusts of men. People who dismiss biblical sexual ethics as being quaint or chauvinist traditions of a bygone era have not really wrestled with what the Bible really says about sex. The goal of God's rules for sexual behavior isn't to erect false boundaries of social propriety, but to foster life and happiness. Sex lies close to the heart of God's program.

Of course there are many ways to break from God's design for sex. Many variations, from polygamy to bestiality, fail to reflect and promote God's priorities for building the relationships that make up human cul-ture and civilization. None of these relational configurations support and promote the interpersonal foundations of the new heavens and new earth.

Perhaps the thorniest issues of our day are questions surrounding sex outside of marriage and sexual orientation. Can't sex be casual and recreational without being destructive? Why can't same-sex people who are devoted to one another enjoy marriage and sex in God's program? Is gender itself simply a state of mind?

The problem with so-called casual sex is that sexual intimacy, even when it is consenting and intended to be recreational, creates interpersonal union that is spiritually and psychologically sticky. It is like human superglue whether or not we want it to function that way. Sex without lifetime commitment or with multiple partners fragments and breaks apart people's souls. Pieces of the heart and mind become left behind in a series of uncommitted unions. The capacity to fully bond with a spouse becomes severely numbed because the personal superglue is being applied and ripped off.

Sexual promiscuity and pornographic lust are ultimately depersonalizing and dehumanizing because they make enduring primary one-flesh union with a spouse harder to achieve and enjoy. The ability to responsibly and exclusively experience the most fundamental relationship in society is severely eroded when sex is trivialized and abused.

Casual sex and pornography also transform people into mere objects for selfish pleasure rather than neighbors to serve. Human relationships become easier to break and harder to sacrifice for. Our own perspective of self-giving and receiving becomes warped. This degradation of God's design for sex contributes to the undermining of His relational program on earth.

A poster child of the sexual revolution in the 1960s is the founder of *Playboy*, Hugh Hefner. Even though he has only been officially married three times, according to his own testimony he has slept with over a thousand women. Every few years he has a new rotation of female "bunnies" that come to live in his mansion to model a culture of casual sex.

Perhaps I am projecting my own psyche onto this situation, but it seems to me that the hedonistic path Hefner has chosen is relationally disastrous at best and downright disgusting at worst. What kind of legacy is his life leaving for the sake of others? Has he promoted a pattern of love or of selfish pleasure seeking? Is this kind of sexual revolution really the model we want to embrace as a culture?

This is not to say that sex within marriage cannot be recreational. Quite the contrary, sex is profound recreation in the most literal sense of the word. Far from being casual, it is a re-creative activity that joyfully renews the bond between spouses. It is re-creative in its power to refresh and in its potential for procreation. Sex may very well be the highest form of interpersonal recreation there is.

But the more volatile center of the debate in our culture is now over same-sex marriage and sexual orientation. The reasoning tends

to be that if people have an innate sexual preference that is not monogamous and heterosexual, they should be able to behave and live
accordingly without being discriminated against legally or otherwise.
What is the problem if people want to do something different in their
private and personal lives?

Lady Gaga's hit song "Born This Way" is a popular expression of the
prevailing attitude that our culture has embraced regarding sexuality. It
may be hard for some to believe, but here is a sampling of the lyrics that
are being bought and celebrated by the next generation:

> No matter gay, straight or bi
> Lesbian, transgendered life
> I'm on the right track, baby
> I was born to survive.
>
> I'm beautiful in my way
> 'Cause God makes no mistakes
> I'm on the right track, baby
> I was born this way.

This stands in stark contrast to the teaching of the Bible concerning
sexuality. The Apostle Paul portrayed sexual orientation and homosex-
uality as a willful exchange. Speaking of the sinful brokenness of all
humanity, Paul wrote to the church in Rome,

> Claiming to be wise, they became fools, and exchanged the glory of the
> immortal God for images resembling mortal man and birds and animals
> and creeping things.
>
> Therefore God gave them up in the lusts of their hearts to impurity, to
> the dishonoring of their bodies among themselves, because they exchanged
> the truth about God for a lie and worshiped and served the creature rather
> than the Creator, who is blessed forever! Amen.
>
> For this reason God gave them up to dishonorable passions. For their
> women exchanged natural relations for those that are contrary to nature; and
> the men likewise gave up natural relations with women and were consumed
> with passion for one another, men committing shameless acts with men and
> receiving in themselves the due penalty for their error. (Rom. 1:22–27)

Looking beyond the nature and explicit condemnation of the act itself
for the moment, it is clear that Paul frames homosexual behavior as a willful
choice rather than an inborn orientation or personality trait. It is portrayed
as a decision to act "contrary to nature" rather than being a natural condition.

To the extent that Paul does depict nonheterosexual relations as a willful decision, we must see that within the complex prism of human decision-making and preference. In other words, our choices and desires are not one-dimensional or simple—especially when it comes to something as profound as sexuality. There is not simple on/off switch that people can press in the depth of their heart.

Without meaning to be trivial, think of all the complex pre-conditions and experiences that cause someone to strongly prefer a fine restaurant crème brûlée to a carnival funnel cake. I'm not being facetious. Understanding a seemingly simple preference or desire is quite an exercise into the development of human inclination and perceptions of normalcy. Understanding a far more complicated preference for various nonheterosexual relations requires massive patience and grace.

Some activist homosexuals and scientists are backing away from the notion that nonheterosexual desires and behaviors are biologically determined or inborn. Human sexuality, while complex, is like so many other human desires—it is somewhat plastic. We may have some innate appetites and leanings, but they can morph with circumstances and time. It is probably more accurate to think of human sexual desires existing along a flexible continuum rather than a fixed binary system.

Irrespective of the way we nuance the issue of sexual orientation and choice, the Bible is very emphatic that various sexual behaviors outside of monogamous heterosexual marriage are out of accord with God's program. Whatever we believe about our internal orientations, we still have the ability to make conscious decisions about our sexual behaviors.

Jesus Himself taught that a marriage is between a man and a woman, and He even quoted Genesis 2 as his primary reference point. We can argue whether or not we would have done it differently, but it is futile to argue that the biblical design for sex is somehow unclear or open to debate. It is quite clear on these matters.

I recently read an ironic critique of homosexual sex on the basis that it was too safe. In other words, men intrinsically know how to please other men and vice versa, but to please someone of the opposite sex requires learning a foreign body. Heterosexual sex is more risky because we must focus on giving to another in ways that are alien to us. It means we have to focus more on serving another person who is unlike

216 Man in the Middle

ourselves than simply doing what we would have done to ourselves. Heterosexual sex thus reinforces the principle of self-giving.

The question isn't a pragmatic consideration about whether same-sex couples can be monogamous, mutually caring, or even effective parents. And certainly not every heterosexual marriage is a model for others to celebrate or emulate. What's at stake here isn't a pragmatic or relativistic question for a study committee to research, but the relational matrix that God has erected for the purpose of heavenization. True love has a shape and a context by God's design—it doesn't exist in a vacuum irrespective of relational boundaries.

None of this suggests that it is easy to change the way our preferences have developed, especially when it comes to sexuality. It is simply an acknowledgment that people's inclinations and resulting behaviors are not necessarily fixed by physiological mechanisms. The ability to adapt and change our deepest desires is part of being human.

For people who want to take God's program seriously, and yet find their sexual desires out of accord with its message, there is no easy path. However, there is an easy beginning—trust God for life and fruitfulness. Like all of the inclinations that we develop in our hearts, we must forge them in the context of God's love and mercy. We are called to pray and persevere in the fellowship of God's people, immersing ourselves in His priorities.

There may be lifelong sacrificial choices of abstinence or celibacy that come with following Christ. Sex is about mutually giving ourselves away in love, not taking what we can get for our own purposes. Love is not rooted in a personal perception of individual rights. If our sexual desires cannot be fulfilled in the context of God's design, then we are called to submit our wills to God's will. This may be difficult, but it is not bad or unreasonable. This is how we become more like God Himself.

The nature and gravity of sin

Adam's job as the garden's keeper implied that humanity was tasked with a defensive and protective role. So when we encounter the wicked serpent in the Genesis 3 narrative we can surmise that God allowed an adversary as a means of training Adam to be the guardian of the heavenization agenda. God permitted Satan's fall and presence in the garden in order to help humanity mature into caretakers who would unflinchingly function in the face of wicked options.

Adam's posture toward Satan and the forbidden fruit would reveal whether or not humanity would attain and employ a righteous knowledge of good and evil. If he continued in faith and obedience, humans would mature into their role of kings and queens and be confirmed in righteousness.

On the other hand, the penalty outlined in Genesis 2 for prematurely eating from the tree of knowledge was a death sentence. That may seem like an unduly harsh punishment for Adam and humanity for eating a piece of fruit, but it was entirely appropriate. Breaking fellowship with God was an act of high-handed betrayal. The Bible frames it as a spiritual crime that leaves us all guilty of offending an infinitely holy God. Our sin condemns us and leaves us subject to divine judgment.

But sin doesn't merely condemn—it also corrupts. It damages our souls and turns our priorities inside-out and upside-down. Instead of being oriented toward others and our work in the world, we become obsessed with how others and the world can serve us. Sin warps humanity into something it was not intended to be.

Death not only satisfies God's holy commitment to extinguishing evil, it intentionally disrupts humanity's destructive power. Because humanity is made in God's image to transform the world, we are powerful and therefore dangerous. By not trusting and obeying God, humanity would collectively undermine and destroy God's heavenization project. Disobedience is not only a moral offense against God's holiness that demands justice, it is also a deadly hazard for creation. Condemned and corrupt humanity would not only fail to heavenize earth, it would also throw it into chaos.

The point of the death sentence in Genesis 2 is therefore clear. If humanity would not live according to God's good agenda, humanity would have to be eliminated. Failure to eradicate generations of fallen humanity would result in a veritable hell on earth. Earth would descend into an apocalyptic nightmare. Undying humanity was too dangerous to perpetuate.

Unfortunately, Adam did not succeed in defending the garden sanctuary or his bride when the subtle intruder made his move. Satan's core strategy in Genesis 3 was to attack Adam's faith by portraying God as a lying tyrant who wanted to hold humanity back from their full potential. Satan said to Eve, "Did God actually say, 'You shall not eat of any tree of the garden?'" (Gen. 3:1). In other words, "So God has placed a burdensome restriction on you, huh? You can't any of this good food, can you? God must be such an oppressive bully. What a terrible and enslaving situation for you to be in."

Of course, God had not said that at all. There was only one tempo-rary prohibition from one tree. Adam and Eve were free to eat from any tree except one.

Satan pressed further, completely twisting God's creational intent and said that if they would break God's single prohibition, "You will not surely die. For God knows that when you eat of it your eyes will be opened and you will be like God, knowing good and evil."

Do you see the nature of the lie here? God had *already* made Adam and Eve like Him. They were already made in God's image. And His plan was for them to eventually come to a mature and righteous knowl-edge of good and evil that would allow them to rule effectively. But Sa-tan portrayed God as a liar and His plan as an oppressive burden on hu-manity. Satan distorted God's design, portraying it as a twisted means to enslave humanity, when in fact God's design was to exalt humanity.

In the face of this tragic logic the Bible tells us that Eve was tricked, but Adam sinned. Adam was humanity's designated representative who believed the lie about God's malicious intent. Instead of trusting in God's progressive plan to promote humanity from glory to glory, he decided it would be better to take the reins into his own hands. Adam's sin was a grab for power on his own terms.

Sin is not merely about eating a poison apple, being naughty, or breaking God's arbitrary scruples of personal propriety. The seriousness of sin is breaking away from the holiness of God that is reflected in His good program and design for creation. It is about self-centered unfaith-fulness that destroys loving relationships between God and neighbor.

At its root, sin refuses to acknowledge the majesty of God's glory and the breadth of His goodness, and it fails to enact God's heavenly initia-tive. Instead of giving thanks, we grumble and complain. It is no trifling thing that deserves a mere slap on the wrist.

To grasp the magnitude of Adam's transgression we must see the incredible context of goodness and privilege he was born into. Adam's sin may seem trivial on the surface, but it was egregious and extremely serious. It was like a newlywed committing adultery on the way from the wedding ceremony to the honeymoon. Every good gift and grace had been given, but was abandoned for grossly selfish reasons.

The Apostle Paul ultimately attributes sin to a failure to give thanks to God. Humanity is supposed to be uniquely characterized by an overflowing celebration of gratitude. The very heart of sin is our unwillingness to live in a posture of thanks. Paul says in Romans 1:22, "For although they knew God, they did not honor him as God or give thanks to him, but they became futile in their thinking, and their foolish hearts were darkened."

Sin means being out of step with God's love and His gracious program. It twists the human soul inward upon itself. Instead of facing outward to God, our neighbors, and our work in the world, our souls collapse and descend into selfish inwardness and idolatry. We find cheap and toxic substitutes for the true and living God. The prisms of our souls' faculties are out of alignment and blurred. Our intellect, emotion, and will no longer serve their intended purpose.

Humanity's new clothes

Clothing is symbolic by its very nature. Police officers wear uniforms and badges, doctors wear lab coats, and businesspeople wear suits. We don't wear tuxedos to the circus unless we're the ringleader. Even when we're not dressing for a particular vocation, we try to choose clothing that communicates something about ourselves.

Throughout history, people in leadership are often described as being "vested" with power. This figuratively means that they have been given the vestments—or clothing—that signifies their role. Some vocations still have investiture ceremonies that don the recipient with their new clothes of office. Newly minted graduates are often given a uniquely colored hood to denote the discipline they have mastered.

While there is little doubt Adam and Eve's initial nakedness suggested a kind of psychological and sexual innocence, it was also symbolic of their immaturity and unpreparedness to be vested with the mantle leadership. They were not ready to be robed with kingdom authority yet.[43]

I think the work of C. S. Lewis is brilliant at almost every turn. However, there is something slightly amiss in his book *The Great Divorce*. He writes about a man who has the opportunity to take a trip from hell to heaven—and there he encounters perfected saints who are naked—suggesting they have returned to their original state of purity. The problem with this kind of storytelling is that it does not comport to what the Bible teaches. The glorified Christ and His people do not look forward to an eternity of nudity, but of investiture with kingly robes of light.

43 Jordan, *Through New Eyes*, 265.

We know for certain that perpetual nakedness is not the ideal state of mankind because the saints pictured for us in the book of Revelation are not naked, but instead are clothed in glorious robes. In the Bible, being robed is a sign of glory, authority, priesthood, and kingship. Even in the Genesis narrative we can think of Joseph and his multicolored coat. The coat wasn't a fashion statement for fashion's sake; it was his father's way of symbolizing the authority he gave his young son. It was this investiture along with Joseph's dreams of grandeur that finally drove his brothers to mutiny.

When Jesus was transfigured before Peter, John, and James, His robe became white and glowing to communicate His future exaltation as King of kings. He didn't become nude. According to the book of Revelation, Jesus, the reigning Lord of Lords, now rules in a glorious robe of white, dipped in blood.

With all of this in mind, we can surmise that Adam and Eve's nakedness indicated they had not yet been fully vested as rulers of God's kingdom. They could not wear royal robes until they matured into them. The intended destiny for humanity was not shorts and flip-flops or permanent nudity; it was to be properly robed when the kingdom of heaven was fully realized.

This greater context about the nature of vestments and sin also sheds light on Adam's curious act of tailoring clothes out of fig leaves. Immediately after eating from the forbidden tree of knowledge, Adam became self-conscious of his nakedness in a new way. Once he had broken fellowship with God, he saw himself in a different and distorted light.

Adam wanted clothes not only to conceal his personal vulnerability connected to sexuality, but also to leave the nakedness of immature childhood behind. His fig leaf clothes were a lame attempt at self-glorification and self-investiture. Picture a tribal chieftain decked out in face paint and elaborate garb made of various plants. It was a pitiful effort to clothe himself in power.

Shortly after donning his new dress, Adam heard God coming "in the cool of the day." This translation almost suggests that God was casually strolling through the garden on his daily walk. But the force of the Hebrew is more suggestive of God coming in the wind or spirit of the day. In other words, there was a frightful wind that whipped up as God came to judge his fallen creatures.

This explains why Adam was so quick to strip naked and hide in the bushes. He was feeling pretty good about his new uniform until he realized that eating the tree of knowledge didn't change who was in charge. It was still God's world after all. Parading around the garden as the new world ruler while decked out in fig leaves was suddenly a very bad idea. Under pressure of examination, Adam claimed that he had always been naked to begin with.

The drama over nakedness and clothing was not yet over for Adam and Eve. Before exiling them from the garden, God fashioned new clothes for them. He didn't use fig leaves, cotton, or wool—He used the skin of a dead animal. This infers that God made a substitutionary sacrifice for them and postponed their inevitable physical death. Their sin required justice, and their shame required a symbolically appropriate covering. God righteously and mercifully provided both as evidence of His love and long-suffering.

Immature nakedness and ego-driven fig leaves were thus replaced with a symbol of substitutionary sacrifice. No robes of glory were issued to Adam and Eve. Instead of progressively and fruitfully working to extend a garden-city throughout the earth, humanity was relegated to survival in the uncultivated fields as quasi-beasts. We had exchanged robes of glory for a stupid lie.

When we read about Adam and Eve in Genesis 2 and 3, we begin to see the true tragedy of our human condition. God's plan for humanity is incredibly rich and full of joy, but we have chosen our own way. We have made ourselves lords of our own destinies and have reaped a legacy of corruption and death in return.

What was the answer to this cosmic dilemma? How could this state of affairs be reversed and the curse of death be overturned so that the merger of heaven and earth could be put back on track? God's answer was simple—He would demonstrate His righteousness by doing it Himself on our behalf. He would send His son, Jesus Christ, as the new Man in the middle. He would establish a new humanity, and His robe would be red.

CHAPTER NINE

Christ's Heroic Framework and Backstory

Most of us spend too much time on the last twenty-four hours and too little on the last six thousand years.

—*Will Durant*

One of the many deficiencies of my parenting is that I have not made a consistent commitment to sports in the lives of our four boys. Sure, we have dabbled in a little soccer, a bit of baseball, and some Tae Kwon Do, but in general we have been lackadaisical in our approach to formal athletics. You see, we're not really a sports family—we're more of a superhero family.

Instead of throwing the ball in the backyard, I would have the boys pick three superpowers and draw a new character with a cool name. We would watch superhero movies and cartoons rather than learning how to read box scores. There used to be a basket in the family room full of superhero capes and costumes in the place of shin-guards and helmets.

I'm not defending this as a particularly noble or good approach; I'm just telling it like it is. I enjoy watching sports and believe in keeping in shape, but fantastic stories about saving the city or the world by battling monsters have always inspired me. Being faster than a speeding bullet and able to leap tall buildings in a single bound just seems way cooler to me than dunking a basketball.

Some of my psychology may be the result of being a bit of a late bloomer in the gross motor skills department. I was usually the last to be picked in neighborhood and schoolyard sports teams. It wasn't unusual for the other kids, in a kind gesture of pity, to make me the team manager. I never quite knew what that meant, but it seemed like a respectful title that I could live with. It was certainly better than the humiliation of not connecting with the ball or routinely fumbling on the field of play.

My mother likes to tell a story about me as precocious three-year-old. All of a sudden she couldn't find me in the house, and when she looked out the window she saw me running into the street. After an adrenaline-filled sprint out the door to grab me, she asked what I would have done if a car had been driving down the road. I readily responded, "I would just jump over the car like Superman, Mom!" Between my space pants and delusions of superpowers, I'm surprised I made it to age six.

I'm not completely on the lunatic fringe. I've never been to Comic-Con, a convention for the extreme devotees of various fantasy genres. I would probably enjoy it, but I'm not quite at that level. I'm just a run-of-the-mill fan who looks forward to the summer blockbusters and enjoys character backstories.

Superheroes through the Ages

My personal attraction to superheroes is not unique or novel. This genre has been around in various forms for millennia. Part of the reason Greek mythology has been so enduring is because it captured the imagination of generation after generation with its scheming gods, powerful villains, and ferocious monsters. Who can forget characters like Poseidon, Hades, and Medusa?

The ancient Greeks established hero cults and shrines devoted to these fantastic legends. It may seem silly to us, but their religious commitment was an outworking of a deep thirst for eternal life. They believed that immortality was won through valiant acts of redemption.

Our own vocabulary still has remnants of this Greek ideal. The Greek word *pathos* expresses the essence of virtuous suffering and emotion. It is the root for the English words *empathy*, *sympathy*, and *telepathy*. They all convey a profound sense of shared feeling and experience in the challenges of life. Pathos is alive and well thanks to the Greeks' religious philosophy.

The greatest example in Greco-Roman mythology of heroic pathos was Hercules. As the story goes, the supreme god, Zeus, angered his goddess wife, Hera, by impregnating a human woman. To appease Hera's wrath, the baby was named Herakles, which means *glorious gift to Hera*, but this only incited her to greater fury. She promised to spitefully spend her days tormenting her partially human namesake.

Hera's first vengeful act was to try and kill the infant hero in his crib with lethal snakes. But they could not kill baby Hercules (his Romanized name), the son of god. The divine offspring of Zeus simply strangled the snakes with his own hands and used their dead carcasses as toys.

When Hercules was growing up, two nymphs, Pleasure and Virtue, visited him and offered him two pathways in life—comfort and pleasure, or glory through suffering. True to his heroic nature, Hercules wisely chose to win glory and immortality through trials and hard work. Anyone familiar with the story of Hercules knows that he received his wish.

One of his greatest challenges was battling the Lernean Hydra—a nine-headed dragon filled with poisonous venom. That sounds vicious enough, but this dragon was particularly difficult to kill because the heads would grow back when they were cut off. As Hercules battled the Hydra, it coiled around one of his feet so that he could not escape or easily maneuver.

In the end, Hercules finally prevailed with the help of a friend who cauterized the necks before they could grow new heads. Despite seemingly impossible odds and one foot caught by the enemy, he prevailed as the supreme dragon-slayer and premier hero of ancient Greece.

Interestingly, evil snakes and heroic dragon-slayer myths are not exclusive to Greco-Roman mythology. Many ancient cultures from Asia throughout Europe feature serpentine beasts. The *Epic of Gilgamesh*, a

Sumerian poem dating from around 2500 BC, includes an episode in which the hero, Gilgamesh, had the opportunity to obtain eternal life by acquiring a particular tree branch. However, a conniving snake snatched the life-giving branch from Gilgamesh and left him with the mere possibility of becoming a perpetual memory in the minds of other people.

And who can forget that standard high school English text, *Beowulf*? According to the narrative, the kingdom-feasting center of the Danish king Hrothgar had been under attack by the monster Grendel. In desperate response, the king commissioned Beowulf to the rescue. He successfully overcame a series of three monsters—culminating with a great dragon. But as fate would have it, Beowulf finally succumbed to death while batting the dragon in his deliverance of the kingdom.

The Source of the Snake Myths

These ancient dragon-slaying legends don't spring from a vacuum. It is not hard to connect the dots between godlike heroes defeating serpents by risking their lives and Jesus defeating the serpent-dragon of the Garden of Eden, Satan. These primal cultural myths and stories are derivative of a greater story that is actually true. Humanity's dragon enemy could only be defeated by a divine hero, the true Son of God.

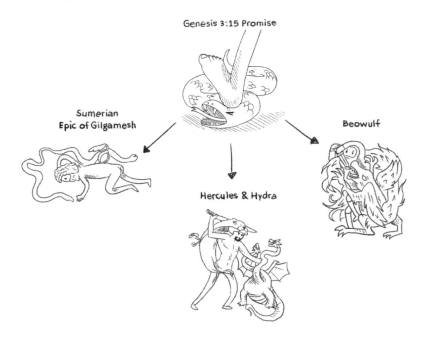

It is probably worth repeating what we briefly reviewed several chapters back regarding God's curse on the serpent in Genesis 3:14, 15:

> Because you have done this, Cursed are you above all livestock
> And above all beasts of the field;
> On your belly you shall go,
> And dust you shall eat
> All the days of your life.
> I will put enmity between you and the woman,
> And between your offspring and her offspring;
> He shall bruise your head,
> And you shall bruise his heel.

The hero humanity needed and looked forward to would be a dragon-slayer. We needed someone to destroy Satan's agenda of lies, destruction, and the greatest enemy of all, death. History as we know it is actually framed in terms of our need for a great hero to defeat the terrible and evil snake, Satan himself.

The final book of the Bible, Revelation, further reinforces this storyline by portraying Satan as a fierce red dragon that is conquered in heaven and thrown down to be defeated in earth:

> Now war arose in heaven, Michael and his angels fighting against the dragon. And the dragon and his angels fought back, but he was defeated, and there was no longer any place for them in heaven. And the great dragon was thrown down, that ancient serpent, who is called the devil and Satan, the deceiver of the whole world—he was thrown down to the earth, and his angels were thrown down with him. And I heard a loud voice in heaven, saying, "Now the salvation and the power and the kingdom of our God and the authority of his Christ have come, for the accuser of our brothers has been thrown down, who accuses them day and night before our God. And they have conquered him by the blood of the Lamb and by the word of their testimony, for they loved not their lives even unto death. Therefore, rejoice, O heavens and you who dwell in them! But woe to you, O earth and sea, for the devil has come down to you in great wrath, because he knows that his time is short!" (Rev. 12:7–13)

The presence of the garden snake and the ultimate downfall of the evil dragon serve as bookends to the entire Bible in the same way that the motifs of heaven and earth do. Beating the dragon-enemy is integral to the whole story of Scripture. It simply cannot be glossed over as a minor detail.

Serpentine monsters also play a significant role throughout the rest of the Bible. The staff that Aaron wielded in Exodus could become a snake-eating serpent on command. This signaled the superiority of Moses' God over the magic of the Egyptian pantheon. God ruled serpents and the serpent, not vice versa.

In the Old Testament book of Numbers, Israel was exiled to the wilderness for forty years, and they incurred God's fierce wrath by grumbling and complaining. To chastise them, God sent a plague of fiery serpents and the only way for them to be healed was to look at a bronze serpent that Moses held up on a staff. Unless they faithfully looked to the crucified and defeated serpent on a pole, they died in judgment.

Centuries later, Jesus alluded to this Old Testament episode with the bronze serpent in his conversation with Nicodemus: "And as Moses lifted up the serpent in the wilderness, so must the Son of Man be lifted up, that whoever believes in him may have eternal life" (John 3:14,15). In this one obscure sentence, Jesus predicted that his future crucifixion would function as a parallel to the bronze serpent upon a pole did in the wilderness. If people would look in faith to his death on a tree and see it as the place where the dragon was slain and death was defeated, they would live.

While the connection is not entirely certain, some have speculated that the mythological rod of Asclepius has its origins in this Old Testament wilderness incident. Many medical associations still use the symbol of a snake on a rod as a sign of healing. The memory and legend concerning a crucified snake lives on to this very day.

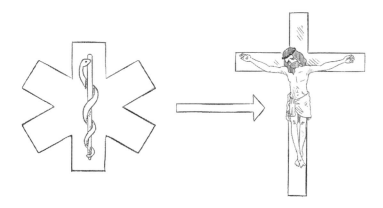

Even the contemporary and fantastically popular Harry Potter series by J. K. Rowling pivots around the defeat of the House of Slytherin, which is represented by snakes. Harry Potter shares an inextricable tie with the villain, Voldemort, because they both speak Parseltongue, the language of snakes. The boy-hero of Rowling's series is a serpent-killer who sacrifices his life to conquer the world's great enemy.

The bottom line is that from Genesis 3 forward, the whole scope and sweep of the Bible becomes focused on undoing the destructive consequences of our mortal dragon-enemy, Satan. The terrible scheme that disrupted the heavenization of earth had to be overcome before God's project could continue. Death itself had to be reversed so that humanity could fully engage with its work. The hero we needed would have to crush Satan to secure new life for humanity.

Defeating Satan to Save the World

You may think this mythology about serpents and dragon-slaying is fascinating yet strangely remote and possibly ridiculous. Today the very notion of Satan is generally derided as superstitious and intellectually backward. It is hard for me to think of Satan without remembering Dana Carvey's "Saturday Night Live" character, the church lady. Who can forget his hilarious parody of the prototypical uptight church secretary who scolded people by asking if they were possibly under the influence of "Mmmm could it be...Satan?"

Angels and demons

But the biblical narrative does include a class of sentient beings called angels. They are different from humans because they do not have bodies, but they can inhabit bodies—both animal and human. Since angels do not procreate they are collectively referred to as a *host*, not a *race*. Angels are ancillary servants in God's world. They worship in heaven, deliver messages from God's throne, animate certain physical realities, and minister to humanity in mysterious ways.

At some point a group of rebellious angels revolted against God's "man in the middle" agenda and attempted to derail it by condemning humanity. These fallen angels are now called demons. This all speaks to a transcendent dimension of humanity's struggle that is unseen, but real. In the New Testament we read, "For we do not wrestle against flesh and blood, but against the rulers, against the authorities, against the cosmic powers over this present darkness, against the spiritual forces of evil in the heavenly places" (Eph. 6:12).

The horrific tribulations of poverty, disease, and injustice exist against a background of spiritual evil and warfare. Humanity's relationship with God is broken, and a demonic accuser seeks to undermine and destroy us. There are still otherworldly forces of evil at work in the world. We need to acknowledge them even if we can't fully understand them.

When I was a freshman at Indiana University, a novel about angelic and demonic forces, *This Present Darkness*, was very popular. The author, Frank Peretti, told a compelling behind-the-scenes tale of angelic warfare as it played out in the world. Spiritual forces animated every aspect of life in his story. Even though he took some very imaginative and dramatic theological liberties, it was just the ticket for anyone into escapist fantasy literature.

Unfortunately for me, I was not particularly well grounded in my theology when I waded into Peretti's book. On a long Thanksgiving weekend I was left alone in a huge darkened dormitory waiting for my ride home to Cleveland. To pass the time, I started reading the novel and was riveted until the wee hours of the morning. I remember being so freaked out and on edge that I began casting demons out from under my bed in the name of Jesus. Peretti's tale had transformed me into an amateur exorcist. It wasn't one of the proudest moments of my faith journey.

What Frank Peretti and I failed to grasp is that the ministry of Jesus had massive and lasting cosmic repercussions that impacted angelic and heavenly realities. There are demonic forces at work today, but they don't function at the same intensity or level that they did prior to Christ's victory over death. In fulfillment of the Genesis 3 promise, Satan's head has been crushed by the death and resurrection of Jesus. The demonic leader's scheme has been defeated and his powers have been seriously diminished and restrained.

As the new "man in the middle," Jesus ushered in a new era in the history of humanity, heaven, and earth. One of the reasons Jesus casts out demons in the Gospels is to demonstrate the vast and penetrating scope of His redemptive project. He came to put the world back together again by driving out and conquering the transcendent forces and consequences of evil.

This heavenly dimension of Christ's work was hotly contested in Jesus' own day. After performing an exorcism, some leading religious authorities actually accused Jesus of being a demon Himself. He responded,

How can Satan cast out Satan? If a kingdom is divided against itself, that kingdom cannot stand. And if a house is divided against itself, that house will not be able to stand. And if Satan has risen up against himself and is divided, he cannot stand, but is coming to an end. But no one can enter a strong man's house and plunder his goods, unless he first binds the strong man. Then indeed he may plunder his house. (Mark 3:23–27)

This profoundly significant verse shows the consequences of Jesus' ministry: He came to ransack Satan's house—which is what armies do in conquest. He threw Satan down to earth and tied him up before plundering and taking the spoils of victory. When Jesus overcame death through His resurrection, He crushed Satan's fundamental threat to God's heavenization program. Christ made it possible for humanity to be reinstated to their man in the middle work and inherit eternal life.

Humanity's global mop-up operation

But even though the rabid hellhound's influence and doom were sealed by the work of Jesus, humanity was still badly broken, and the total renovation of the world hadn't been consummated. It was therefore fitting for God to leave the extended mop-up operation for His redeemed people to accomplish. Near the end of his letter to the Romans, the Apostle Paul refers to this ongoing reality with yet another allusion to dragon-slaying in Genesis 3. In the final words of his letter to church in Rome he wrote, "The God of peace will soon crush Satan under *your* feet. The grace of our Lord Jesus Christ be with you" (Rom. 16:20).

Jesus figuratively crushed Satan under His heel at His crucifixion, and now His people participate in the enemy's destruction by collectively trampling his body back to dust. Jesus secured the path for His people to plunder the world and share in his triumph. It is our privilege and calling to reclaim the context for God's kingdom feast as Beowulf did for Hrothgar.

The arc of human history is thus characterized as a comprehensive global rescue effort because of humanity's fall into sin. Human brokenness and death have to be dealt with before the full grandeur of heaven can be realized on earth. One of my favorite passages that references this dynamic is Romans 8:19–23:

For the creation waits with eager longing for the revealing of the sons of God. For the creation was subjected to futility, not willingly, but because of him who subjected it, in hope that the creation itself will be set free from its bondage to corruption and obtain the freedom of the glory of the children of God. For we know that the whole creation has been groaning together in the pains of childbirth until now. And not only the creation, but we ourselves, who have the firstfruits of the Spirit, groan inwardly as we wait eagerly for adoption as sons, the redemption of our bodies.

The redemption the world needs includes people's souls, but it does not end there by any means. Oceans and forests, schools and business-es, families and cultures—all of them need to be redeemed because the world been subjected to warped humanity. The whole creation has been groaning under the weight of our destructive power and awaits God's people to progressively deliver it back to its true purpose.

The early church was so alert to this cosmic and earthly dimension of Christ's impact that its theology of Christ's death and atoning sac-rifice is often framed as the "Christus Victor" theory. In other words, the nascent church emphasized Jesus as humanity's epic hero who van-quished the schemes of its mortal enemy, Satan. Abstract theological terminology that emanated from legal and judicial constructs was over-shadowed by the basic story of humanity's hero, King Jesus.

There is a strong biblical basis and place for more theologically ab-stract conceptions of Christ's sacrifice that we will briefly explore later in the book. However, it is critical to remember that these are all tools to explain the basic story and work of Christ. At the most basic level, Jesus is the champion who slew the dragon. Jesus wasn't merely a moral teacher, and He achieved far more than securing forgiveness of sin for individuals. Jesus Christ was the hero who came to save the world.

Joel Salatin of Polyface Farms is a fantastic embodiment of this truth. He is a Christian farmer who believes that humans are called to be thoughtful stewards of this world. His conviction is that we can have healthier food and a healthier earth when we farm in ecological-ly responsible ways. Instead of using an array of chemicals to control pests and grow massive crops, he strategically rotates different kinds of livestock through the fields to naturally fertilize the land and feed the animals. The result is a beautiful example of humanity's power to be good and fruitful curators of the land and animals.

But the thing I love most about Joel Salatin is the way he speaks about his work. In an interview he was asked to describe what he does for a living. He quickly replied, "I'm in the redemption business." He didn't say, "I'm an organic farmer," or, "I'm a holistic practitioner of agricultural ecology." No, he simply described himself as someone who is here to heal and bless the world through his farming techniques. He sees himself as someone sent to free the creation from the futility of broken humanity.

Christ's Extensive Backstory

Like any good superhero legend, the story of Jesus starts with an extremely extensive and detailed backstory. Who can really appreciate Superman without knowing something about Krypton? How can we truly understand Batman unless we know his tragic family history in the city of Gotham? In a similar way, the Old Testament covers thousands of years before Jesus ever comes on the scene. Messiah's origins are absolutely critical to fully understanding his true identity. Familiarity with the context is essential to making sense of the mystery of Christ.

A family of faithful superheroes

A cover-to-cover reading of the Bible shows that Jesus stands on the shoulders of a special family of heroes. There is a very real sense in which the whole Old Testament traces the history of a particular family as the communal vehicle that carried the redemptive seed-line of Messiah. Jesus is the climactic and crowning character in a long series of faith-filled spiritual champions.

We can't take the time to look at each significant forerunner to Christ, but it will be helpful to take a brief glance at Abraham and Moses. Seen together, they are the dual pillars of the Jewish context into which Messiah was born.

Abraham served as the chief patriarch and founding hero of Judaism. God called this very wealthy and elderly man to leave his Mesopotamian home to establish a new nation in a faraway land. God invited Abraham with a fantastic promise that his progeny would literally save the world: "Go from your country and your kindred and your father's house to the land that I will show you. And I will make of you a great nation, and I will bless you and make your name great, so that you will be a blessing. I will bless those who bless you, and him who dishonors you I will curse, *and in you all the families of the earth shall be blessed*" (Gen. 12:1–3).

Abraham already very rich and comfortable in his homeland, so it wasn't just the prospect of inheriting a new land flowing with milk and honey that attracted him. No, he was inspired and motivated by the prospect of having a family that was in the global redemption business. Theologians refer to this fantastic promise as the Abrahamic Covenant.

But there was a hitch. Abraham and his elderly wife, Sarah, didn't have children. Although he was a well-established man with many re- sources at his disposal, he had no heir. For God to make good on His promise to aged Abraham, God would have to provide a miracle son. Abraham inquired of God in Genesis, saying,

> "O Lord GOD, what will you give me, for I continue childless, and the heir
> of my house is Eliezer of Damascus?" And Abram said, "Behold, you have
> given me no offspring, and a member of my household will be my heir."
> And behold, the word of the Lord came to him: "This man shall not be your
> heir; your very own son shall be your heir." And he brought him outside and
> said, "Look toward heaven, and number the stars, if you are able to number
> them." Then he said to him, "So shall your offspring be." And he believed the
> Lord, and he counted it to him as righteousness. (Gen. 15:2–7)

Against all physiological and philosophical odds, Abraham believed in God's promise of an heir. Abraham was many things, but most of all he was a man of heroic faith. In the face of a seemingly impossible situation, he chose to believe in God's good plan to save the world. This faith in God's cosmic salvation put Abraham in a right relationship with God. He was considered by God to be a "righteous" man.

This all sounds really nice and rosy, but then the story takes a grit- ty soap-opera-like turn. Abraham's wife, Sarah, was getting a little antsy with this whole plan and the time it was taking to evolve. She was not getting pregnant and was certainly not getting any younger, so she made a decision that was fairly common in ancient times.[44] She decided to make her maidservant, Hagar, a surrogate mother. Sure enough, Abraham suc- ceeded in impregnating Hagar, and she gave birth to a son, Ishmael.

But God made it clear that Ishmael was not the son He had prom- ised, despite Sarah's well-intended plan. God reiterated that Abraham and Sarah would have a biological child of their own—even at their ex- tremely old age. And in a fascinating twist, God commanded Abraham to mark himself and his male descendants with a sign to remember this promise. God told Abraham to circumcise them—to cut off the fore- skins of their penises.

---

44 Jordan, *Primeval Saints*, 67.

It is kind of humorous to consider in these terms, but you know how superheroes usually have a special emblem or outfit that marks them as special? Batman has his mask, Superman has an "S" on his chest, and Wonder Woman has a tiara and golden lasso. Well, Abraham's heroic family also had an emblem marking out their identity—it just happened to be on their genitalia.

But why? Why circumcision? Some people have conjectured that it is a sign of cleanliness, as if removing the foreskin from a penis is somehow more sanitary. Perhaps it has something to do with blood. But this doesn't fit with the Genesis narrative at all. Circumcision is given right in the middle of the crisis of faith Abraham and Sarah were having concerning getting pregnant. The context is crucial—after the story about impregnating Hagar and immediately prior to the birth of their true biological son, Isaac.

Circumcision was not an arbitrary sign of cleanliness; it was a sign of faith in God's promise to save the world. The Apostle Paul—a former teacher of Judaism, says so himself: "For we say that faith was counted to Abraham as righteousness. How then was it counted to him? Was it before or after he had been circumcised? It was not after, but before he was circumcised. He received the sign of circumcision as a seal of the righteousness that he had by faith while he was still uncircumcised" (Rom. 4:9b–11).

Circumcision is an incredibly profound fleshly sign of faith in God's covenant that a family of superheroes would come by His divine power, not by the devices of men. Circumcision is an illustration that the heroic seed-line of Messiah was not ultimately dependent on the procreative power of men's penises, but on the power of God's purpose and promise. Therefore, God had his family of superheroes symbolically emasculate themselves as a reminder that God's family of superheroes was contingent on God's faithfulness alone.

This is important because the core identity of Abraham's family and of the nation of Israel was supposed to be fundamentally characterized by a life of faith in God. But we're not talking about a generic faith. No, it was a profound faith in God's promise to save the world. Circumcision was the deeply ironic and poignant sign of God's grand plan to propagate a miracle Seed. Jesus even said that Abraham's faith looked forward to the future Messiah: "You father Abraham rejoiced that he would see my day. He saw it and was glad" (John 8:56).

Perhaps the most overwhelming evidence of Abraham's incredible faith came when God called him to sacrifice his only son and heir, Isaac. Such an act is almost inconceivable. But the context of the story raises the stakes to another level. Abraham believed so deeply in God's promises that he was willing to offer up the only hope he had for those promises to be fulfilled.

In the end, God intervened and provided a substitutionary animal to be sacrificed in the place of Isaac. Nevertheless this episode is designed to make us stop and wonder what kind of faith behaves like this. If we're honest with ourselves, this kind of faith looks borderline crazy. Moving to a new land is understandable. Adopting circumcision as the family's religious badge is strange, but digestible. Sacrificing the only miracle son you have as an act of obedience to God seems psychotic.

Thankfully, the Bible gives us some commentary on this to help us understand Abraham's rationale and mindset. In the book of Hebrews we read, "By faith Abraham, when he was tested, offered up Isaac, and he who had received the promises was in the act of offering up his only son, of whom it was said, 'Through Isaac shall your offspring be named.' He considered that God was able even to *raise him from the dead*, from which, *figuratively speaking*, he did receive him back." (Heb. 11:17–19).

This passage is one of my favorite in the Bible. It tells us that Abraham's faith was very special because it was a *resurrection* faith. Abraham did not obey with the blind and unthinking faith of an automaton. Abraham's faith reasoned that God would bring Isaac back from the dead in order to fulfill His promises.

This also subtly underscores the concept that sacrificial death is inextricably and fundamentally connected to new life and resurrection. Bloody sacrifice is not an end unto itself, but the pathway toward renewed life. In God's economy, sacrifice ultimately leads to total transformation, not utter annihilation.

And while Abraham did not ultimately sacrifice Isaac, the Bible says that he figuratively did. This is critical to understand. The ram that God provided symbolically stood in Isaac's place as a legitimate representative. God accepted a substitute so that Abraham would not have to make the sacrifice of his only son.

Of course, this defining moment in the life of Abraham revealed more than the nature of his faith. This figurative episode also foreshadowed the divine Father's willingness to give up *His* only Son as the necessary sacrifice for humanity. Father Abraham's faith was great because it emulated the ultimate faithfulness of God.

God's strategy for raising Abraham's family

But what about all of the laws in the Old Testament? The faith of Abraham is one thing, but what about Moses? How do we piece together God's global promises to Abraham with God's laws to Israel?

First, it is critical to understand that the Ten Commandments and the Law given by Moses came centuries *after* God's promise to Abraham and the emblem of circumcision. The primary root of biblical Judaism is *not* living an ethical and moral life in devotion to God according to Torah; it is sharing an Abrahamic faith in God's redemptive purpose to bless all the families of the earth.

The Mosaic Law was given as a progressive and provisional teaching tool to help God's heroic family mature into its redemptive role and better anticipate the world's Messiah. The Mosaic Law was never intended to be an end unto itself or the ultimate basis for being right with God. Otherwise it would have preceded God's promise as a condition, rather than coming later as an aid to covenantal life.

The preamble to the Ten Commandments shows the dynamic between the Abrahamic promise and the Mosaic Law. Moses delivered the Ten Commandments from Mount Sinai *after* the Exodus from Egypt, not before. God's holy law wasn't framed as an if-then statement: "If you live a moral life, then you will be considered righteous, God will make you His people, and deliver you from slavery in Egypt." Quite the opposite. The first sentence of the Ten Commandments says, "I am the LORD your God, who brought you out of the land of Egypt, out of the house of slavery. You shall have no other gods before me. You shall not make for yourself a carved image . . . . " (Exod. 20:2).

Notice that God puts His saving grace *first* and the law *second*. When Israel cried out to God in their Egyptian bondage, God remembered His promissory covenant with Abraham. God essentially said, "Because I have *already* made you My covenant people based on my promise to Abraham, and because I have *already* saved you from Egyptian bondage, this is how I want you to live in My presence and behave before a watching world."

Saving Grace First ⟶ Law of Life Second

I am the Lord your God
Who brought you out
Of the land of Egypt,
Out of the house of slavery

You shall have no other
Gods before me...

There was admittedly a conditional if-then component to the Mosaic epoch that offered national blessings for obedience and curses for disobedience. In fact, God threatened Israel's very geopolitical existence if they failed to live according to His law. Nevertheless, the initial and eternally abiding relationship between God and Abraham's family was not rooted in law or complex regulations, but in God's gracious and global promise of redemption.

It is very helpful to think of God's strategy with Israel in terms of a parenting metaphor. Part of being an effective parent to young children is providing an environment with clear boundaries and routines, consistent discipline, and predictable outcomes. When a young child is brought up in this kind of context, they internalize a pattern of life that is not easily broken.

As parents of four boys involved in various educational and social environments, my wife and I have witnessed many puzzling parenting approaches. Some parents actually turn matters upside-down and are extremely lax and hands-off when their children are young. Then they try to impose strict rules on their teenagers as a way of protecting them from making horrible life choices. This backward tactic almost always blows up in their faces, and their unrestrained and untrained children rebel. Do you know any teenagers who want to progressively lose their freedom and independence as they become young adults?

When he was two years old, our strongest-willed and most stubborn son would constantly fight us at the dinner table. If he didn't want something, he would obstinately clamp his mouth shut and throw the food on the floor and tuck his hands under the tray on his highchair. He was going to take control of his own diet, period. I can still remember the incredible look of self-determination on his face. Two-year-olds are fully human, for sure.

Now this may not seem like a big deal. After all, it is just food and he was well nourished through other means. So as parents we had to decide whether to battle his toddler rebellion by tackling his table tantrums on a nightly basis. Why push him to eat food he didn't like and make a big scene? Wouldn't it be better to just let him eat what he wanted when he wanted and skip the drama to avoid hurting his emotions and self-esteem? Surely he would come to better dining decorum later in life. Shouldn't we just let the whole food thing resolve itself as he grew up?

In a word, no. For him, eating what was on the menu became more than a matter of physical nutrition—it became a matter of soul nurture. Gina and I were convinced that we needed to instill certain patterns of authority, choice, and behavior early on so that they would take hold later. These patterns start with the small and mundane things of life, not the big ones. If children can learn how to follow our lead in the little things of life, they will not find it hard to follow our lead in the big things of life. Rules about small issues are like training wheels that help us learn how to achieve mature balance and stability.

What we were really trying to teach our son at the dinner table was how to exercise appropriate self-rule. Good decision making outside of external regulations was always the goal. Our aim was not to make him subservient, but to teach him self-mastery and the ability to override his base impulses. These are learned behaviors, and good parenting makes use of rules and boundaries to progressively help children get control over their emotions.

Now I won't lie—this is not always a particularly fun or easy approach to childrearing. For many months there were almost nightly episodes that nearly ruined every family dinner. There were moments when we wondered why we were going through so much emotional trauma for the sake of getting a child to eat against his will.

Years later, I can tell you that we have very few rules around our dinner table or in our home. Healthy boundaries are now unspoken assumptions about daily living. Nevertheless, the strong will and self-determination of our son has not disappeared or dissipated. Rather, it has been gradually trained and pointed in the right direction. He makes consistently good choices about his diet, education, and friendships because his internal compass has been set. Instead of becoming more entangled and frustrated by new layers of parental interference, he is making more independent decisions. He is functioning more and more like a young man, and we couldn't be prouder.

When Abraham's redemptive family was young, God taught them the basics of redemption and how to behave in His holy presence. He gave them many life-shaping boundaries that would point them toward His coming kingdom. There were detailed laws about food, clothing, lending money, worship, and holidays—every aspect of life.

But even though the Mosaic Law is quite complex in many respects, it boils down to two overarching principles: loving God and loving other people.

When Jesus was asked what the Mosaic Law was all about, He responded, "Love the Lord your God with all your heart and with all your soul and with all your mind…. You shall love your neighbor as yourself" (Matt. 22:37, 39).

This teaching about love and the so-called Golden Rule was by no means novel. Jesus was actually paraphrasing the well-known words of Moses. Before Israel entered the Promised Land after their wilderness wanderings, Moses reiterated the Law in the book of Deuteronomy. In the prologue, Moses wrote the words that would become Israel's slogan, "Hear, O Israel: The LORD our God, the Lord is one. You shall love the Lord your God with all your heart and with all your soul and with all your might" (Deut. 6:4,5).

So on the one hand the Mosaic Law was quite intricate and overwhelming, and on the other hand its purpose was quite simple. In many respects it is parallel to the household rules parents have for their children. Some theologians have summarized the complex structure and single purpose of the law by recognizing three main features:

- *Moral Law*—Permanent instructions about how to love and worship God and love other people. Examples: You shall have no other gods before Me. Do not make idols. Do not commit adultery. Do not murder.

- *Ceremonial Law and Holiness Codes*—Temporary instructions during the Mosaic era about the priesthood, tabernacle, and sacrifices to teach humanity about their need of a suffering substitute for atonement of sin. Unique and provisional behavioral regulations that physically distinguished Israel from surrounding Pagan nations.

- *Civil Laws*—Temporary national laws for Israel during the Mosaic era that demonstrated principles of retributive and penal justice.

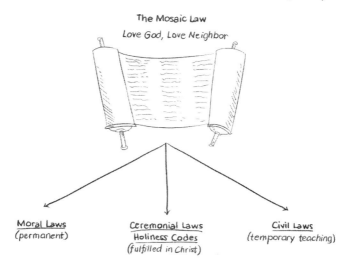

Along with the three parts of the Mosaic Law, they also see three applications or uses of the Law. Like a good parenting strategy, each rule could be applied with multiple effects:

- *Restraining evil*—The law of God guides human culture to curb the extent of our potential for evil. It helps to direct our civic formation by establishing behavioral boundaries and principals of retributive justice.

- *Convicting of sin*—When we encounter God's laws we see that we fall short of His holiness and desperately need His forgiveness. We learn that God extends mercy and brings us back into His presence through substitutionary sacrifice.

- *Teaching holy living*—God's laws guide His people to live a life of love toward God and neighbor. It trains us how to remain in fruitful and joyful community.

These paradigms help us to see that the Mosaic Law was not about earning God's favor so much as it was about learning God's pattern for life. God's plan at this stage of humanity's development was to give laws that would help teach the basics of a life filled with love, devotion, and anticipation of His saving grace.

The relationship between Abraham and Moses shows that the true character of biblical Judaism is rooted in having Abrahamic faith that leads to a legacy of obedience and fruitfulness. A Jew is not properly identified as someone who is a racial descendant of Abraham. After all, the tribe of Abraham that was initially circumcised in Genesis 17 included foreigners who were not biologically connected to Abraham. There was no strict racial purity in the covenantal line to begin with.

And contrary to some modern thinking, Judaism was never permanently intended to be about a narrow geopolitical expression of God's kingdom in the Middle East. Biblical Judaism is a faith that believes in God's covenant promise to Abraham to save the world. True circumcision of the heart and spiritual Judaism are about trusting in God's messianic program and a thankful life of love that emanates from that reality. This is the heart of the Old Testament.

Consider these prophecies that speak to that reality:

A new covenant (better than the Mosaic covenant)
Behold, the days are coming, declares the LORD, when I will make a new covenant with the house of Israel and the house of Judah, not like the covenant that I made with their fathers on the day when I took them by the hand to bring them out of the land of Egypt, my covenant that they broke, though I was their husband, declares the LORD. For this is the covenant that I will make with the house of Israel after those days, declares the LORD: I will put my law within them, and I will write it on their hearts. And I will be their God, and they shall be my people. (Jer. 31:31–33)

Christ's birth in Bethlehem
But you, O Bethlehem Ephrathah,
   who are too little to be among the clans of Judah,
from you shall come forth for me
   one who is to be ruler in Israel, whose coming forth is from of old,
   from ancient days. (Mic. 5:2)

Christ's miraculous birth and divine name (Immanuel = God with us)
Therefore the Lord himself will give you a sign. Behold, the virgin shall conceive and bear a son, and shall call his name Immanuel. (Isa. 7:14)

Christ's identity as the Son of God
I will tell of the decree: The LORD said to me, "You are my Son; today I have begotten you." (Ps. 2:7)

Christ's suffering as a sacrifice for sin

Who has believed what he has heard from us? And to whom has the arm of the LORD been revealed? For he grew up before him like a young plant, and like a root out of dry ground; he had no form or majesty that we should look at him, and no beauty that we should desire him. He was despised and rejected by men; a man of sorrows, and acquainted with grief; and as one from whom men hide their faces he was despised, and we esteemed him not.

Surely he has borne our griefs and carried our sorrows; yet we esteemed him stricken, smitten by God, and afflicted. But he was pierced for our transgressions; he was crushed for our iniquities; upon him was the chastisement that brought us peace, and with his wounds we are healed. All we like sheep have gone astray; we have turned—every one—to his own way; and the LORD has laid on him the iniquity of us all.

He was oppressed, and he was afflicted, yet he opened not his mouth; like a lamb that is led to the slaughter, and like a sheep that before its shearers is silent, so he opened not his mouth. By oppression and judgment he was taken away; and as for his generation, who considered that he was cut off out of the land of the living, stricken for the transgression of my people? And they made his grave with the wicked and with a rich man in his death, although he had done no violence, and there was no deceit in his mouth.

Yet it was the will of the LORD TO CRUSH HIM; he has put him to grief; when his soul makes an offering for guilt, he shall see his offspring; he shall prolong his days; the will of the LORD SHALL PROSPER IN HIS HAND. Out of the anguish of his soul he shall see and be satisfied; by his knowledge shall the righteous one, my servant, make many to be accounted righteous, and he shall bear their iniquities. Therefore I will divide him a portion with the many, and he shall divide the spoil with the strong, because he poured out his soul to death and was numbered with the transgressors; yet he bore the sin of many, and makes intercession for the transgressors. (Isa. 53)

Putting the whole backstory together

Of course the heroic ancestry of Jesus is larger and more diverse than Abraham and Moses. We haven't even touched upon prominent figures such as King David or the prophet Daniel. Is there a way to summarize the whole story that will help us grasp Christ's backstory?

One of the best biblical ways to piece it together is seeing how God progressively used promissory covenants throughout human history. Even though the Old Testament can feel foreign, overwhelming, and haphazard, there is a narrative element that gives it shape.

Specifically, God made special promises known as covenants with some of the most preeminent figures of the Bible: Noah and his family, Abraham and his family, Moses and the people of Israel, and King David and his dynasty. Each covenant builds upon the other in a redemptive crescendo that anticipates the New Covenant with Christ and His followers.

Think of it this way:

Covenant Crescendo of Biblical History

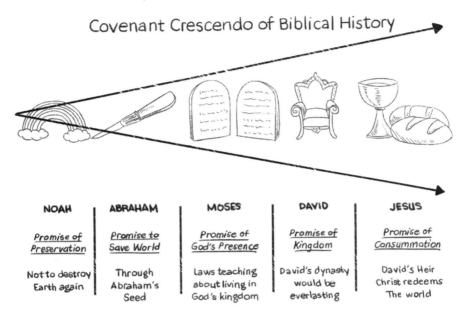

NOAH	ABRAHAM	MOSES	DAVID	JESUS
Promise of Preservation	*Promise to Save World*	*Promise of God's Presence*	*Promise of Kingdom*	*Promise of Consummation*
Not to destroy Earth again	Through Abraham's Seed	Laws teaching about living in God's kingdom	David's dynasty would be everlasting	David's Heir Christ redeems The world

This covenant scheme reveals a simultaneous continuity and discontinuity in God's plan.[45] The continuity flows from a unified succession of redemptive promises that build on one another. But the New Covenant ratified by Jesus puts some of the features of preceding covenants to rest because He fulfills them.

The Apostle Paul recognized this unity and diversity of the historical covenant structure in his letter to the Ephesian church. Addressing a group of Gentiles who had converted to Christianity he wrote,

> Therefore remember that at one time you Gentiles in the flesh, called "the uncircumcision" by what is called the circumcision, which is made in the flesh by hands—remember that you were at that time separated from Christ, alienated from the commonwealth of Israel and *strangers to the covenants of promise,*

---

45 For further study on the covenants, see Palmer O. Robertson, *The Christ of the Covenants* (Grand Rapids: Baker Book House, 1980).

having no hope and without God in the world. But now in Christ Jesus you who once were far off have been brought near by the blood of Christ. (Eph. 2:11–13)

The whole Old Testament builds in anticipation of the singular promise that God would put the world back together again. Each hero from Noah to David played their role but could not finish the job. Everything in God's program led to the covenant of Christ.

This is one of the reasons why Christians are no longer bound to the peculiar holiness codes of the Mosaic Law. Even the fleshly mark of circumcision is no longer necessary as an emblem of the community of faith because water baptism has replaced it. The Passover meal of the Exodus has been more fully realized and transformed into the Lord's Supper. It is no longer necessary to keep repeating the temple sacrifices because of Christ's final sacrifice. The nation of Israel's distinct role in redemption has been fulfilled because of Messiah's arrival. Jew and Gentile are no longer separated because Christ is knitting humanity back together as one.

The point isn't that the covenants before Christ were somehow tangential or did not fulfill their purpose. The point is that they all led to the consummation of the New Covenant in Christ Jesus. He is the cornerstone and the capstone, the alpha and the omega of God's whole plan.

I am not only asking my modern Jewish friends to seriously reconsider the scriptural narrative and theological foundations of their faith tradition, I am also asking my fellow Christian brothers and sisters to reconsider their approach to the Old Testament. The Old Testament should not be read as a mere tome of moral instructions or stories. It is a progressive preparation of God's people to recognize the ultimate human hero, Jesus Christ, when He arrived in history.

Because I have had young children I have been quite involved in Christian education and Sunday school at my church. I have wanted to make sure our children are approaching the Old Testament Scriptures with a Christ-centered framework. When I see curriculums that focus solely on the moral attributes of certain characters—the integrity of Daniel or the bravery of Esther—I am disheartened. Daniel had incredible integrity and Esther was amazingly brave, but that approach leaves too much off the table because it misses the messages about the coming Messiah.

I remember once sitting in a church committee meeting, reviewing various Sunday school curriculums. When I said that I wanted to make sure the Old Testament teaching was focused on Christ and not mere moralizing, there were a lot of blank stares around the table. Some people were actually quite upset. Many people on the committee were stuck on the simplistic notion that the Old Testament was about *law* and the New Testament was about *gospel*.

The problem is that Jesus Himself did not interpret the Jewish Scriptures this way. He actually said they were all about *Him*, and, frankly, that is part of what got Him in trouble. He said the temple was about Him, the Mosaic Law was about Him, the prophets were about Him—all of it.

In fact, after his resurrection He mysteriously appeared to two disheartened disciples walking along the road to Emmaus who did not recognize Him and were speaking about His crucifixion. Jesus asked what they were talking about and they said,

> "Are you the only visitor to Jerusalem who does not know the things that have happened there in these days?" And he said to them, "What things?" And they said to him, "Concerning Jesus of Nazareth, a man who was a prophet mighty in deed and word before God and all the people, and how our chief priests and rulers delivered him up to be condemned to death, and crucified him. But we had hoped that he was the one to redeem Israel. Yes, and besides all this, it is now the third day since these things happened. Moreover, some women of our company amazed us. They were at the tomb early in the morning, and when they did not find his body, they came back saying that they had even seen a vision of angels, who said that he was alive. Some of those who were with us went to the tomb and found it just as the women had said, but him they did not see." And he said to them, "O foolish ones, and slow of heart to believe all that the prophets have spoken! Was it not necessary that the Christ should suffer these things and enter into his glory?" And beginning with Moses and all the Prophets, he interpreted to them in all the Scriptures the things concerning himself. (Luke 24:18–27)

The point should be clear enough. Jesus said that his identity as the suffering Savior of humanity was deeply and pervasively embedded in the Old Testament. Yes, there are moral lessons to be learned there, but that was only one dimension of the story. The whole Old Testament is designed to reveal the full context and backstory of the Jewish Messiah who would come to save the world.

God Becomes the Hero

But perhaps the most amazing part of the overall biblical narrative is that God Himself came to play the part of humanity's hero. According to Scripture, the second person of the Trinity, the eternal Son of God, took on human flesh to reestablish humanity and the new heavens and new earth. God did not remain distant from or uninvolved in the brokenness of the world, but became broken for its sake.

This is the heart of Christianity's answer to the philosophical and theological problem of evil, often referred to as "theodicy." The notion that an infinitely good and great God can permit the existence of suffering, sin, and evil seems quite incongruent. Doesn't the existence of evil suggest that God must be tainted by evil in some respect?

Consider that the whole message of the Bible—indeed the whole case for Jesus Christ—is a response to this conundrum. The philosophical "problem of evil" is not imagined or manufactured. It is real and it is all around us. The extent of human pain and exploitation is an inescapable and deplorable part of our world. Raging against its very existence and struggling with its implications are entirely rational and absolutely necessary reactions. What kind of God would allow this kind of world to exist?

The answer is that the kind of God who would allow it is the kind of God who would personally come to reverse it. God is good because He came to solve and heal it. God is loving because He cared enough about humanity and the world to provide the way of redemption. This is precisely the argument of the Apostle Paul in his lengthy letter to the Romans. He wrote, "For I am not ashamed of the gospel, for it is the power of God for salvation to everyone who believes, to the Jew first and also to the Greek. For in it the righteousness of God is revealed from faith for faith, as it is written, 'The righteous shall live by faith'" (Rom. 1:16,17).

To paraphrase, Paul is not embarrassed or shy about the good news of Christ because it reveals the very "righteousness of God." Christ is the philosophical key that unlocks our deepest philosophical and existential dilemma. The message about Christ's global redemption vindicates God's good character and holy purpose. The gospel of God coming in human flesh is the answer to the problem of evil.

Christ as the God-man

I recently had a discussion with a Jewish friend about Jesus, and his chief concern was that the whole concept of God becoming human seemed like a form of idolatry. It felt to him that considering God in this manner was similar to fashioning an idol and reducing Him to some kind of object.

But I urged him to remember that according to the Jewish Scriptures, God made humans in His image. Humans are already legitimate pictures and likenesses of God. So it only makes sense that the fullest revelation of God would be manifest by a man. Taking on human flesh does not obscure who God is, it brings God into clearer view. This is the mystery of Christ.

Throughout the centuries, the philosophical and theological mechanics of the God-Man have been disputed and debated. Is Christ half God and half man? Is He some third kind of being that combines them? It is beyond the scope of this book to delve into all the derivations of this centuries-long discussion. Suffice it to say that the Bible does not work through the details of how the incarnation works. It simply posits that Christ is and must be both fully divine and fully human with no confusion, division, or dilution.

When it comes to the incarnation, the Scriptures focus on the why, not the how. Humanity needed a new representative in order to fully escape their Adamic condemnation. Therefore, the Savior needed to be fully human. But humanity also needed an infinitely good and powerful Savior to overcome death and evil. Therefore, humanity needed God Himself. The incarnation is the necessary solution to both of these needs.

Jesus Christ is consequently not an idol, but the very image and glory of God. In the New Testament we read,

> He is the image of the invisible God, the firstborn of all creation. For by him all things were created, in heaven and on earth, visible and invisible, whether thrones or dominions or rulers or authorities—all things were created through him and for him. And he is before all things, and in him all things hold together. And he is the head of the body, the church. He is the beginning, the firstborn from the dead, that in everything he might be preeminent. For in him all the fullness of God was pleased to dwell, and through him to reconcile to himself all things, whether on earth or in heaven, making peace by the blood of his cross. (Col. 1:15–20)

Jesus is the ultimate hero because He is the ultimate Man in the middle between heaven and earth. He slew our mortal enemy, Satan, and He reconciles all things to Himself through his life and sacrifice. The ancient legends of a hero with true pathos are realized in none other than Jesus Christ, the Son of God, whose mission was to save the world.

CHAPTER TEN

The Heroic Work of God's Son

Jesus does not give recipes that show the way to God as other teachers of religion do. He is himself the way.

—*Karl Barth*

A couple of years ago I was very excited to buy Gina her first Dutch oven for Christmas. If you're not familiar with this particular piece of cookware, you are missing one of life's true joys. These heavy-duty enamel coated cast iron pans are made for slow cooking and braising. You can brown meat and sauté vegetables on the stovetop first and then pop the pot in the oven to simmer for hours. It is, hands down, our favorite way to cook.

Since it was Christmas, I decided to go whole hog and get a large and rather expensive five-and-a-half-quart Le Creuset oven. It came in a big box that weighed over twelve pounds. I couldn't find a place to hide it, so I decided to gift wrap it and put it under the tree with Gina's name on it. I was very pleased with myself.

Now the main point of having wrapped presents under a Christmas tree is to create emotional anticipation and joyful tension. Everyone can see that there are potentially amazing gifts to open, but they don't know what they will be. The goal of the gift wrap is to create mystery by concealing the coming surprise.

So you can understand my disappointment when Gina came to me a week before Christmas and said, "So you got me a Dutch oven for Christmas! Is it a Le Creuset?" I couldn't believe it. She had poked around under the tree, taken out the large box in her name, and picked it up and shaken it. Due to its weight and size, she concluded that it could only be the heavy cast iron pot that we had been aspiring to own.

I was not amused. I expect such things from a four-year-old. Of course they will take out every box and shake it around—listening for sounds that might tip them off on the identity of the gift. But behavior like this from my grown-up wife? I was shocked. How could she ruin my big surprise? I guess some of us can't stand to wait.

Can you imagine Gina's reaction if she had been wrong in her guess? What if I had bought her heavy fitness equipment instead? Not only would her hopes have been unmet, but I would have risked a real tongue-lashing. There are few things more dangerous in life than intense hopes that are out of alignment with reality.

The Expected and the Unexpected

The ancient mystery of Christ worked a little like a wrapped present that didn't immediately meet popular expectations. While the Old Testament built a sense of palpable anticipation that God was going to redeem Israel and the world, it left many details out of focus. The mystery wasn't so much whether a Redeemer would come, but how. It was an immense truth that was partially concealed until the day of unveiling arrived.

Of all the Israelites filled with anticipation of the resolution to the mystery of Christ, John the Baptist must have felt it most acutely. He was the first prophet Israel had seen for centuries, and his specific call was to announce Messiah's arrival. He knew that Christ's time had come; he just wasn't sure how it would all unfold.

The one thing that John the Baptist knew for certain was that Israel needed to get its spiritual house in order. If the Day of the Lord was nearing, then the Jews needed to come clean with God and prepare for a radically new reality. Therefore, John set up his ministry as a symbolic reenactment of Israel's deliverance from Egypt into the Promised Land.

Since God led Israel into the wilderness after leaving Egypt, John led Jews into the wilderness. In the same way that Israel crossed through the Jordan River to enter the Promised Land, John baptized Jews in the Jordan River. His ministry of baptism was a ritual cleansing from the dirtiness of sin that would allow the Jews to venture back into the place of God's promise and presence.

John the Baptist certainly envisioned a future that involved imminent and serious judgment for those who were out of step with God's program. He even compared them to Satanic snakes who would be consumed by fire. When the religious leaders of the day came to see him, John said,

> You brood of vipers! Who warned you to flee from the wrath to come? Bear fruit in keeping with repentance. And do not presume to say to yourselves, 'We have Abraham as our father,' for I tell you, God is able from these stones to raise up children for Abraham. Even now the axe is laid to the root of the trees. Every tree therefore that does not bear good fruit is cut down and thrown into the fire.
>
> I baptize you with water for repentance, but he who is coming after me is mightier than I, whose sandals I am not worthy to carry. He will baptize you with the Holy Spirit and fire. His winnowing fork is in his hand, and he will clear his threshing floor and gather his wheat into the barn, but the chaff he will burn with unquenchable fire. (Matt. 3:7–12)

So it is no surprise that John was deeply confused and conflicted when Jesus showed up to be baptized. John immediately asked why the long-awaited Christ wasn't baptizing *him*, instead. Without giving a full explanation, Jesus cryptically answered that His baptism was necessary to "fulfill all righteousness." It was what God wanted, and no other justification was given.

John's confusion intensified later on when he was wrongfully imprisoned and facing death. He actually sent messengers to Jesus asking if He was the Messiah or not. Things weren't going according to John's expectations, and he wanted to know what was going on. Where was Christ's judgment? Where was the apocalyptic end of evildoers? Why was he in prison facing death instead of enjoying the new Promised Land? This did not seem to be going according to plan.

Jesus told the messengers to go back to John and say, "Go and tell John what you hear and see: the blind receive their sight and the lame walk, lepers are cleansed and the deaf hear, and the dead are raised up, and the poor have good news preached to them. And blessed is the one who is not offended by me" (Matt. 11:4–6).

Unfortunately, we don't have record of John's reaction to Christ's message. And while we can't know for sure, I think it helped John immensely. In these few words, Jesus selectively quoted from the Old Testament prophet Isaiah about Messiah's mission. These scriptural excerpts would have reminded John that the final apocalypse and fullness of the new heavens and new earth would come later in the story.

Christ wasn't coming in immediate judgment, but to heal the world and preach about God's coming kingdom.

Like John the Baptist, we have to bring our thoughts about God's Redeemer into alignment with God's plan. Otherwise we may miss the full impact of Christ's ministry and feel a sense of disappointment and confusion.

We know from the last chapter that the Christ had heroic work to do. And in keeping with our superhero theme, we know that every superhero has a special set of super powers. Some of them can fly, some are super strong, some can control elements of nature. But what about Jesus? What were His super powers and what kind of superhero would He become?

If we read the heroic patterns and offices of the Old Testament carefully and juxtaposition them against the life of Christ we see that Jesus would be humanity's hero by becoming the *premier Prophet, supreme High Priest*, and *conquering King*.

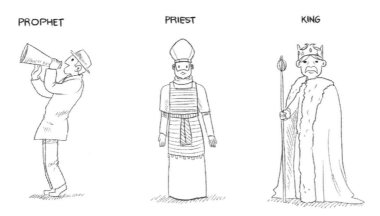

Premier Prophet

We often think of prophets as having the ability to foresee and predict the future. But in the Old Testament, a prophet is defined as someone who is "mighty in word and deed." Sometimes they did tell the future, but that was only part of their role. Their core calling was to deliver God's word with authority, and that authority was proved and authenticated by the miraculous deeds they performed.

It is important to put these concepts together because they are inter-related. If I were to tell you that I have a word from the Lord for you concerning your career, you would be right to be suspicious. I can say whatever I want or feel moved to say, but if there is nothing to prove that it is from God Himself, then why should you believe it? However, if I give the word and then perform a miracle or series of miracles, you are likely to pay much closer attention. You may still choose not to believe me or may think I have performed fancy tricks, but you will be more likely to stop and consider it.

On the other hand, if I perform miracles with absolutely no words of explanation, what is their meaning? Entertainment? Are they good for a circus act or magic show in Vegas? Would they prompt people to exalt me or medically examine me to figure out my abilities? Miracles without corresponding words would be empty and void of significance.

In the Old Testament, prophets came proclaiming God's Word and performing mighty acts of deliverance and judgment. They were preachers who comforted God's people in their distress and warned them of the consequences of disobedience. They manifested God's powerful presence among His people.

When Jesus asked his disciples who people thought He was, they answered that people universally recognized Him as a prophet. Who could say and do the things He did unless He was sent from God? While Jesus was more than a prophet, He was the premier prophet the world had been waiting for, and His message would change the world.

Mighty in (Kingdom) Word

But what was the message of Jesus? Was it universal love and toler-ance or the pursuit of personal enlightenment? Was He a forerunner of Gandhi-like peace or Malcolm X-style social resistance? Should we view Him as a supreme moral teacher or spiritual guide? How should we understand His prophetic message?

The teachings of Jesus are so profound that it is hard to summarize them in such a short space. However, there are a couple of features that rise to the surface. First and foremost, Jesus came to announce the arrival of the kingdom of heaven through the establishment and presence of his kingdom people. Second, He came to subversively reinterpret and challenge the major cultural and religious symbols of his day.

Over and over again we encounter the theme of God's heavenly kingdom in the teaching of Jesus. He told story after story to proclaim that God's ruling presence had definitively come to earth in order to reclaim and redeem it. As one of his final commissions to his followers makes clear, the goal of Jesus was to fulfill the Abrahamic promise of transforming every nation of the world. He said to them, *"All authority in heaven and on* earth has been given to me. Go therefore and *make disciples of all nations,* baptizing them in the name of the Father and of the Son and of the Holy Spirit, teaching them to observe all that I have commanded you. And behold, I am with you always, to the end of the age"* (Matt. 28:18–20).

Notice the deliberate language Jesus used about heaven and earth. He was tying the Genesis 1 framework together with God's global promise to Abraham. His ultimate goal was clearly to bring all the families and nations of humanity back into communion with God so that they could do the cosmic work they were designed to do.

In the United States, when we elect a new president, the installation into office is followed by a highly publicized inaugural speech. The point of the speech is to outline the philosophy and goals of the new administration. Who can forget some of the great quotes that captured the hearts and imaginations of Americans:

Ask not what your country can do for you—ask what you can do for your country. —*John F. Kennedy, 1961*

Let me assert my firm belief that the only thing we have to fear is fear itself. —*Franklin D. Roosevelt, 1933*

Government is not the solution to our problem; government is the problem. —*Ronald Reagan, 1981*

With malice toward none, with charity for all, with firmness in the right as God gives us to see the right, let us strive on to finish the work we are in, to bind up the nation's wounds, to care for him who shall have borne the battle and for his widow and his orphan, to do all which may achieve and cherish a just and lasting peace among ourselves and with all nations. —*Abraham Lincoln, 1865*

Television pundits pore over inaugural speeches, analyzing them for clues about the president's agenda and psyche. The whole nation stops to listen to the new leader of the free world in hope that the nations might be enriched by fresh vision of freedom.

Jesus also gave an inaugural speech of sorts toward the beginning of his ministry. Many of us know it as His famous Sermon on the Mount, primarily recorded in Matthew 5–7. Like the prophet Moses before Him, Jesus ascended to a mountaintop to deliver God's kingdom message. But He didn't deliver new laws or talk about Himself. The fascinating thing to notice is that Jesus focused on His followers. Jesus focused on heavenizing earth through man in the middle, if you will.

The opening speech began with the a set of blessings called the Beatitudes. I like to remember these as the "beautiful attitudes" of God's people. You may recall some of them:

> Blessed are the poor in spirit, for theirs is the kingdom of heaven.
> Blessed are those who mourn, for they shall be comforted.
> Blessed are the meek, for they shall inherit the earth.... (Matt. 5:3–5)

It is critical not to understand these sayings as a series of if-then statements that promise subjective or psychological blessings. The grammar does not suggest that being blessed is an internal future reward based on personal performance. Rather the passage describes someone who is already blessed by the smile and approval of God due to his or her current spiritual posture of waiting and anticipation.

The poor in spirit aren't people who lack energy or self-esteem; they're people who know their spiritual poverty, who recognize that they are spiritual beggars who desperately need God in their life. They mourn and yearn for spiritual satisfaction at the deepest level, and they recognize Jesus as the solution. God's people are characterized by an attitude of hunger and thirst for being made right with God and Jesus satiates them.

In this objective sense, Jesus was saying that the followers of his kingly administration were already blessed. Because God's kingdom people are starving for the world to be made right and unbroken, Jesus will more than satisfy them. God has come in Christ to put heaven and earth back on track.

Continuing with His man in the middle theme, Jesus said,

> You are the salt of the earth, but if salt has lost its taste, how shall its saltiness be restored? It is no longer good for anything except to be thrown out and trampled under people's feet.

You are the light of the world. A city set on a hill cannot be hidden. Nor do people light a lamp and put it under a basket, but on a stand, and it gives light to all in the house. In the same way, let your light shine before others, so that they may see your good works and give glory to your Father who is in heaven.

Do not think that I have come to abolish the Law or the Prophets; I have not come to abolish them but to fulfill them. (Matt. 5:13–17).

Describing His followers as salt may strike us as a bit curious. However, salt was an incredibly valuable commodity in ancient times for its culinary and medicinal qualities. In the absence of refrigeration and modern antibiotics, it cured meats and helped to heal flesh-wounds. We still gargle salt-water today to try and heal sore throats. The phrase, "He is worth his salt," came about because salt was often used as currency.

We tend to take salt for granted in modern times, but try to imagine life without it. If you've spent any time in the kitchen, you know what I mean. Salt isn't just a flavor, it's an enhancer for every other flavor. In the same way that salt brings savor to food, God's people exist to bring joy and meaning to the world. We are called to provide a depth of flavor to life that is unachievable without knowing Christ. If we don't, then we are only good as gravel.

Jesus also said that His people are a light in a dark world. The illuminating presence of God's people helps humanity see things as they truly are. Good works that seek to heal the world's wounds reveal God's redemptive agenda for humanity. When God's people live their lives as agents of love and service, the watching world will see the handiwork of God Himself.

Man in the Middle

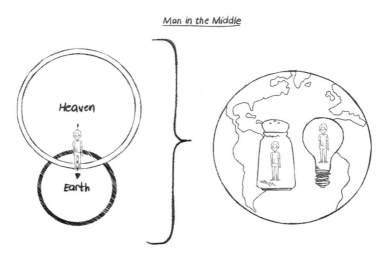

Again notice that up to this point in the inaugural address, Jesus has said nothing about Himself. Not a thing. Everything is about the role of His people in the world. He picked up on the redemption and heavenization project of humanity immediately.

It is no accident that Jesus next turns His attention to the Law and the Prophets—two major sections of the Old Testament Scriptures. His teaching so far sounded quite different than much of the Jewish tradition of His day, and Jesus wanted to disabuse people of the thought that He was a theological radical. Rather, He was showing the true intended spirit of the Mosaic Law.

The agenda of Jesus wasn't intrinsically revolutionary, but it felt that way because Israel was functioning so far off-script, biblically speaking. Much of His teaching ministry was aimed at bringing the Jewish community back into proper alignment with the heart of its own Scriptures. As Jesus said, He did not come to abolish the Mosaic Law, the temple, or the priesthood, but to fulfill them. He said they all pointed to and anticipated Him.

Of course, that didn't mean His message wasn't deeply unsettling to the reigning establishment, because it was. In His stories, Jesus often alluded to the unfortunate reality that the Jewish leaders of His generation, the King's own people, did not recognize their Messiah. The Jews who did have Messianic expectations thought Christ would reestablish Israel as a world power, but Jesus came as the suffering Savior who would reverse the human condition of sin and death. Only after He had accomplished that could the nations be progressively redeemed through the agency of His kingdom followers.

If we think that message is a hard sell in today's world, it was no easier back then. There were several significant theological and political factions at that time, and they each had their own ideas about how God would redeem Israel and the world. Few of them would have immediately resonated to Jesus because of their own theological and ideological precommitments.

Before we chew on the way this manifested in the prophetic ministry of Jesus, let's look at our own day. In America we tend to split into certain ideological camps that reflect different approaches to pursuing a better future. Each ideology also embraces certain cultural symbols that represent their position.

For example, Republicans and conservatives tend to promote individual responsibility, freedom, and opportunity as the pathway to prosperity. They see government as an inhibiting variable that diminishes personal initiative and liberty. Many conservatives embrace gun ownership, militarism, and free enterprise as staple symbols of their framework. There is not necessarily an overt desire to be violent or greedy, but these cultural elements convey their commitment to the defense of happiness and the creation of prosperity.

On the other hand, Democrats and liberals tend to emphasize communal cooperation through government agency as the means to peace and social justice. They are often suspicious of unregulated powers that can exploit and control minorities and the weaker members of society. This is why they tend to align behind initiatives that emphasize greater commitment to areas like public education and civil rights.

Without going too far into this, try to imagine the way Jesus might confront American conservatives and liberals today. How might He do it? If we take the Gospels as a guide to his strategy, we can surmise that He would rarely challenge their ideologies head-on. Rather, He would cleverly confront their symbols as a way of probing their whole worldview.

Instead of candidly antagonizing conservatives for being greedy people that needed to be more concerned with their struggling neighbors, Jesus might tell subversive and insightful stories about Wall Street. He might show up at the Pentagon to tell enigmatic parables that allude to our failure to bring abiding peace and prosperity to Afghanistan through force and coercion.

Rather than directly telling liberals that their social agenda is ironically counter-productive in fighting poverty, Jesus might go to a public school and ask how many children came from broken homes. Maybe He would go to a gay rights parade to inquire how that activity lifts up the poor people of the city.

I am obviously taking some liberties here. I don't know what Jesus would do in our day; however, we can see what Jesus did in His day. While there were times when He confronted the behavior and thoughts of the established factions of his contemporaries directly, He usually did it by taking enigmatic action and telling subversive stories that confronted and reinterpreted cultural symbols.[46]

One of the Jewish factions in the first century believed that keeping the Mosaic Law very carefully was the key to reestablishing the Kingdom of

---

46   N.T. Wright, *Jesus and the Victory of God* (Minneapolis: Fortress Press, 1996), 369.

Israel and ushering in peace and prosperity. Perhaps the most significant symbol of this approach was properly keeping the Sabbath. The thought was that if faithful Jews were careful to observe the Sabbath by not working, God would finally honor Israel and intervene on their behalf.

So what did Jesus do to confront this partisan view of pursuing God's agenda in the world? He merely picked grains of wheat from a field on a Saturday. This outraged the Sabbath-keeping religious establishment because it looked like Jesus wasn't committed to keeping the Mosaic program. Jesus cryptically responded that man was not made for the Sabbath, but that the Sabbath was made for man. He went so far as to say that He was the Lord of the Sabbath.

Think of how brilliant this strategy was. Without directly denouncing the dogmas of his opposition, Jesus symbolically said, "The Sabbath is about resting in God's work, and I am God's work in the flesh. I am the Sabbath rest you're looking for, and the Mosaic Law is about me." Jesus could have explicitly declared, "Hey folks, let me explain how the Mosaic Law works and what the Sabbath is all about. I'll break it down to you in a series of ten easy-to-understand lectures." But no, Jesus took carefully calculated action paired with obscure stories to put people off-balance and make His point stick for generations to come. It also served to prolong His life and ministry as long as possible.

But Jesus didn't just play around the edges. There was another powerful faction that believed keeping the Temple sacrifices running—even if it meant compromising with pagan governing authorities—was the key to Israel's kingdom revival. The temple in Jerusalem was at the very epicenter of Jewish identity and hope.

So when Jesus visited the temple and turned over the tables of the moneychangers, it was a very big deal. He wasn't attacking business or money in principle, He was shutting down the operation of the temple itself. If people couldn't buy sacrificial animals, they couldn't make the atoning religious transaction that supposedly made them right with God. Jesus was pointing out that their whole concept of worship and being made right with God was off base. He came to put it right.

In fact, Jesus said, "Destroy this temple, and in three days I will raise it up" (John 2:19).

While Jesus was subtly prophesying about the inevitable end to the temple system, He was also clearly talking about his own death and resurrection. In the same way that Jesus confronted the law-keeping faction with the Sabbath, Jesus confronted the temple faction by claiming to be the true temple. He was the true sacrifice, the true High Priest, and the true house of God. It all pointed to Him.

To be sure, Jesus did teach about prayer, fasting, love of neighbor, and a multitude of other topics. However, it is important to step back and locate these teachings within the greater context of His prophetic words. They were not random teachings on a variety of topics. They announce and describe the nature of his heavenly kingdom.

I have often heard people object to this heavenization interpretation of Christ's teaching because He said that his kingdom was "not of this world" and was "in our midst." But those utterances don't mean that his kingdom is restricted from earth or only in our hearts. Not at all. Jesus meant that his kingdom came from heaven and was now landing smack dab in the middle of our world. Jesus was picking up on the heaven-and-earth theme that we explored in chapter seven.

Otherwise, the Lord's Prayer would not make sense. Jesus taught his disciples to pray, "Your kingdom come, your will be done on earth as it is in heaven" (Matt. 6:10).

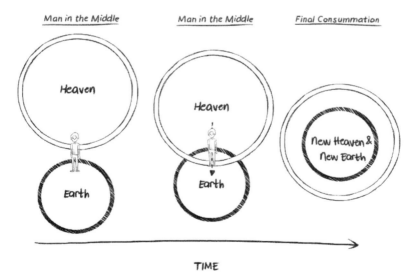

The kingdom is not just a spiritual reality that we experience internally and subjectively. It is the outworking of Christ's reign on earth through His redeemed people. It is not yet entirely visible in every circumstance, but it will become progressively evident over time because that has always been God's plan. This was the heart of his prophetic word.

In fact, the very word *gospel* was a political term to announce the good news of a new emperor. When a new Caesar would ascend to the throne, heralds would go throughout the empire proclaiming the gospel of the new king. The subjects of the kingdom were encouraged to look forward to his new reign as a fresh way to provide peace and prosperity. The ascent of the new ruler was supposed to be good news.

When Jesus and His disciples used the word *gospel* to describe His kingdom message, it would have stopped people in their tracks. Who would dare to declare a new Gospel and risk confronting Caesar? What kind of man would be that provocative unless He really saw Himself as the rightful King?

Think about it. If Jesus really only spoke abstractly about peace, love, and individual spiritualism, He wouldn't have been killed. People who try to completely depoliticize Jesus are not seriously grappling with the provocative heart of his kingdom message. Jesus was ultimately killed because He was a political problem and a threat to the establishment. His brutal death on a cross demonstrates that He was more than a moral teacher. He was executed because His kingdom message was not welcomed by the entrenched powers of his day.

Mighty in (Kingdom) Deed

President Thomas Jefferson famously used a razor to eliminate the miracles from the Gospel narratives in order to purify them of supernatural superstition and reveal the true heart of Christ's ethical system. He then compiled parts of the four Gospels into a single narrative to present a chronological ordering of Christ's life and teaching. He would even cut the texts mid-verse to exclude any reference to the miraculous if he deemed it necessary.

We may think Jefferson's approach was somewhat overboard, but I believe many people try to mentally filter out the miraculous dimension of the Gospel narratives to seek an understanding of Christ. Jefferson was just being more honest with himself and more diligent in his approach.

Despite Jefferson's best intentions, Christ's deeds spoke just as loudly as His words. If we leave them on the cutting room floor, we will miss much of who Jesus was as a prophet. His miracles were not simply

262 The Heroic Work of God's Son

magic acts to confirm His deity and power. They purposefully and symbolically conveyed the goals of His heroic agenda.

My favorite has to be Jesus' first public miracle at the wedding reception in Cana of Galilee. When the reception host ran out of wine, Jesus' mother, Mary, asked Jesus to solve the problem. With some hesitation about overplaying his hand too early in his ministry, Jesus went ahead and instructed the servants to fill six stone jars with water. These particular jars were large jars used in Jewish purification rituals, and each held twenty to thirty gallons. We're talking about a lot of water.

Jesus then proceeded to turn all of the one hundred plus gallons of water into fine wine. When the master of the feast tasted it he was pleasantly shocked that the groom had saved the best stuff for last. Usually, they would let people get buzzed on the good wine first and then trot out the cheaper stuff because people wouldn't be able to tell the difference as the party wore on. Jesus did the opposite.

There is no doubt that turning water into wine would be an awesome party trick. But Jesus wasn't just accommodating his mother or trying to impress his disciples. Throughout the Bible, wine carries massive symbolic weight. It was a staple beverage that communicated life (blood) and a theological symbol of deep rest and celebration. Far from being prohibitionist against alcohol or advocating teetotalism, the Bible is thoroughly pro-wine.

Producing fine wine from stone jars designed for Jewish purification rites showed that the ministry of Jesus would go beyond mere ritual cleansing. The spiritual purification of Jesus would lead to a rocking party.

Think of it this way. When a sports team wins the championship, what do they do? They go to their locker rooms and douse one another with champagne. They not only drink it, they shower each other in it. It is not unusual to see players and reporters wearing plastic bags to avoid getting drenched in a celebratory booze bath.

There is a very real sense in which Jesus' first miracle parallels this scenario, but the irony is that He reveled at the beginning of his ministry instead of the end. He took the vessels meant for giving religious baths and transformed the water into celebratory wine. His kingdom was going to be so much greater than the Mosaic era that the participants in His party would have enough wine to bathe in.

Jesus was in the business of putting the world back on course so that humanity could enjoy their fellowship with one another and God. What better way to convey his purpose than providing an abundance of fine wine to celebrate with? Jesus was no prohibitionist or teetotaler, that's for sure.

Of course not all of Christ's miracles were intended as a reason to party. Some were meant to be deeply provocative. A great example was his feeding more than five thousand people from two fish and five loaves of bread. Unfortunately, people then and now are slow to appreciate the point of this prophetic deed. It was not done to reveal His supernatural abilities or to demonstrate his deep concern for human hunger. It wasn't a spiritual lesson about the way He can use something small and meager and make it significant. Instead, it was an ingenious setup for His prophetic teaching.

In John 6, we read that when the crowds fully internalized what Jesus had done in feeding them, they wanted to "take him by force to make him king." He was the answer that they had been looking for. Jesus was a human gravy train who could care for their physical needs!

When they predictably reacted with that rationale, Jesus turned the situation into an opportunity to clarify his agenda. He famously said to them, "I am the bread of life; whoever comes to me shall not hunger, and whoever believes in me shall never thirst." In other words, "Don't just look at me as your meal-ticket. What you really need and what I offer is far greater. You need to feast on me as the true sustenance of your life."

This didn't make the crowds happy at all. In fact, they started to grumble and complain, "Is not this Jesus, the son of Joseph, whose father and mother we know? How does he now say, 'I have come down from heaven'?" The story continues:

> Jesus answered them, "Do not grumble among yourselves. No one can come to me unless the Father who sent me draws him. And I will raise him up on the last day. It is written in the Prophets, 'And they will all be taught by God.' Everyone who has heard and learned from the Father comes to me— not that anyone has seen the Father except he who is from God; he has seen the Father. Truly, truly, I say to you, whoever believes has eternal life. I am the bread of life. Your fathers ate the manna in the wilderness, and they died. This is the bread that comes down from heaven, so that one may eat of it and not die. I am the living bread that came down from heaven. If anyone eats of this bread, he will live forever. And the bread that I will give for the life of the world is my flesh."
>
> The Jews then disputed among themselves, saying, "How can this man give us his flesh to eat?" So Jesus said to them, "Truly, truly, I say to you, unless you eat the flesh of the Son of Man and drink his blood, you have no life in you. Whoever feeds on my flesh and drinks my blood has eternal

life, and I will raise him up on the last day. For my flesh is true food, and my blood is true drink. Whoever feeds on my flesh and drinks my blood abides in me, and I in him. As the living Father sent me, and I live because of the Father, so whoever feeds on me, he also will live because of me. This is the bread that came down from heaven, not like the bread the fathers ate, and died. Whoever feeds on this bread will live forever." (John 6:43–58)

To fully appreciate what Jesus did and said here, you have to remember the link between food and faith that was established way back in Genesis 2. God set up the world so that we would be utterly dependent on His provision, but we lost access to the tree of life. We were banned from the Garden of Eden and its life-giving sanctuary.

Jesus was picking up on this theological reality and identifying Himself as the ultimate tree of life. He was God's heavenly provision for humanity. Eternal life is contingent on participating in Him through a feasting faith. He didn't just come to provide daily meals, He came to become our true life source. We need the life that only He can provide.

The point should be clear enough. Christ's miracles weren't devoid of kingdom meaning or detached from His teaching. His words and deeds interpenetrated one another. Attempts to strip the miracles out of the narrative leave us with a truncated view of Jesus. Following Jefferson's skeptical path doesn't give us more of Christ, it gives us far less.

Of course Christ's greatest prophetic deed was to conquer death by rising from the dead. But to fully grasp the meaning of this we need to understand the other heroic role He played as the Supreme High Priest.

Supreme High Priest

Of all the facets of Jesus' heroic ministry, His priesthood may be the hardest for people to swallow. It is one thing to acknowledge Christ's prophetic teaching about God healing a broken world. Conceptually understanding His claim to be the King of kings isn't too hard, even if it is hard to accept. However, really digesting the necessity of a personal Savior is a major stumbling block for many people. Why do we collectively and individually need the priestly death and resurrection of Christ?

To fully grasp why Jesus' death and resurrection are so central to the gospel message, we have to revisit our basic understanding of God and humanity. If we bring misconceptions about God and humans to the discussion, our interpretation of His sacrifice will be off-target.

There was an interfaith panel discussion a few years ago between a very prominent Jew and a Roman Catholic that serves as a convenient example. At one point in the discussion, the Jewish man said something along the lines of, "I try to be a good person. I'm not a murderer. I'm faithful to my wife. I worship God and try to be generous with people. Why do I need your Jesus?" In other words, "I have my own righteousness and personal sacrifice to offer God. Why would I need the righteousness and sacrifice of someone else—especially Jesus?"

The pivotal issue on the table was how humans come into a right relationship with God, and the Jewish man's question was absolutely spot-on. He could not have articulated the theological sentiments any more clearly. Many religious adherents would ask the very same question.

Unfortunately, that line of questioning doesn't fully account for the internal logic of the Old Testament Scriptures. It simultaneously exaggerates the role of our morality and discounts the impact of our sin. As we observed in the early chapters of Genesis, human relationships with God were never rooted in raw moral achievement or ethical earning. In addition, the offense of sin could not be repaired without satisfying God's commitments to extinguishing evil and renewing humanity. Individuals need Jesus because only He can provide what we need.

The basis of a right relationship with God

Many religions and individuals envision God with a divine morality score-card, individually tracking and weighing our good deeds versus our bad deeds. It is almost like the blindfolded Lady Justice who holds out a scale in her hand to see which side is heavier—the case for righteousness or for guilt. The approach to God becomes about piling up good works to gain His favor.

This position is very understandable and reasonable on the surface. If God is good, then He obviously cares about moral behavior and a life in accordance with His program. It would therefore seem only natural that our individual relationship with God comes down to our overall performance as moral agents. No personal Savior is necessary if we are each tasked with paying our own way, so to speak.

One of the hitches with this conception is that good deeds do not erase or counterbalance guilt. Let's chew on a scenario to help illustrate the point. Imagine someone who was in charge of a Nazi concentration camp that killed scores of innocent men, women, and children. After the war ended, that person escaped to South America and started a new life that saved an equal number of lives through the establishment of various orphanages and hospitals. We might agree that such a transformation is laudable, but that he must still be held to account for his murderous deeds. The good deeds in and of themselves could never wipe away the guilt of his previous sins.

So even though the idea of Lady Justice weighing good and bad deeds in the balance has a kind of logic, it isn't a cogent way of dealing with the issue at hand. It is definitely not consistent with the way the Bible nuances the relationship between our morality and our relationship with God. On the one hand, God's program wasn't designed so that humans would merit and earn his love by accomplishing a moral task list. On the other hand, the relational breach of evil and guilt has to be dealt with. Our relationship with God was never fundamentally or initially based on a series of ethical transactions.

When I was growing up, a group of Christians initiated a ministry to combat this belief in independent spiritual bootstrapping. Their program, Evangelism Explosion, took a quite simple and interesting approach. They encouraged Christians to create a dialogue with people by using a prefabricated scenario. They would ask people to imagine dying and appearing before God's judgment throne. Then they would ask, "If God asked you why He should let you into heaven, what would you say?"

Of course, many people would be intrigued enough to engage and would often say, "I should be admitted to heaven because I am a good person." The ministry's strategy was then to cite Bible verses that show we are saved by faith in Christ, not our moral works. A favorite Bible reference they would point to reads, "For by grace you have been saved through faith. And this is not your own doing; it is the gift of God, not a result of works, so that no one may boast" (Eph. 2:8, 9).

They were substantially on the right track, but with one problem. Their scenario about the way divine judgment plays out is unbiblical. When we die and appear before the judgment seat, we don't get to make an individual verbal case for ourselves. As intriguing as Evangelism Explosion's approach was, it is potentially misleading because God's judgment won't happen this way. Our eternal life is not hanging in the balance of a theological *Jeopardy* question. There will be no quiz.

Jesus taught something about the final judgment and it serves as a fascinating and enigmatic glimpse into how God's judgment works. He said,

> When the Son of Man comes in his glory, and all the angels with him, then he will sit on his glorious throne. Before him will be gathered all the nations, and he will separate people one from another as a shepherd separates the sheep from the goats. And he will place the sheep on his right, but the goats on the left. Then the King will say to those on his right, 'Come, you who are blessed by my Father, inherit the kingdom prepared for you from the foundation of the world. For I was hungry and you gave me food, I was thirsty and you gave me drink, I was a stranger and you welcomed me, I was naked and you clothed me, I was sick and you visited me, I was in prison and you came to me.' Then the righteous will answer him, saying, 'Lord, when did we see you hungry and feed you, or thirsty and give you drink? And when did we see you a stranger and welcome you, or naked and clothe you? And when did we see you sick or in prison and visit you?' And the King will answer them, 'Truly, I say to you, as you did it to one of the least of these my brothers, you did it to me.'
>
> Then he will say to those on his left, 'Depart from me, you cursed, into the eternal fire prepared for the devil and his angels. For I was hungry and you gave me no food, I was thirsty and you gave me no drink, I was a stranger and you did not welcome me, naked and you did not clothe me, sick and in prison and you did not visit me.' Then they also will answer, saying, 'Lord, when did we see you hungry or thirsty or a stranger or naked or sick or in prison, and did not minister to you?' Then he will answer them, saying, 'Truly, I say to you, as you did not do it to one of the least of these, you did not do it to me.' And these will go away into eternal punishment, but the righteous into eternal life. (Matt. 25:31–46)

Notice a few things here. First, we will be judged in some respect according to our works. Did we seek to serve the needy through acts of mercy? Did we serve others instead of being self-serving? Jesus clearly says that our love for our neighbor will serve as the evidence of our love for God.

But there's a puzzling catch in the story. The people who do the good works are oblivious to them. When the King commends them for their acts of service, they will be confused and bewildered. Contrary to expectations, they will think they have nothing to claim. In fact, they will honestly dispute their own commendation. They will come to God empty-handed and in need of mercy.

In contrast, the cursed people will make claims for their own righteousness. They will be indignant and surprised that the King is not recognizing their philanthropic contributions.

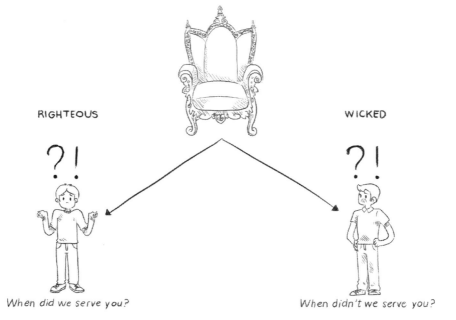

RIGHTEOUS   WICKED

When did we serve you?   When didn't we serve you?

This kind of story telling shows the subtle genius of Jesus. He takes something that seems so easy and inserts details that turn it completely on its head. What is going on here? Are we judged by our works or not? Are the righteous and the wicked lying about their respective conditions?

I don't believe either party is lying about their confusion or indignation. The emotions happening at the final judgment will not be feigned. It will be an incredibly raw and revealing moment of our deepest inner realities.

The shocking revelation of Jesus is that righteous people do not trust in their own worthiness before God. In fact, they deny it outright. Being right with God is therefore not a straightforward function of living an ethical life. Rather, the divine assessment approves of those who come in a posture of spiritual poverty. Righteous people don't attempt to weigh their acts of service in the scales of God's justice. In the final analysis, they know that they have no claim before God and need His mercy.

On the other side, the wicked are exceedingly self-aware. They are ready to defend themselves as people who served others in order to love God. Ironically, this shows that their core motivation is devotion to self, not to God. The wicked have God's priorities completely backwards despite passionately feeling that their intentions are noble.

What we're encountering here is the intricate and fascinating interplay between faith and obedience. There is no question that our behavior matters to God. However, it does not flow from an attitude of moral earning. For sinners, a right relationship with God begins with coming to Him empty-handed. This is what Jesus meant when He said, "Blessed are the poor in spirit for theirs is the kingdom of heaven" (Matt. 5:3).

But how does this point to our need of a Savior? Can't we simply have this humble attitude without needing Jesus? How does Christ enter the spiritual equation at all?

One of the most beautiful teachings of the New Testament is that faith in Christ spiritually disconnects us from the first Adam and reconnects us to Jesus as the new Adam. In theological terms, we become spiritually "united" to Christ and share His life and identity. Instead of being condemned and corrupted to death by our association with the first Adam, we attain a new life. The unbroken fellowship of love that the Son of God has with the Father and the Spirit becomes ours.

This is why Paul's statement about not being saved by works remains consistent with Christ's teaching about the judgment. We are not saved by our own deeds. However, our life serves as evidence of our faith and connection to Christ. Saving faith is not a mere attitude or generic belief in a higher power—it is trust in God's merciful endowment of a Savior.

Christ's unbroken fellowship with the Father is what we need, not a list of moral achievements. Humans weren't made so that they could strive to be made in God's image or fellowship. We were created in His image and part of His family from the beginning. Humanity's relationship with God was established around a posture of faithful trust and love. Therefore, the Savior we need is not a moral wage slave, but the Son of God who has eternal communion with the Father and the Spirit.

This is one of the reasons why the Creator of humanity is predominantly portrayed as a Father. He does not love His children because of moral performance any more than I love my children because of their moral performance. He loves His children because they share His image and share His joyful fellowship. Of course, obedience and right behavior are part of honoring and maintaining the relationship, but they do not *create* the relationship. Obedience happens in a preexisting matrix of love and care, not through raw moral achievement.

By analogy, my sons do not come into a relationship with me by virtue of their moral accomplishments. Their behavior does not make them any more or less my sons. The rationale for righteous behavior is not to earn or attain a status of sonship to me—it is to further enjoy the filial relationship they already have.

Think of it another way. If I buy my wife flowers or wash the dishes as a way to gain her love, I think we would all concede that our relationship is flawed. However, if I buy her flowers and wash dishes as an expression of the love and delight I already have for her, we would acknowledge that as healthy and beautiful. There is little doubt that gift giving and acts of service build our relationship. But the minute our relationship becomes merely transactional there is little hope of true fellowship.

The preexisting and confirmed relationship of Christ to God as the faithful Son is what Jesus provides for his followers. We can be at peace with God and enjoy His love because of the status we have in Christ. We do not have to earn God's favor by piling up good works, we simply need to rest in the gracious provision of God's Son.

Extinguishing evil humanity and raising it to new life

While all this seems reasonable enough in the abstract, I can imagine my Jewish friends saying, "But what should we do with verses like the one from the prophet Micah that seem to suggest the opposite principle?"

> He has told you, O man, what is good; and what does the Lord require of you but to do justice, and to love mercy, and to walk humbly with your God? (Mic. 6:8)

On its face, this verse and others like it do not seem to comport with our need of an individual Savior. It appears quite clear that being in a right relationship with God is defined by our success or failure as moral agents, not our union with Christ. The tension between God's explicit moral requirements and the need of a Savior is palpable.

To solve the riddle of these paradoxical concepts it is helpful to look at the admonition of Micah 6 more carefully. Simultaneously doing justice and loving mercy presents a profound conundrum because they pull in opposite directions. How can we vanquish evil and pursue forgiveness with equal vigor? It isn't quite as easy or as clear as it sounds.

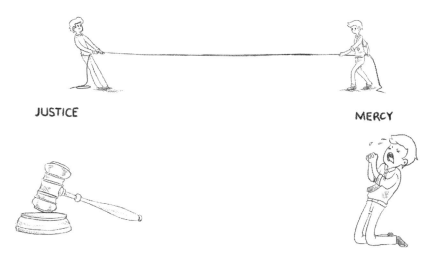

JUSTICE   MERCY

Whenever I think about the competing priorities of justice and mercy, I think of my good friend Mike. In his early thirties he courageously married a widow with four young children. The challenge was even bigger than you might expect, because the deceased husband had severely traumatized the family. His drug addiction and severe abuse had left a devastating mark on the children. For many years, Mike and the family were tormented by the previous husband's legacy.

The oldest son, in particular, started to become quite a handful as a teenager. He even had to leave the home for a time because he was a threat to the safety of the other children. When he was in his early twenties, he was involved in a carjacking that ended up in a high-speed police chase caught on television. This was obviously bad enough, but it got even worse as he attempted to flee the stolen car on foot. Upon exiting the vehicle he committed a very serious felony by firing a weapon at authorities. No one was injured or killed, but it was viewed as attempted murder of a police officer.

I will never forget going to the son's sentencing to support Mike's family. Many people from their church had written letters to the judge pleading for mercy on the troubled young man. They retold the story of his traumatic childhood and the abuse that he had been subjected to. Dozens of people came to the courtroom in an impassioned attempt to reduce his punishment. The rest of the young man's life was hanging in the balance of the court's judgment.

When the judge finally spoke, he openly acknowledged the heartfelt letters and overwhelming presence of the family's friends in the courtroom. In a grave and empathetic tone, he said that while he understood the appeals for mercy and would like to grant it, his job was to give justice by enforcing the law. His job and role as judge was not to be an agent of mercy. His call was to uphold the laws of the land. With a voice of deep sadness he sentenced the son to twenty-five years in prison without the possibility of parole. The son received justice according to the law of the land, not mercy.

Micah's call to do justice and love mercy should stop us in our tracks. It should humble us. Fulfilling these requirements is not a mere matter of feeling or emotion. These requirements cause us to plumb the very depths of living in a broken world.

Perhaps the best way to penetrate the enigma of these competing priorities is to look to God Himself. How does a holy and righteous God simultaneously satisfy both justice and mercy in the face of real and destructive evil? How can both be accomplished on behalf of fallen humanity? Isn't it a choice between one and the other?

By God's eternal design, the answer is substitutionary sacrifice followed by personal transformation. Since our relational guilt and condemnation is rooted in a representative (Adam), God mercifully allows another representative (Jesus) to satisfy the requirements of justice. Instead of being permanently eliminated from the new heavens and earth through death, God allows Jesus to die in our stead. Without Jesus as our substitute, we would be left to fulfill justice ourselves and would suffer eternal death.

Some may see this as an example of gross injustice. How can someone pay a penalty other people deserve? Doesn't that make that Jesus an abused whipping boy for unworthy evildoers?

The only possible answer to this very legitimate question is the incarnation. This is precisely why God took on flesh and became man. God cannot accept just any substitute. He doesn't simply provide a random individual to suffer on behalf of others. In the ultimate act of mercy, He takes the judgment on Himself. God becomes the solution for fallen humanity by simultaneously issuing and receiving the just penalty we deserve.

All of this helps to explain why the Old Testament is full of repetitive animal sacrifice. During the Mosaic era, people were instructed to come to God's house, the temple, to worship. But they could not come simply as they were because of their sin. They needed to come with a substitutionary sacrifice as a way of dealing with their broken relationship with God.

In one of the most important rituals, the worshiper would stop at the front door of the temple and lay their hands on the head of sacrificial animal before personally slaughtering it. This symbolic procedure was the way of transferring their personal sinfulness to a substitute. The figurative conveyance and consequence of their guilt met the demands of justice in God's presence.

Once the death sentence had been satisfied, the temple priest would take over because the worshiper was symbolically dead. The priest would take the dead carcass from the front door of the Temple directly to an altar of fire—often referred to as God's feasting table. Think of it as God's barbeque pit.[47] After sprinkling blood as evidence of justice being fulfilled, the priest would place the dead body on the altar.

Contrary to many misconceptions, this action was not symbolic of further judgment. The fire was not representative of hell. Rather, it was the place of radical transformation and fellowship with God. In temple lingo this step was not the sacrifice; it was the offering. God said that the smell of the smoke was pleasant in His nostrils. The priests were even allowed to eat some of the meat at the altar-table as a sign of celebrating renewed fellowship with God.

Now obviously God does not need to eat, and He is not ultimately satisfied with the death of animals. However, the temple ritual repeatedly told the story of God's priorities. Sinful humanity needed a sacrificial substitute so that they could come into His presence. As they were transformed at His table, the people in God's house could feast with Him again. Israel rehearsed this pattern over and over again for centuries to internalize their need for the once-and-for-all sacrifice that would fulfill all of the temple symbolism.

---

47 Joshua Appel and Peter J. Leithart, *A House for My Name: Questions & Answers*. Moscow, Idaho: Canon Press, 2009), 83.

The priestly work of Christ brings us back into the feasting sanctuary of God that we were meant for. Jesus brings us back full circle to the Garden of Eden so that we can enjoy friendship with God and neighbor. Instead of being left to die, we are invited back into God's house.

Jesus was the supreme high priest because He became the sacrifice *and* the offering for us. The awe-inspiring irony of Christ's death on a cross is that it alone achieves the divine fusion of justice and mercy. Jesus went so far as to say that his execution as a criminal revealed the very glory of God. Christ's substitutionary sacrifice shows God's glory because it simultaneously demonstrates both God's thirst for bringing justice and His astonishing love of giving mercy and forgiveness to sinful humanity. The cross of Christ surprisingly gives both at once. It is the place where justice and mercy meet.

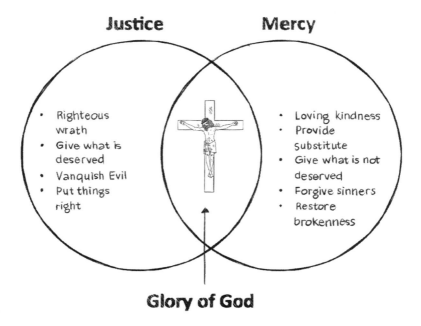

Justice

- Righteous wrath
- Give what is deserved
- Vanquish Evil
- Put things right

Mercy

- Loving kindness
- Provide substitute
- Give what is not deserved
- Forgive sinners
- Restore brokenness

Glory of God

Think about it. If God merely judged sinners, He would not exhibit his tremendous and overflowing love for fellowship and mercy. If God merely forgave sinners without seeking justice, God would be capricious and unrighteous. Either way, His divine holiness would be compromised. But the cross of Christ holds these divine priorities together. This is why it is where the glory of God is revealed.

Bloody sacrifice is the means of meting out justice because the penalty for sin is death. Good deeds cannot assuage guilt. Guilt can only be removed when the penalty of guilt has been realized.

In theological terms, a bloody sacrifice provides *propitiation* (fulfilling God's justice) and *expiation* (fulfilling God's mercy). As a propitiation for sin, death quells God's holy wrath and satisfies His justice. As expiation for sin, death releases and acquits the guilty party from the stain of sin. When a bloody sacrifice is made on behalf of the guilty party, God's justice and mercy are simultaneously enacted.

The centrality of the resurrection

But substitutionary death alone does not solve humanity's problem. We also need to be given new life so that we can participate in the new heavens and new earth. This is why the physical resurrection of Christ is so critical. If Jesus had stayed dead, His death would be no good to us. Resurrection vindicated Jesus—proving that He was the Son of God who could not be held by death. He took us down with Him into death and brought us back up through resurrection. It thus secured the personal transformation and renewal humanity so desperately needs.

Like the sacrificial animal carcass that was transformed into food and smoke on the altar, Christ's body rose from the dead. His body was renewed and glorified so that He could bring new life to his people.

The Apostle Paul was quite emphatic that Christianity is utterly meaningless if the resurrection of Christ is not true. He went so far as to say that Christians should be pitied as the most delusional people on earth if Christ did not rise from the dead. It is not an ancillary matter that can be easily dismissed. The resurrection of Christ lies at the very center of the whole theological and philosophical system.

Paul said this because without the resurrection, the whole aim and goal of the Bible remains unmet. God's glorious plans for man in the middle of the new heavens and new earth cannot be realized without it. The scope and sweep of the whole biblical story is unfulfilled if humanity cannot overcome death.

When Jesus rose from the grave on the third day, He conquered and overcame humanity's ancient death penalty. He reversed the curse so that we would not be forever eliminated from God's heavenization program. Those who are united to Christ by faith receive the full benefits of

His unbroken fellowship of love to the Father, His sacrificial death, and the promise of new life.

The salvation that Christ offers is not merely spiritual. The salvation Christ accomplishes for His people is holistic and total. It involves our bodies and souls. It renews our intellect, emotion, and will. It restores our ability to work according to our call and to enjoy the fruits of our labor.

Christ's achievement as the supreme high priest does not bring us to a mere break-even point with God. His death and resurrection secure everything on our behalf. In the place of guilty condemnation we receive a pardon and full declaration of righteousness. In the place of corruption we receive a new life and identity.

The amazing teaching of the Bible is that people are united to Christ and saved by grace through faith. We cannot earn union to Christ's death and resurrection any more than we can earn God's favor to begin with. As it was from the beginning, it is faith and trust in God's provision that saves us. One of the great passages of the Bible says,

> Therefore, if anyone is in Christ, he is a new creation. The old has passed away; behold, the new has come. All this is from God, who through Christ reconciled us to himself and gave us the ministry of reconciliation; that is, in Christ God was reconciling the world to himself, not counting their trespasses against them, and entrusting to us the message of reconciliation. Therefore, we are ambassadors for Christ, God making his appeal through us. We implore you on behalf of Christ, be reconciled to God. For our sake he made him to be sin who knew no sin, so that in him we might become the righteousness of God. (2 Cor. 5:17–21)

Conquering King

At this point in the heroic work of Jesus, we might expect some victory laps around the globe to celebrate His victory over death. If I were scripting history, I would make sure He personally took the time to confront those who had condemned him to death. It would have been so cool for him to show off and take on Caesar and Pontius Pilate head to head. What a great finale it would have been.

But that's not the way the narrative works. There was no ticker-tape parade in Jerusalem or partying in his hometown. After a period of a mere forty days from His resurrection, Jesus left the scene. Why?

Before his crucifixion, Jesus prophesied that He would soon depart to the Father and leave His followers with the help and power of the Holy Spirit. He said,

> These things I have spoken to you while I am still with you. But the Helper, the Holy Spirit, whom the Father will send in my name, he will teach you all things and bring to your remembrance all that I have said to you. Peace I leave with you; my peace I give to you. Not as the world gives do I give to you. Let not your hearts be troubled, neither let them be afraid. You heard me say to you, 'I am going away, and I will come to you.' If you loved me, you would have rejoiced, because I am going to the Father, for the Father is greater than I. And now I have told you before it takes place, so that when it does take place you may believe. (John 14:25–29)

Jesus pressed his prophecy further by teaching three successive parables of delay recorded in Matthew 24 and 25. Each story intimated that He would be gone much longer than anyone might expect. The message was unmistakable—Jesus was not planning on sticking around or coming back anytime soon. He instructed his followers to patiently and faithfully do their work during His extended absence.

And this is precisely what occurred. After his resurrection, Jesus spent several weeks instructing His faithful core followers about the kingdom of God and then ascended to heaven in a cloud. While this may seem like a dodge of responsibility that calls the credibility of Christ's resurrection into question, it fits perfectly with God's initial program.

The goal of history was always for the community of God's image-bearers to transform and glorify the world. Once Jesus reestablished humanity to the "man in the middle" program through His death and resurrection, the work of heavenization passed back to others.

Christ's ascension was not an abdication of His duties; it was actually the pathway to His cosmic coronation. He did not vanish into the ether; He went to take His seat on the kingly throne of heaven and earth. From there, Jesus would empower and direct His followers by the power of His Spirit.

Christ's followers were a little fuzzy on this agenda before the Spirit came to them on the day of Pentecost. In fact, right before Jesus left they asked if He would restore the kingdom to Israel in their day. Even though Jesus had taught them about his imminent and prolonged departure, they were still waiting for an immediate conclusion to history. Jesus firmly pushed back on this with his final words: "It is not for you to know times or seasons that the Father has fixed by his own authority. But you will receive power when the Holy Spirit has come upon you, and you will be my witnesses in Jerusalem and in all Judea and Samaria, and to the end of the earth" (Acts 1:8).

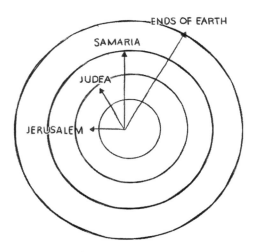

I find this episode to be absolutely fascinating. The disciples of Jesus were so hungry for the new heavens and new earth that they wanted to see it happen in their day. And while that deep longing was on target, it skipped over humanity's kingdom role. By the authority and power of Christ, our job is to take His kingdom message to out in the whole world. That is why the geographic trajectory of Christ's instructions worked almost like concentric circles. This would clearly not happen in one generation. The global realization of Christ's directive would take millennia.

A global monarchy

Concepts such as animal sacrifice and the priesthood are hard for us to grasp because they disappeared from the scene when the temple was destroyed in 70 AD. But the paradigm of monarchy and kingdom is somewhat closer to our collective consciousness because it has only been gone from American politics for a few hundred years. Nevertheless, a quick refresher course is in order.

The unique political innovation of the original founders of the United States was to split the role of king into three branches in an effort to avoid the tyranny and corruption that often comes with the concentration of these powers. The founders went to great lengths to make sure that the executive, legislative, and judicial aspects of government were not in the hands of a single individual.

We will consider modern political science later in the book, but for the moment it is helpful to recognize that the monarchy of Jesus encompasses all of these roles and responsibilities. Christ defines the agenda and arranges the pieces on the board as the chief executive. He issues legislation because He is the final law of the land. And Jesus provides justice because He in the business of vanquishing evil and making all things right.

In previous sections we have considered quite a bit about the way Christ's final judgment works. His kingdom legislation concerning mutual love, service, and healing is fairly familiar to us. However, we probably need to revisit His executive agenda again because it is so widely misunderstood.

In the United States, when the president is overwhelmingly elected by popular vote, pundits like to say that the president has a mandate. This means that he has the clear consent of the governed to act authoritatively to enact the promises of his platform. Political negotiation and compromise are overlooked because of the common consensus to achieve certain goals.

While Jesus does not rule the world by the consent of the governed, His kingdom mandate is very clear. As we saw in the beginning of the chapter, He stated it in his Great Commission: "*All authority in heaven and on earth* has been given to me. Go therefore and *make disciples of all nations,* baptizing them in the name of the Father and of the Son and of the Holy Spirit, *teaching them to observe all that I have commanded you.* And behold, I am with you always, to the end of the age" (Matt. 28:18–20).

Many Christians in modern times have interpreted this to mean that Jesus wants every ethnic people group of the world to be exposed to the gospel message. But merely garnering a few converts from each ethnicity falls short of the true impact of these words.

First, a disciple is not simply a learner or student of a subject matter. A disciple is someone who seeks to copy the total life pattern of his or her mentor. Discipleship does not imply a pupil-teacher relationship; it establishes an apprentice-master relationship. Making disciples means bringing deep personal transformation through imitation.

Second, the word *nations* includes but is not semantically restricted to *ethnicities.* A nation is a definable entity with geographical and political boundaries. Jesus didn't merely have individuals in view. He could have said that if He wanted to communicate that, but He didn't. He clearly said that He wants to bring the various governments of the world under the banner of his kingdom.

Taken on its face, Christ's royal mandate is a command to pervasively spread the gospel of the kingdom to the point where entire governing authorities explicitly pattern themselves by it. It is far from being an anemic call to convert a few people from everywhere.

Over the centuries, Christians have been deeply conflicted and confused about the outworking of this program. The violence of the medieval crusades, the forced baptisms of conquered peoples, and the domineering extension of the British Empire easily come to mind. It is one thing to talk about individual salvation; it is quite another to talk about geopolitical systems on a global scale.

In reaction to the historical abuses of Christians in the name of Christendom, many have tried to interpret Christ's kingdom along strictly populist lines. They narrowly emphasize individual transformation from a grassroots level. Larger organizational systems or top-down authority structures are often considered to be inappropriate targets that are beyond reach. Such aims smack of power-hungry elitism.

Unfortunately, this posture has fed what some have referred to as the Christian ghetto or cul-de-sac. Since Christians have not had a clear view of the what and how of the kingdom of God, they have retreated into their own insular communities. Instead of being global agents of healing and enlightenment, Christ's followers have become increasingly sidelined from the machinery of the world's affairs.

I believe this overreaction to Christian abuses related to global discipleship fails to grasp the nature of God's program to begin with. The whole point of the creation is for God's image-bearers to fruitfully labor on the earth to glorify it. The project was initially derailed by sin, but Christ's core mission was to restore humanity to its purpose. Erecting inward-looking Christian ghettos was never God's intent.

Four common views

The bottom line is that our understanding of Christ's lordship shapes the nature of our engagement with the world. While all Christians agree that Christ will physically return for the final judgment to finally consummate the new heavens and earth, we tend to disagree what happens in the intervening time.

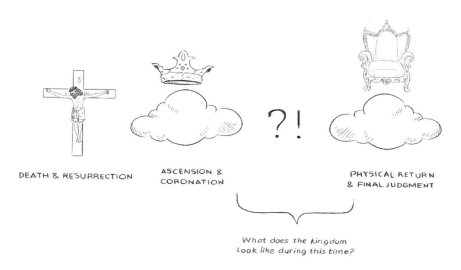

DEATH & RESURRECTION   ASCENSION & CORONATION   PHYSICAL RETURN & FINAL JUDGMENT

What does the kingdom look like during this time?

People have generally subscribed to one of four views concerning the state of the world during Christ's absence:

1. *Pessimism*—The world will gradually get more and more corrupt in Christ's absence until He returns in cataclysmic judgment. Many modern Evangelicals even believe His kingdom is literally postponed until His physical return. Strategic engagement in culture and institutions is largely futile and polishing brass on a sinking ship. The main objective should be to save souls from imminent judgment—and there may not be many who are ultimately saved.

2. *Stalemate*—Evil corrupts the world at roughly the same rate righteousness transforms it. The kingdom is provisionally and spiritually expressed through true converts and the church. This creates a basic stasis in the affairs of men. Cultural and institutional transformation are achievable only in a limited sense. There will be masses of people who perish and masses of people who are saved.

3. *Indifference*—We will not know the nature of the degeneration or transformation of the world until Christ returns. We

shouldn't worry about it too much and should focus solely on our personal obedience and evangelizing those within our immediate spheres of influence.

4. *Optimism*—The kingdom of God will massively transform the entire world during Christ's long departure. While humanity's heavenization project will not be complete or easy prior to Christ's return, it will be visibly and markedly advanced over the long course of his absence. We can expect the number of converts to Christianity to be vast.

4 VIEWS OF THE KINGDOM PRIOR TO CHRIST'S RETURN

Pessimism	Stalemate	Indifference	Optimism
things will	things will roughly	we don't know	heavenization
get worse	stay the same	who cares?	is slowly happening

As you might imagine, the practical ramifications of these divergent views are huge. Whenever I talk through this with people, I am surprised when they think this is an irrelevant or merely academic subject. Expectations are everything, and the Bible is by no means silent on this matter. Christian obedience is never done in the absence of expectations. Christ's followers are supposed to be deeply animated by hope.

At this point in the book it should be obvious that I'm a firm adherent of the fourth category of kingdom optimism. I am fully aware of many texts that seem to support the other views, but I think they have to be interpreted in the total context of the scope and sweep of the biblical story. The gospel isn't about worldwide judgment. The gospel has always been about God's redemption of the world.

Jesus taught that heaven was playing offense and that hell would lose on defense. He said, "...I will build my church, and the gates of hell shall not prevail against it" (Matt. 16:18).

Note that Jesus didn't say that the gates of heaven would hold up against the advances of hell. Quite the contrary, His church will advance against Satan's program of sin and death. The best defenses of hell will collapse under the weight of God's grace and love.

Of course, no one knows the day or hour of Christ's return. My suspicion is that his return is far off because the Great Commission concerning the nations is yet to be fulfilled. Irrespective of the timing of Christ's return, we should labor in hope. It has been rumored that Martin Luther was once asked what he would do if he knew Christ was returning tomorrow in judgment. He brilliantly responded that he would plant a tree. He understood that the destiny of the world is not destruction, but glorification. The fire that awaits the world according to Biblical prophecy is not annihilating, but purging and purifying.

Concerns about utopianism, triumphalism, and power

Christians who hold different views of the kingdom often have very grave concerns that an optimistic posture leads to naive utopianism or strident triumphalism. The progressive success of Christ's kingdom in the world almost seems to be in conflict with the very narrative of Christ's life. Some theologians disparage those with optimistic convictions for having a "theology of glory" instead of clinging to a "theology of the cross." The criticism of more pervasive cultural impact and development is that Christ's ultimate mode of battle was martyrdom. That doesn't sound particularly successful in worldly terms.

But this contrast is a classic false dilemma. It is almost like saying sweet and savory flavors don't mix. As one of my favorite theologians likes to point out, Christians are called to be "limping victors." Will Christians suffer ridicule, severe persecution, and even martyrdom for their convictions? Of course they will. Will Christians or the world be perfected this side of Christ's return? Of course not. But that doesn't suggest that our suffering service or sacrificial presence will be in vain. Quite the contrary, they will bear much fruit. Jesus said the faith of his followers would move mountains, figuratively pointing to our impact on the largest features of human enterprise.

Perhaps the biggest apprehension regarding kingdom optimism is that worldly expressions of power appear to be contrary to Christ's own paradigm. Didn't Christ abandon and forsake formal power structures in favor of taking on the form of a humble servant, born in a feeding trough? The example of Jesus seems to point away from top-down or quasi-elitist models of global transformation. The Apostle Paul even said that his "strength was made perfect in weakness."

It is absolutely true that Christ and the testimony of his apostles should deeply nuance our understanding of strength, power, and authority. However, we must be careful not to confuse power with the abuse of power. Taken to its logical end, this kind of thinking would lead to anarchy by denying the very concept of authority itself. There is nothing inherently evil about the power that authority figures or formal institutions wield. In fact, formal power is a vital part of boundary setting within complex communities.

In the presence of evil and sin, forceful coercion is not only necessary, but also good. Police aren't meant to carry weapons to terrorize or bring tyranny, but to keep the peace and uphold the laws that make for peace. There is a tyranny that comes from abusive authority, but there is also a tyranny that comes from the absence of authority as well.

So the issue isn't that power itself is wrong or must be eschewed, but that it must be wisely sought and handled. Christ's followers are not called to naively abandon and neglect various power structures of leadership that manifest in government, education, and business. Rather, they are called to exhibit Christlike power and position wherever they find themselves. This means that they must lead as self-sacrificing servants, not belligerent masters.

The Bible teaches that the kind of power Christians are given by the Holy Spirit is resurrection power. That means that we will suffer persecution and death in this life, but those sufferings alone will not hold or define us. We will persevere through them with the strength to carry on and keep striving in our work to serve others. As the world watches our selfless and loving struggle for global redemption they will come to know who Jesus really is.

Jesus taught that a fruitful life follows a death and resurrection pattern. He said, "Unless a grain of wheat falls into the ground and dies, it abides alone. But if it dies, it brings forth much fruit" (John 12:24).

Clearly, the so-called theology of the cross (death) and theology of glory (resurrection) go hand in hand. That's the way it worked for Jesus and that's the way it works for His followers. Paul wrote,

> For this reason, because I have heard of your faith in the Lord Jesus and your love toward all the saints, I do not cease to give thanks for you,

remembering you in my prayers, that the God of our Lord Jesus Christ, the Father of glory, may give you the Spirit of wisdom and of revelation in the knowledge of him, having the eyes of your hearts enlightened, that you may know what is the hope to which he has called you, what are the riches of his glorious inheritance in the saints, and what is the immeasurable greatness of his power toward us who believe, according to the working of his great might that he worked in Christ when he raised him from the dead and seated him at his right hand in the heavenly places, far above all rule and authority and power and dominion, and above every name that is named, not only in this age but also in the one to come. And he put all things under his feet and gave him as head over all things to the church, which is his body, the fullness of him who fills all in all. (Eph. 1:15–23)

It is no accident that the writers of the New Testament repeatedly describe the church as Christ's body. While Jesus did ascend to his heavenly throne, He is still immanently present through His people. The world has not been discarded to the dust heap of eternity. It is being progressively and slowly enriched and reconciled through the salt and light presence of his disciples.

But what does this really look like in practical terms? Beyond a fifty-thousand-foot view of these matters in the abstract, how shall we then live? What is Christ's kingdom strategy? How does the mystery of Christ work in the real world?

EXPLORING THE PRACTICAL IMPLICATIONS OF THE KINGDOM

CHAPTER ELEVEN

Christ's Kingdom Strategy

Baseball is like church. Many attend, few understand.

—*Leo Durocher*

I will never forget the day that I was introduced to my future wife, Gina. A mutual acquaintance thought we should meet since we were both transfer students from large universities. Between Gina's stunning beauty and my friend's endorsement, I was immediately infatuated. My mind raced, thinking of ways to connect with her. We were at a fairly small college so I didn't think it would be too hard to cross paths.

But we didn't cross paths at all. We weren't in the same classes and we didn't run into each other along the way. I couldn't believe it. How could I get to know her better? The answer might seem pretty obvious: I needed to call her up and ask her out on a date, right? There were only two problems—I didn't know her last name and I didn't have her phone number. It wouldn't normally be a big deal to acquire that information, but I didn't want to risk broadcasting my feelings by sharing my intent with anyone. So I did what any rational guy would do; I went to the student center and carefully combed through the school roster for every Gina in the school.

I found three Ginas: Gina Clark, Gina Johnson, Gina Mangiarelli. To be honest, I can't remember precisely what the first two Ginas' surnames were, but my heart skipped a beat. The brunette, dark-eyed beauty that I wanted to get to know could only be a Mangiarelli. And that meant she could only be of Italian heritage and was probably even

Roman Catholic. I couldn't believe it. I had fallen for someone who was sure to be extremely intense, loud, and a bit wild.

Now to fully appreciate my reaction to Gina's maiden name, you have to understand my personal history. I grew up in a very middle-of-the-road white Anglo-Saxon Protestant environment. My brother and I like to joke that the only Mexican culture we encountered or knew of was Taco Bell. It couldn't have been any more WASPy except for one small thing—we lived next door to the Castiglione family.

The Castigliones epitomized what it means to be both Italian and to be Roman Catholic. There are Irish Catholics, Mexican Catholics, and so forth, but let's get real—if you want to meet someone who has authentic Catholicism down to their actual DNA, you need to brush shoulders with an Italian Catholic. These people are representing the home team.

Suffice it to say that I did more than brush shoulders with the Castigliones. They had two boys and a girl all around the same age as my younger brother and me. We were on the same little league teams and constantly played together in the neighborhood. We were very close for many years.

During that time I encountered things in the Castigliones' lives that I didn't understand. Strange, weird things. They didn't go to the local public school that my brother and I attended. Instead, they wore uniforms and went to St. Rita's to be taught by nuns. They regularly missed little league practices for something called *catechism*. Their china cabinet held a large red family Bible that was revered as a sacred object—almost like a relic. They didn't call going to church *going to church*, they called it *mass*. And sometimes they went there on Saturday. Once a week they sat in a mysterious and dark closet to tell their sins. After they prayed they made motions over their head and torso. And most puzzling of all, they didn't eat meat on Fridays. It was all very foreign and confusing.

As you might guess, the description doesn't end there. I remember a lot of yelling—often in close proximity. Wine was not merely an evening beverage, but was openly imbibed during the day. They frequently introduced new vocabulary words to me that I had never heard before—most of them with four letters. I learned new hand and body gestures to communicate with people. In the Castiglione home there was far more raw emotion, more laughter, more food, more parties (with more relatives), more sports…more everything. It even seemed to me that these flamboyant people of an unfamiliar faith were possibly more *alive*.

But I was too young to put this all together. These were just impressions that I carried with me, not things that I puzzled over. All I knew was that these non-Protestant, Italian Roman Catholics were a deeply committed bunch the likes of which I had never seen before. Their serious devotion alongside their larger-than-life behavior felt intriguing and incongruent. It was too big for me to put my arms around.

So maybe you can appreciate why I hesitated when I saw the Mangiarelli name on the college roster. Not because it was bad, but because it was so much bigger than me. It conveyed something deep that I wasn't sure I could connect to. I was genuinely afraid.

As it turns out, I was right about Gina Mangiarelli. Her heritage was obviously Italian, she was raised as a Roman Catholic, and her family was very much like the Castigliones. They were boisterous party people with a penchant for acts of deep devotion. Gina came out of that family with an iron will, a sharp mind, and serious skills in the kitchen. And despite my initial trepidation, within nine months of our first date we were married.

I was deeply conflicted about the nature of Roman Catholicism for quite a few years. Its inconsistencies with my Protestant faith and identity seemed like a bridge too far. Many people in my Evangelical tradition would not even refer to Catholics as Christians. Some saw Catholicism as a cult. There is no doubt that from a theological perspective, I was digesting the notion that Roman Catholicism was a deceptive counterfeit.

This line of thinking extended to the Orthodox Church and Church of England, as well. Pentecostals were increasingly suspect, as were mainline Protestant denominations. Serious theological errors and massive indifference to biblical precision seemed to be rampant throughout the whole world. I was drinking some serious partisan Kool-Aid.

The irony was that the Reformed tradition I embraced liked to claim a couple of things. First, it liked to assert that we prioritized going back to the source. We were all about being historically orthodox. We weren't nondenominationalists who were arrogantly wrote their own statements of faith. No, we harkened back to the basic truths of the Bible as expressed through the Apostles', Nicene, and Chalcedonian Creeds. Our faith was biblical and historically ancient—free of the perversions of later tradition.

Second, we had these slogans from our theological forebears: Faith alone. Scripture alone. Christ alone. Grace alone. To God be the glory alone. These were powerful words that seemed to truly convey the distinctive and crucial truths of Scripture. Traditions that didn't adopt these principles were likely beyond the pale of true Christianity.

SLOGANS OF THE PROTESTANT REFORMATION

SCRIPTURE ALONE
The Bible has ultimate authority over matters of faith and practice

FAITH ALONE
We are made right with God through faith, not our moral works

CHRIST ALONE
We are made right with God through Christ's death and resurrection

GRACE ALONE
Redemption is accomplished by the gift of God's grace, not our worthiness

TO GOD'S GLORY ALONE
All of life and creation exists for the purpose of glorifying God

During this season the music minister at my church in Austin, Texas, encouraged me to memorize the Nicene Creed. I wasn't sure how I would benefit from the exercise, but I played along. It is a great summary of the Christian faith written all the way back in 381 AD. This is what it says:

> I believe in one God, the Father Almighty, Maker of heaven and earth, and of all things visible and invisible.
>
> And in one Lord Jesus Christ, the only-begotten Son of God, begotten of the Father before all worlds; God of God, Light of Light, very God of very God; begotten, not made, being of one substance with the Father, by whom all things were made.
>
> Who, for us men for our salvation, came down from heaven, and was incarnate by the Holy Spirit of the virgin Mary, and was made man; and was crucified also for us under Pontius Pilate; He suffered and was buried; and the third day He rose again, according to the Scriptures; and ascended into heaven, and sits on the right hand of the Father; and He shall come again, with glory, to judge the quick and the dead; whose kingdom shall have no end.
>
> And I believe in the Holy Ghost, the Lord and Giver of Life; who proceeds from the Father and the Son; who with the Father and the Son together is worshiped and glorified; who spoke by the prophets.
>
> And I believe one holy catholic and apostolic Church. I acknowledge one baptism for the remission of sins; and I look for the resurrection of the dead, and the life of the world to come. Amen.

You may notice a few things about the way the Nicene Creed flows. First, it is structured by past, present, and future time. It clearly emphasizes that the Christian faith is deeply embedded in history and real events. Christianity is not a meditative religious abstraction. Time and history are moving toward the goal of the world to come.

Second, the creed revolves around the one God who mysteriously exists as three Persons—Father, Son, and Spirit. This Triune God acts as a community of love from the beginning of time to create and redeem humanity for His purposes. The eternal Son of God was even made man and subjected to death and resurrection to enact God's plan.

And finally, this creed is quite short. Let's face it. We're looking at about 223 words compared to the English Bible's nearly 775 thousand. The creed isn't even a fraction of one percent of the content of the Christian faith, and yet it is the most widely adopted creed summary of the Christian faith in the history of Christianity and has stood the test of time for almost two thousand years. Amazing stuff.

Have you ever experienced a pivotal moment when your perspective radically and permanently shifts? About three months after I memorized the Nicene Creed I was reading a devotional magazine from a Reformed ministry. That month's issue included an exposé on the Orthodox Church, and one of the articles pointed out that their tradition is deeply committed to the Nicene Creed. The writer acknowledged that the claims of the Nicene Creed essentially shape Orthodox identity. But then the article went on to vigorously condemn the Orthodox Church as fundamentally idolatrous because of its use of religious icons in worship.

And that's when something in me snapped. On the one hand, the magazine was recognizing the Orthodox Church's deep and devoted commitment to who God is, what Christ did for humanity, and the goal of history. But on the other hand it was saying that the Orthodox Church is an idolatrous sect and false church. So ... we can agree on some of the most astounding core beliefs about the nature of God, humans, and history, but disagree on icons and it is game over for the Orthodox Church?

It didn't make sense. In that moment it struck me how inconsistent my tradition was with itself. If we really believed in "Grace alone" as a slogan, then we should be characterized by grace. And grace doesn't cast aspersions on people who deeply believe in "Christ alone" or "one

Lord Jesus Christ…God of God, Light of Light, very God of very God." Surely grace doesn't behave that way.

I didn't swing the other direction and leave the Reformed branch of the Christian church. I still believe that many of our theological convictions are biblical and helpful. I think we have significant resources and internal examples to help move the kingdom ball down the field. My distinctive theological views haven't been scrapped, but I hold them differently now. They are not reasons for division, but truths to earnestly, patiently, and winsomely contend for among the brethren for the sake of unity.

Christ's Kingdom Strategy: Christian Unity

What I started to realize as I went through this experience was that Christ's kingdom strategy was not merely about proclaiming a message. Christ's core kingdom strategy was also the embodiment of His message in the lives of His people. The heart of Christ's mission was to establish His followers as a loving and transformative family. As we grow together as a community, we will accomplish His purposes.

The night before Jesus was crucified, He prayed these words:

> I do not ask for these only, but also for those who will believe in me through their word, *that they may all be one, just as you, Father, are in me, and I in you, that they also may be in us, so that the world may believe that you have sent me.* The glory that you have given me I have given to them, that they may be one even as we are one, I in them and you in me, that they may become perfectly one, so that the world may know that you sent me and loved them even as you loved me. Father, I desire that they also, whom you have given me, may be with me where I am, to see my glory that you have given me because you loved me before the foundation of the world. O righteous Father, even though the world does not know you, I know you, and these know that you have sent me. I made known to them your name, and I will continue to make it known, that the love with which you have loved me may be in them, and I in them. (John 17:20–26)

Please notice the portion of Christ's prayer that I have italicized. He connected the conversion of the world to the unity of his people. Discipleship of the nations will not be achieved by merely trumpeting words. The truth of the message has to be manifested by a people who have been reconstituted to their true image. We were made to be like God in our communal relations and we must live that way to accomplish our mission.

On the surface it would appear that Christ's prayer has gone unanswered. His followers are deeply divided on both an organizational and individual basis. We disagree on everything from doctrine to the color of carpet in the church foyer. Unity is one thing Christians seem to lack the most.

All of this raises the thorny question of how Christian unity should be defined. Is unity primarily expressed in institutional terms, or is it successfully expressed in heartfelt principle? Must Christians be part of the same ecclesiastical group, or are common convictions enough?

I believe that the Apostle Paul substantially answers this question in his letter to the Ephesians. He wrote,

> I therefore, a prisoner for the Lord, urge you to walk in a manner worthy of the calling to which you have been called, with all humility and gentleness, with patience, bearing with one another in love, *eager to maintain the unity of the Spirit* in the bond of peace. There is *one body and one Spirit*—just as you were called to the *one hope* that belongs to your call—*one Lord, one faith, one baptism, one God and Father of all*, who is over all and through all and in all. But grace was given to each one of us according to the measure of Christ's gift....
>
> And he gave the apostles, the prophets, the evangelists, the shepherds and teachers, to equip the saints for the work of ministry, for building up the body of Christ, until we all *attain* to the unity of the faith and of the knowledge of the Son of God, to mature manhood, to the measure of the stature of the fullness of Christ, so that we may no longer be children, tossed to and fro by the waves and carried about by every wind of doctrine, by human cunning, by craftiness in deceitful schemes. Rather, speaking the truth in love, we are to grow up in every way into him who is the head, into Christ, from whom the whole body, joined and held together by every joint with which it is equipped, when each part is working properly, makes the body grow so that it builds itself up in love. (Eph. 4:1–7, 11–16)

In this crucially important passage, Paul affirms a both/and perspective regarding Christian unity. Christians share a true spiritual unity now because of the common faith that roots them in one Lord. Since they are part of Christ's one body by the power of the one Spirit, Paul urges them to recognize and *maintain* that unity.

But there is a sense in which he openly acknowledges the immature divisions between Christians. While they have a spiritual unity in principle, they are solemnly urged to *attain* further unity in practice. Christians need to grow up and grow beyond different doctrines and schemes in order to fully manifest the unity of their one baptism.

Water baptism conveys many things, but one that all Christians agree on is that it is the visible entry rite into the institutional church. Christians are invisibly united to Christ by the power of the Spirit and God has provided a communal ceremony to mark out that reality. Faith in Christ isn't a matter of individual navel-gazing; it visibly brings people into the fellowship of God's family.

And even though we might like to avoid it, this means that the function and unity of the visible and organized church matters as a central part of God's redemptive program. By definition, a Christian disciple cannot be his or her own master and apprentice. This is precisely why Christ's Great Commission gives the dual mandate of discipleship with baptism. Faith in Christ and membership in the church go hand in hand.

Christians absolutely and unequivocally need the community of the church in order to mature. As we just read in the passage from Ephesians, the organized church is the God-ordained institution through which evangelists, shepherds (pastors), and teachers equip the disciples of Christ to grow. The church is not just an unseen idea or hyperlocalized religious association; it is a globally identifiable group of people who are specially organized for a particular purpose.

This is why I can gladly confess the sentiments of the Nicene Creed regarding the "one holy catholic and apostolic church." The word *catholic* is an extremely useful term that conveys universality and oneness. It means that the church is not ultimately defined by partisan or geographic boundaries, despite the fact that those boundaries exist. This is one of the reasons why the label *Roman Catholic* is an unfortunate oxymoron. Ascribing a territorial descriptor to a word conveying universality betrays the kind of partisan spirit Christians are called to rise above.

The one baptism Paul cites does not merely join people to a particular branch or denomination of Christianity; it marks people out as disciples of the body of Christ wherever it may be found. Roman Catholics, Eastern Orthodox, Episcopalians, Presbyterians, and Baptists all attach different nuances to the practice, meaning, and effect of baptism, but they all practice baptism in the name of the Father, Son, and Holy Spirit. There aren't many baptisms; there is one baptism.

Different Christians simply emphasize and exaggerate different aspects of the one baptism Christ instituted. For example, Roman Catholics tend to stress the relationship between baptismal water and the impartation of God's Spirit in the life of a disciple. Baptists typically focus on the new life that is started by being identified with Christ's death and resurrection. Presbyterians often point to the covenantal and promissory dimension of baptism that parallels Old Testament circumcision. The list goes on, but the point remains. There is still only one baptism.

In the early church there was a fascinating controversy over baptism and church membership that demonstrates this principle. Before Emperor Constantine politically protected and promoted the church, Christians were often persecuted in brutal ways. One of the nagging questions that arose during this season was whether a person's baptism was invalidated if the pastor who administered the baptism apostatized under persecution. In other words, if a "false" pastor administered baptism, was the baptism any good or should it be re-administered?

The wise answer of the church was that baptism is ultimately God's action, not the action of a particular person. Therefore, because there is only one baptism providentially given by God's grace, the baptism was legitimate irrespective of the person who administered it. This decision was a theological triumph for church unity that has stood until this very day.

I am very aware that this kind of ecumenical perspective concerning the church may smack of being somewhat Pollyannaish and romantic. It almost feels like I am promoting an adolescent ignorance of the theological chasms that divide many Christians. However, I think this attitude overlooks the both/and teaching of maintaining and attaining unity. There were different factions and churches in Paul's own day, but he still taught about the essential unity Christians shared.

I also think our perception of increasing unity is a function of where we identify ourselves in history. If we think history is imminently drawing to an apocalyptic close at any moment, then hoping for greater institutional and ecumenical unity is a hard thought to swallow. But what if we take Christ's teaching about his extended delay to heart and consider that we may still be in the earlier stages of church history? Perhaps then we can imagine that God's redemptive program is still at the beginning or middle of the development process. Our hope concerning more organizational unity is largely a matter of perspective on where we stand in the story.

However we see our place in the unfolding of time, the Bible clearly teaches that Christians must work to maintain and unity in spirit and strive to attain unity in practice. Christians should joyfully labor toward those goals, and not remain content with stasis or degeneration.

But how does this happen? How do the designated evangelists, pastors, and teachers of the institutional church accomplish the ministry of equipping disciples? What does it look like to go about the business of maturing so that Christians can effectively pursue their work in the world? In short, how can people become more transformed in order to bring transformation?

Reflecting on several paradigms of personal change

Throughout history, the prospect of deep personal change and development has been a central concern across cultures and religions. And while the particulars have changed as modern science has brought various therapies and medications to the fore, there is nothing new under the sun when it comes to the broad approaches to this topic. In principle, people of various worldviews have tackled the project of individual change through a couple of basic paradigms.

The first primarily seeks transformation from the inside out. Personal change is thought to begin with inward illumination and erudition, so various strategies are employed to properly organize and align the mind. The key is to attain an enlightened internal state that eclipses external conditions and shapes bodily passions.

An inside-out approach is often manifested in Eastern meditative traditions that pivot around disciplines of mental stillness and emotional balance. But it is also very well represented by Western traditions that propose higher education or professional psychotherapy as the keys to personal change. Both East and West are heavily invested in an inside-out model of individual and collective transformation.

The second paradigm primarily stresses an outside-in strategy through bodily regimens and practices. It strives to purify and tame the inner self through the outward health and discipline of the body. Configuring certain environmental and physical inputs is understood as the pathway to transformation.

The outside-in model is often expressed through the adoption of special diets, exercise routines, and specially prescribed behaviors. Obvious examples of this include things like Veganism, insanity workouts, and Feng Shui home design. But we would be seriously remiss if we blindly omitted the culture of consumerism we are immersed in. The attainment of luxury vehicles, fashionable clothing, and the like all promise to deliver a good life.

Modern and alternative medicines are also significant manifestations of the outside-in strategy. While both are legitimate in their own right, many people believe that the physical manipulation of biological brain mechanics and chemistry holds the key to change. Of course, it is undeniable that scientific advances have led to pharmaceutical therapies that address true organic afflictions, but I think we can all agree that prescription drugs are overused and often abused in our culture. Many people are chasing happiness and fulfillment in a pill bottle.

If you think this inside-out and outside-in analysis is oversimplified, look no farther than your local bookstore. Comb through the physical fitness, diet, self-help, and psychology sections. Examine the way different authors frame the prospect of personal transformation. You will find that the promises and approaches of personal change keep boiling down to a selective emphasis on inside-out or outside-in models.

I don't necessarily intend to be dismissively critical in my assessment. There is a legitimate reason for this dynamic, and it lies at the heart of being human. We are composed of body and soul (or body and mind, if you prefer), so there is a duality inherent to the business of personal change. Both halves of the human equation must be addressed. It just so happens that most people tend to emphasize one half over the other, and almost all of them degenerate into individual initiatives.

Interestingly, in the midst of the self-help boom of our day there has been a creeping awareness that personal change is deeply limited by "self." People are recognizing that go-it-alone tactics tend to fail, and this has led to an explosion in the professional coaching business. Coaching is no longer restricted to the realm of athletics or physical training. It is now available to almost every profession and walk of life you can think of. The self-help movements of popular psychology have morphed into a world filled with personal gurus.

My most intense experience of this phenomenon came several years ago when I was invited to a four-day "Unleash the Power Within" conference led by Tony Robbins. I went at the behest of my business partners even though I was quite skeptical and reticent. Motivational speakers have never really appealed to me very much, and doing Robbins's famous fire-walk seemed kind of cultish.

But I ended up enjoying the experience very much. First, the level of hunger and thirst many people have to radically improve their life struck me very deeply. People from all walks and stations of life came in the hope of gaining some insight that would enable to them to lose weight, fix their marriage, or find a more rewarding career. Rich and poor, fat and thin—people are desperate for change.

Second, I was simultaneously impressed and shocked that Tony Robbins laid out a sophisticated paradigm of personal transformation that was remarkably close to that of Christianity. His whole premise is based on a triadic framework that hits almost all of the notes the Bible addresses. He spent four full days teaching how personal change is a three-fold function of our story, state, and strategy.

Robbins insightfully observed that our lives are first and foremost a function of the stories we have about reality and ourselves. If we want to change, then we have to recognize our internal narratives and change them. Second, personal change is linked to our physical and psychological state because "motion is emotion." The health of our bodies and energy of our minds are critically important to our ability to realize our potential. Finally, our actual strategy for reaching our goals must be wise and appropriate. If we have great ideas for ourselves and maintain good health, but don't act in wise ways, we will find our lives in ruin.

But although Tony Robbins's three-fold priorities are profoundly in sync with the message of the Bible, there is a critical hole in his approach. Namely, like almost every other transformation paradigm, he benignly divorces personal change from the truth of Christ and the work of God's Spirit through the church.

This massive omission places the ultimate onus of transformation back onto the self. Even with the assistance of coaches trained in Tony Robbins's techniques, people are saddled with imagining their own story, finding their own state, and fashioning their own strategy. His triadic formula is eerily close to the truth, but falls tragically and fatally short because it completely neglects the specific work and power of Christ through God's Spirit. While Robbins pays lip service to God generically, his teaching deliberately or ignorantly leaves out the specific role of God's Spirit.

Contrary to popular belief, God's Spirit does not work in a random fashion or ad hoc context of our own making. Christ taught that God's Spirit is present in a particular way that is discernible and accessible.

When we connect to God in the manner in which Christ prescribed, we will find the transformation need and we so deeply long for.

Refashioning Our Humanity and the Organized Church

This brings us back to the introduction of the book. Being refashioned into the loving machines we were meant to be involves realigning our bodies and souls to the fullest expression of humanity, Jesus Christ. Our individual and collective hearts need to come back to God's priorities in the way we think, desire, and make decisions. This means that our intellectual, emotional, and volitional capacities require reformation at the deepest levels.

The Faculties of the Human Soul

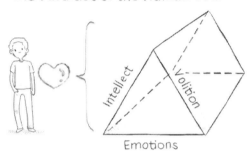

This paradigm is helpful because it reminds us what discovering and regaining our true identity involves. Our cognitive processes need to be deeply informed by the truth of God. Our emotional appetites and aspirations need to be consumed by the wisdom and love of God. And our volition and behavior need to be directed by God's program.

Theologians often call this process of personal change *sanctification*, which means *to make holy*. The more we become like Christ, the closer we draw to God and neighbor. While we never experience personal perfection in this life, we progressively become more mature by the power of God's Spirit working within us.

Various branches of Christianity tend to pursue the path of holiness in different ways. And, frankly, each one tends to emphasize one of the dimensions of our humanity over another. Some accentuate the primacy of the intellect through biblical teaching and doctrine. Others stress emotional engagement through immersion in highly charged environments of worship. Some traditions highlight volition through the establishment of communities that commit to certain standards and missions.

George Marsden, a historian of American Christianity, has observed this kind of dynamic within the Reformed branch of the Protestant church. He says that Reformed churches tend to break down into communities that are characterized by being one-dimensionally focused on doctrine (emphasis on teaching and cognition), liturgy (emphasis on worship), or mission (emphasis on communal participation in service).[48] But I think his observation easily extends to Christianity as a whole, because it springs from the very make-up of humanity itself.

Different traditions emphasize different dimensions

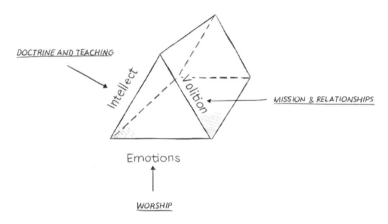

This is not to say that any branch of Christianity completely lacks two of the three emphases. I would say that a vast chunk of my Protestant tradition lifts up doctrine as primary, but it is by no means silent on worship and service. I am merely pointing out that many people in my faith community hold forth cognition as the key to personal transformation. My writing this book serves as Exhibit A.

But the reality that Christians need to strive toward is that each dimension needs careful attention. We cannot thrive as individuals and communities with a truncated view of ourselves. A holistic approach to our renewal in the context of the organized church is necessary for the work God has set before us.

For many people, this is a point of serious resistance. Talking about unity in general is fine, and pursuing our highest individual potential

---

48 See Introduction by George Marsden. David Wells, *Reformed Theology in America* (Grand Rapids: Baker, 1997), 10.

is stimulating to consider, but locating those realities in the organized church seems like a stretch. It might even sound downright depressing.

The institutional church is deeply dysfunctional at global and local levels. It certainly is not the most attractive place to think about regaining one's true self. But we need to soberly realize that despite its inherent and comprehensive brokenness, the church is at the heart of God's strategy for our redemption and the heavenization of earth.

And speaking of earth, let's get specific. If we need to realign ourselves to Christ in the context of his body, the church, then how do we do that? What tools does the church have to make this happen? What kinds of things do evangelists, pastors, and teachers in the church employ?

Fascinatingly, the church has three main tools that roughly overlap with the three facets of our soul. The three tools are the ministry of the word of God, the ministry of the sacraments, and the exercise of church discipline. Let's briefly look at the way each works to calibrate and re-shape the dimensions of our heart.

How the organizational church reshapes our humanity

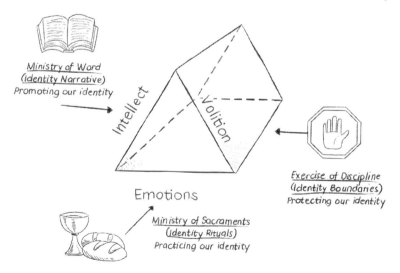

Ministry of Word
(Identity Narrative)
Promoting our identity

Intellect

Volition

Emotions

Exercise of Discipline
(Identity Boundaries)
Protecting our identity

Ministry of Sacraments
(Identity Rituals)
Practicing our identity

Ministry of the Word (recalibrating our identity narrative)

Our identity is deeply rooted in the story we believe about the world and our place in it. Most of the time, people unconsciously inherit a life script from the culture they were raised in—Their family of origin, exposure to popular media, and immersion in certain educational and recreational environments form their idea of what life in the world is about. This dynamic is often invisible because the underlying narrative about life is simply assumed, and alternatives are not known or explored.

I was recently at a party conversing with a young mother who immigrated to the United States from Latin America. She was telling me a story about how she was speaking to her American-born daughter about her family of origin. At one point, she said to her daughter, "Honey, you are a beautiful Latina. Don't forget that." Her daughter shook her head in disagreement and replied, "No, mom. I'm not a Latina. I'm a Leslie."

This small vignette is a great example of the way different narratives compete for the formation of our identity. Like young Leslie, sometimes we unwittingly accept them and adopt them into our perspective. Other times, we reject them in favor of another identity.

Of course some people are consciously aware that narrative shapes identity. And while this depth of understanding is encouraging, I am often surprised by their approach to replacement scripts. Instead of searching for or considering a universally governing narrative, they imagine the world and themselves in a way that feels compelling and set their own direction.

Christianity affirms that our identity is derived from story, but denies our ability to live outside of *God's* story in a script solely of our own imagining. There is a very real sense in which the mystery of Christ is all about explaining the story of the cosmos and our place in it. This is one of the primary reasons why the Bible is structured as an extended narrative.

One of the chief roles of the church is to persuasively proclaim and teach the story of heaven and earth over and over again. By exploring the arc and details of the story through vibrant preaching, instruction, and study, Christ's disciples find themselves and their place in the world. King David wrote that God's word was "a lamp to my feet, and a light to my path" (Ps. 119:105). It reveals where we stand and where we are headed.

This is why good preaching and teaching are so critical for Christians. Biblical illiteracy makes Christian transformation and unity impossible to achieve. We cannot be committed to love if we don't know what love does. Love is not an amorphous feeling, but thoughtful service. If we don't know how God calls us to serve one another we will love each other very poorly. Profound love requires a penetrating wisdom that is learned.

Attaining a love seasoned with wisdom is similar to progressing from basic arithmetic to calculus. It moves from simple relationships toward sophisticated and complex relationships. It requires lots of prerequisite knowledge and practice. It is not an easy endeavor.

What does love look like when a husband and wife have different ideas about raising their children? How does love try to liberate people from generational poverty? What does love do in the face of serious addictive behaviors by beloved family members? How does love function in a maximum security prison?

Too many Christians and churches are too comfortable with a low bar for love and wisdom. We have contented ourselves with addition and subtraction instead of striving toward trigonometry. And this is one of the reasons why Biblical illiteracy is rampant. Until Christians understand their call to be wise, transformational people in the midst of a broken world, we will be satisfied with superficial kindnesses. Christ's disciples must master the story and become mastered by it. The ministry of the Word is God's strategy for telling us who He is, who we are, and what the world is really like.

Ministry of the sacraments (rehearsing identity rituals)

Another key factor that impacts our identity is ritual. Whether or not we realize it, all of us have individual, family, and cultural rituals that reveal and reinforce our desires. At a mundane level, we may begin each day with a shower to reflect our commitment to hygiene. Families celebrate holidays in different ways that manifest their values.

Even being an American is marked with all kinds of rituals. We have ceremonies and protocols for properly raising our national flag. We place our hand over our hearts and sing our national anthem before sporting events. Super Bowl Sunday, Thanksgiving, and Independence Day all feature symbolic behaviors to practice and exhibit our core and cultural character. We don't eat Turkey and cranberry sauce on July 4, and it would be unthinkable to serve cheeseburgers on Thanksgiving.

It may be helpful to make a distinction between ritual and ritualism. Ritual is an unavoidable, necessary, and good part of being human. There are symbolic rhythms to life that frame our identity. However, ritualism is a naive strategy of mindless engagement in external motions

306 Christ's Kingdom Strategy

to attain deep personal change. It expects the soul to be magically transformed through merely physical acts.

A cursory reading of the Bible shows that rituals have always been a part of God's program of transformation. While they have been radically reduced and changed in our current epoch, they still exist and cry out for our implementation. Christ effectively replaced the temple rituals with his own sacrifice. But He also replaced circumcision of the Abrahamic covenant with baptism, and the Mosaic Passover meal with the Lord's Supper. These two communal rituals, sometimes called *sacraments*, now help to form the identity of his disciples.

Like circumcision, the ritual of baptism marks out people who belong to the community of faith. But it establishes even more by communicating that people of faith have been washed clean of sin, anointed by the Spirit, and raised from death to new life. Even those who were born into God's covenant family and have no memory of being baptized can look back on God's gracious calling and work in their lives. Every time we remember or witness baptism we are called back to the reality of our true selves.

I was not baptized as an infant, but as a teenager in a Presbyterian church. I will never forget a conversation I had with my pastor before being baptized. He asked me what it meant to be baptized and I responded that it was a sign that I had faith and had chosen God. He cocked his side to the side and with a somewhat pained expression on his face said, "No, Brett. Baptism isn't about you choosing God. It is about God choosing you."

I was not only deeply offended by his comment, but I was horribly confused. Hadn't I come to faith and decided to be baptized? How could baptism not be a reference to that fact?

What I failed to understand that there was divine agency and grace that was behind my decision. I didn't come to faith in a vacuum or because of my superior moral or intellectual abilities. I came to faith because of God's gracious action in my life. The rite of baptism roots our identity in God's grace, not self-achievement or illumination. We cannot give birth to ourselves, and we cannot baptize ourselves. Inclusion in God's family is an act of sheer grace.

Our faith is our own, but it does not spring to life outside of God's action. There is a very real sense in which the passivity of the baptism ritual reflects this. Salvation is God's work, not our work. He accomplishes redemption for His people; we do not accomplish it for ourselves. That is why the ritual does not allow for self-administration of the water.

In contrast, the second ritual of the Lord's Supper does reflect our ongoing and active participation in God's program. We cannot baptize ourselves, but we can make a decision about feasting at the family meal and partaking of its fellowship. We can choose whether or not to abide and grow into the reality to which we have been called.

Controversies over the meaning and practice of the Lord's Supper abound in Christianity. This may be one of Christianity's most tragic ironies, because the ritual participation in the blood and body of Christ is supposed to be the supreme evidence of our essential unity.

The ancient church in Corinth was abundant in strife and rival factions. Many were even taking on monikers of certain apostolic schools—some were of Apollos and some were of Cephas. Others had the audacity to say that they had no apostolic relationship at all and were of Christ Himself. It was a chaotic situation.

The Apostle Paul had a lot to say to the Corinthians, but one of the ways he appealed to their unity was through the practice of the Lord's Supper. He wrote, "I speak as to sensible people; judge for yourselves what I say. The cup of blessing that we bless, is it not a participation in the blood of Christ? The bread that we break, is it not a participation in the body of Christ? Because there is one bread, we who are many are one body, for we all partake of the one bread" (1 Cor. 10:15–17).

Notice the way Paul puts an emphasis on collective participation in the elements, not on the mysterious nature of the elements themselves. Many Christians get hung up on the mystical qualities or meanings of the elements of the Supper. Is the wine a mere symbol of Christ's blood or is it a miraculous or spiritual manifestation of it? These discussions have their place, but we must be careful not to overlook the overall activity and context of the Supper itself.

If we take a few steps back, we see that the Supper is a ritual wherein the people of God come together as friends who have been reconciled to God and to each other. They are one body because they partake of one bread. No longer cast out of God's place of presence and feasting, His people can now come together to share a friendship meal. This is now possible because of Christ alone, who is our life source, our human tree of life.

Paul gives these instructions to the church at Corinth to make sure they are celebrating the Supper properly:

> Whoever, therefore, eats the bread or drinks the cup of the Lord in an unworthy manner will be guilty concerning the body and blood of the Lord. Let a person examine himself, then, and so eat of the bread and drink of the cup. For anyone who eats and drinks without discerning the body eats and drinks judgment on himself. That is why many of you are weak and ill, and some have died. But if we judged ourselves truly, we would not be judged. But when we are judged by the Lord, we are disciplined so that we may not be condemned along with the world.
>
> So then, my brothers, when you come together to eat, wait for one another— if anyone is hungry, let him eat at home—so that when you come together it will not be for judgment. (1 Cor. 11:27–34)

This is a fairly frightening warning and has caused no small debate within the organized church. What does Paul mean when he tells people to examine themselves to make sure they are discerning the body of Christ? Does it mean we need to have a sound theology of Christ in our heads? Does it mean we need to come without sin in our lives?

Throughout the letter to the Corinthian church, Paul was addressing the problem of their internal their factions and schisms. He wanted them to know that the body of Christ is not divided, but is one. Therefore, the discernment of the body Paul was talking about has to do with community and unity, not a philosophical consideration of Christ's redemption.

What Paul was essentially saying was, hey, if you're coming to the Lord's Supper without a heart for the unity of Christ's church, you are not properly engaging in this ritual. If you don't get this rite right, your lives and your health are at stake.

This peculiar feasting ritual around bread and wine is a realization of our unity now and a rehearsal of our ultimate future in the new heavens and earth. Celebratory feasting is actually the primary mode of world transformation. Christians will be salt and light to the world in direct proportion to the friends they make and meet at God's feasting table.

Christians should not be seen as a dour, morbidly introspective people who are curled up in the fetal position during corporate worship and life. We are called to be people who are full of celebration and thanksgiving. In fact, that is one of the reasons the Lord's Supper is called the

Eucharist, which is the Greek word for *thanksgiving*. It is the regular thanksgiving meal that shapes our day-to-day action in the world.

This brings me back to the Castiglione and Mangiarelli families. I think it is fair to say that their lives are organized around family, celebration, and feasting. Italians don't have a reputation for amazing cuisine and boisterous families without cause. It is actually an emanation of their historic commitment to the centrality of God's thanksgiving meal.

It is too easy to miss the fact that this identity ritual is a paradigm for life. The more vigorously and regularly we participate in the Eucharist, the more it will direct the trajectory of our daily lives. Instead of retreating into states of isolated meditation, we will seek opportunities to break bread and make friends with people. We will connect in ways that make room for the kinds of discussions that allow God's story of heaven and earth to be told and experienced.

Exercise of discipline (reinforcing identity boundaries)

Many Christians are tempted to tackle the identity narrative and rituals in the context of their private domains. Gaining exposure to all kinds of information through online sermons, Bible studies, and the like is easier than ever. All of the options at our disposal make commitment and identification to the organized church seem superfluous.

But this kind of naked individualism is completely contrary to God's plan for humanity. The goal has always been for us to live in close community with one another. If we try to find to forge our identity outside of community, we will completely miss the point and stray from our calling.

Therefore God has given the organized church a dual responsibility. First and foremost, it is supposed to invite people into the fold and minister to them through Word and sacrament. Second, it is tasked with reinforcing identity boundaries through the exercise of discipline.

Before we launch into how this works, we need to look closely at the word *discipline*. It doesn't mean punishment. Parents often confuse this when they are trying to address a child's disobedience. Their role is not to punish for the sake of punishment, but to discipline in order to disciple. Remember that we defined a *disciple* as someone who seeks to copy the total life pattern of his or her mentor. Discipline is fundamentally about mentoring and training, not penal sanctions. The church is in the business of discipleship, not punishment.

When a Christian flagrantly and continually ignores their identity in Christ, the organized church is responsible for taking action. After a series of private conversations and confrontations, if the Christian disavows their faith through either words or actions, the church is tasked with disciplining that person. Such discipline involves officially declaring the person to be no longer a member of Christ's body. The public form of this declaration is a prohibition against eating the Lord's Supper.

This identity boundary is brilliant. The ritual of the Eucharist is the celebration of a family meal. If someone has decided to reject the faith commitments of the family, then having familiar and close fellowship with them is strained at best. They have in essence abandoned the community of God, and this discipline is an acknowledgment of the reality of what they themselves have already done.

The power of excommunication lies in the hope that people thus disciplined will awake to their spiritual and communal starvation. When they realize what they are missing and how empty life is without Christ, they will return home to eat. If they do not return home, then the chances are good that they have brought judgment on themselves.

Practicing Our Identity Narrative, Rituals, and Boundaries

This triadic approach—Word, sacrament, and discipline—sounds fine in the abstract, but how does it actually work out in practice? How does the organized church implement these tools for the sake of our transformation and unity? Is there a nexus where all of these activities are manifested?

The supremacy of corporate worship

The short answer is that it happens in the corporate worship of God's people. When God's people gather together in His presence, a divinely initiated conversation happens by the power of the Holy Spirit. And this conversation between God and His people not only brings great joy and pleasure to God, it puts the ministries of Word, sacrament, and discipline into play.

One of the ways the church can grow toward greater unity is to take a closer look at the rhythm and pattern of the conversation between God and His people in corporate worship. We have not been left to our own devices and imaginations in this matter. In fact, God has given us a wealth of instruction if we are careful to pay attention.

The key is to understand that the bulk of God's teaching about corporate worship is delivered in the Old Testament. Nowhere do we encounter more on the subject of proper worship than in the instructions regarding the tabernacle and the temple. It is unavoidable.

Some people find this quite confusing given the way Christ's sacrifice fulfilled the temple rituals. Aren't we done with temple worship now? How can we pattern our worship according something that has clearly been fulfilled and set aside?

The problem with this line of reasoning is that the New Testament consistently refers to Christians as the Spirit-filled temple. Together, we manifest the new dwelling place of God. Therefore, we must not be too quick to leave the temple instructions entirely behind as if they were irrelevant. Being identified with the temple is not a matter of mere sentimentality.

Without going into exhaustive detail, it is helpful to understand how saints in the Old Testament were supposed to worship. As we briefly discussed in the previous chapter, God would invite them to approach the temple with a heart of praise and thanksgiving. When they arrived at the gate they would acknowledge God's holiness and their sinfulness by bringing a sacrificial substitute to die in their place. The priest would then give them instructions on how to live a holy life and would enact the offering at God's table as a friendship meal. The worshiper would then go home to live out his life of faith in God's world.

Covenant renewal

Several of my favorite theologians have summarized this pattern of temple worship as an exercise in *covenant renewal*.[49] Being invited into God's presence brings us back into the reality of His promise and redemption. There we have a gospel-shaped conversation that reflects our full fellowship with God and neighbor. The corporate dialogue looks like this:

- *Call to worship*—When we gather together it is because God has invited us to His house. This causes us to come in praise and thanksgiving for his amazing grace.

- *Confession of sin*—As we enter God's house, we realize that God is holy and that we are in need of forgiveness for not abiding in His loving agenda.

---

49 For a fuller treatment of this pattern of worship, see Jeffery Meyers, *The Lord's Service: The Grace of Covenant Renewal Worship* (Moscow: Canon Press, 2003).

- *Cleansing from sin*—God assures us that He has provided a sacrificial substitute for our sins. In Christ's death and resurrection we have a full pardon and the righteousness we so badly lack.
- *Consecration by the Word*—In light of Christ's redemptive action on our behalf, God tells us who our true identity through the reading and preaching of the Word.
- *Communion by the sacrament*—After being recalibrated by God's Word, we are invited to celebrate at the Lord's Supper together as family friends.
- *Commissioning into the world*—Finally, God sends us back into the world as ambassadors of His grace.

The beauty of this simple structure is that it captures the overall flow of Temple worship. When Christians gather together as God's house, this flow reveals who we are and what God is doing in heaven and earth. The main part of worship isn't the singing or the sermon—it is the whole gospel of Jesus Christ. The whole worship service is an opportunity to embody and experience this.

Despite all the variations from denomination to denomination, every church has an order of worship, or *liturgy*, whether or not it is explicit. The question isn't whether a particular church has a liturgy; it is whether it is consciously patterned after God's instructions. Some are quite loose and leave out many elements of the covenant renewal pattern. Others are incredibly detailed and intentional.

Whenever I teach this, I inevitably encounter people who are startled and even offended by the notion that God has prescribed a specific pattern for worship. There is concern with the thought that there is a "right" way to worship and that every other way is "wrong." Is that what is at stake?

I don't believe so. God is very patient and long-suffering with us. He knows our hearts. Framing this as right versus wrong is off the mark. The issue here has to do with transformational power. The more the ministries of Word, sacrament, and discipline are practiced in the context of a temple-based covenant renewal conversation, the more power they have to change us.

My mission isn't to explore every facet on the diamond of corporate worship, so I am sidestepping quite a few of issues here. However,

I have found this insight about covenantal renewal worship invaluable. Rather than leaving such critical matters to chance or the musings of an individual, God gives us a timeworn and powerful pattern to practice.

In fact, I believe that the Bible teaches something very special about this. When we gather as God's people and when we are alerted to the way God works in our midst, we find that we are standing at the mystical junction of heaven and earth. Our corporate worship is the powerful and provisional expression of the new creation.

One of my favorite chapters of the Bible is Hebrews 12. Read these words carefully:

> For you have not come to what may be touched, a blazing fire and darkness and gloom and a tempest and the sound of a trumpet and a voice whose words made the hearers beg that no further messages be spoken to them. For they could not endure the order that was given, "If even a beast touches the mountain, it shall be stoned." Indeed, so terrifying was the sight that Moses said, "I tremble with fear." But you have come to Mount Zion and to the city of the living God, the heavenly Jerusalem, and to innumerable angels in festal gathering, and to the assembly of the firstborn who are enrolled in heaven, and to God, the judge of all, and to the spirits of the righteous made perfect, and to Jesus, the mediator of a new covenant, and to the sprinkled blood that speaks a better word than the blood of Abel.
>
> See that you do not refuse him who is speaking. For if they did not escape when they refused him who warned them on earth, much less will we escape if we reject him who warns from heaven. At that time his voice shook the earth, but now he has promised, "Yet once more I will shake not only the earth but also the heavens." This phrase, "Yet once more," indicates the removal of things that are shaken—that is, things that have been made—in order that the things that cannot be shaken may remain. Therefore let us be grateful for receiving a kingdom that cannot be shaken, and thus let us offer to God acceptable worship, with reverence and awe, for our God is a consuming fire. (Heb. 12:18–29)

Notice a few things. First, the writer to the Hebrews tells us that when we come together in worship we have come to the city of the living God, the heavenly Jerusalem. Whether or not we can see it, the reality is that the worshiping community has come to the place where heaven and earth overlap.

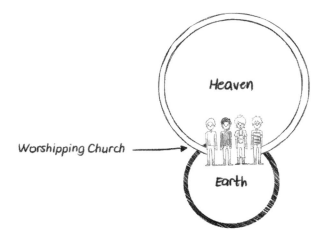

Second, we are not alone in this place. We stand in the presence of innumerable angels and those who have gone before. And, most of all, we stand in the presence of God Himself. There is far more going on in corporate worship than meets the naked eye.

And that is why the writer admonishes worshipers to listen carefully to the words being spoken. God is delivering a kingdom to his people, and that dynamic is shaking the universe. Heaven is on the move. We are receiving a heavenly kingdom on earth that cannot be shaken or removed.

Think of how significant this is. If this is really true, then we can start to understand how Christ's kingdom is extended. It is not through the sword of war or conquest, but through the spiritual sword of God's Word. When God's people gather in covenant renewal the watching world can see and hear the good news of the gospel. They can begin to sense what it means for God to intervene in history to save the world. The flow and fellowship of God's redemptive program is there for them to taste and see.

My deep conviction is that the more people grow in their awareness of this dimension of God's program, the more committed they will be to worship—and they more transformation they will experience. God's program for church unity and transformation is deeply intentional. The Spirit of God works in a context that can be found by those who are seeking it.

Which Christian Tradition?

The frustrating reality at this point in the development of the universal church is that different traditions tend to emphasize one part of the triad over the others. Many churches handle their practice of liturgy sloppily and do not fully embody the principles of biblical covenant renewal. Where can we go to be nurtured and fed?

I want to be clear that while I am a Reformed catholic (Presbyterian), I do not believe we have a corner on practicing the triadic ministries of Word, sacrament, and discipline very well. Frankly, I think we're generally very poor at sacraments and discipline. Our handling of God's Word is often one-dimensional and truncated.

Here is the deal. It really is not for me or anyone else to condemn any particular tradition—whether it be Roman Catholic, Orthodox, Methodist, Episcopalian, Baptist, nondenominational, etc. It seems to me that a better approach is to sketch a roadmap that allows us to better engage and re-form the communities in which we find ourselves.

One way we can do this is to lay the ministry of Word along a vertical spectrum and the sacraments along a horizontal spectrum. (Theoretically we'd need a third axis for discipline, but a church's view of that often goes along with its approach to the sacraments, so we'll leave it out for the sake of simplicity.) At either end of each spectrum, the emphasis on Word or sacrament is alternately high or low, which splits the graph into four quadrants:

The four quadrants can be labeled this way:

- *Low Word and Low Sacrament/Radicalism*—In this quadrant there is little biblical literacy and little practice of the sacraments or church discipline. The church becomes more of a platform for individual causes and ideological movements that are connected to Christ in name only.

- *High Word and Low Sacrament/Rationalism*—In this quadrant, cognition is upheld over communal experience and ritual participation. Missional engagement in the world tends to be low because the focus is individualistic and hyperintellectual.

- *Low Word and High Sacrament/Romanticism*—In this quadrant, ritual participation can sometimes slip into ritualism, but engagement in mission can be quite high. Biblical literacy tends to be low, and mission can suffer from a lack of redemptive knowledge.

- *High Word and High Sacrament/Redemptive Realism*—This is where the three elements of the triad are diligently and consciously upheld. There is a focus that is internal and intellectual as well as external and communal. Preaching and teaching are not pitted against the sacraments or vice versa.

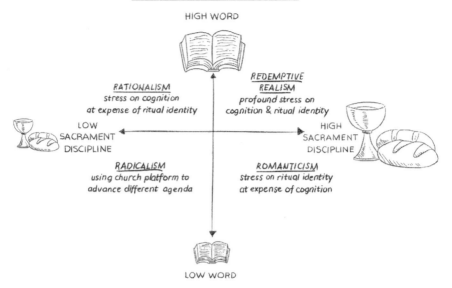

QUADRANT ANALYSIS OF THE CHURCH

HIGH WORD

RATIONALISM
stress on cognition
at expense of ritual identity

*REDEMPTIVE
REALISM*
profound stress on
cognition & ritual identity

LOW
SACRAMENT
DISCIPLINE

HIGH
SACRAMENT
DISCIPLINE

RADICALISM
using church platform to
advance different agenda

ROMANTICISM
stress on ritual identity
at expense of cognition

LOW WORD

My perception is that most Protestant traditions tend to be in the rationalism and radicalism parts of the grid. Roman Catholics and the Orthodox seem to be more entrenched in the romanticism quadrant. Of course this is a generalization, and I know Protestants, Catholics, and Orthodox who escape such characterization. None of us has this all figured out, and, frankly, we need one another. The sooner we recognize this, the sooner we will start mending the rifts that divide.

I am not a sociologist, and I am not going to take the time to try to identify where every specific branch and twig of Christianity belongs in the quadrant analysis. The value of this tool is to reflect on where we each find ourselves. I happen to find myself in a Presbyterian church that is somewhat close to the center of the grid. In my estimation, we can definitely afford to strive after greater biblical literacy and sacramental engagement.

The goal isn't necessarily for each one of us to try to find a church or tradition with the purest expression of these priorities. Rather, it is to try and labor and pray for the community that you are planted in. If you find yourself in a tradition that tends to be more romantic, perhaps you can pursue more biblical training or discipleship in your church. If you are in a more rationalist tradition, perhaps you can work toward more regular practice of the sacraments.

As we strive together toward God's program, using His triadic strategy in the power of His Spirit, unity and transformation will result. We will be salt and light to the world, and Christ's Great Commission will be progressively realized.

CHAPTER TWELVE
Life in the Kingdom

Let your religion be less of a theory and more of a love affair.
—*G. K. Chesterton*

Our family has developed an evening ritual that we generally follow throughout the workweek. Around 6 p.m. we start cooking dinner, and the boys begin working on homework and practicing their musical instruments. While everything is in process, Gina and I like to share an adult beverage with the cable news on in the background. The whole routine helps us transition from the concerns of our busy careers to home.

But sometimes this attempt to calmly shift to a different mode doesn't work as intended. In a flash, Gina will start yelling at the television—arguing with the talking heads. With the full vigor that is especially known to Italian women, she will shake her fist and threateningly wave kitchen utensils at the screen. It is quite entertaining and fascinating to watch her lambaste conservatives, liberals, and anyone else who is unintelligently spewing empty rhetoric.

During a recent election cycle the verbal eruptions from Mount Gina became more frequent and furious. In the middle of a particularly violent episode, one of the boys drifted into the kitchen to gently suggest that the television pundits could not hear what she was saying. As you might imagine, this innocent and obvious observation was not met with immediate agreement.

The bright side of this dynamic is that these outbursts often shape our dinner table conversations. Instead of engaging in small talk, we wade into issues like national security, economics, and education. It is like having our very own family version of *The McLaughlin Group*—albeit with food and wine.

Now I happen to believe that the discussion around our dinner table is a critical kingdom-advancing behavior. After all, Christ's paradigmatic command at the Lord's Supper was to eat and drink together. As one theologian has noted, Jesus' command was to, "*do this* [eat and drink] in remembrance of me," not, "remember me in remembrance of me." Wrestling through issues in the context of a family meal is a key model for world transformation.

But we know that Christ's kingdom is more than talk. Poverty, political injustice, and the like are incredibly complex problems that demand an active response. Beyond participation in the worshiping church and the experience around the family table, what should we do? How should we then live?

There are many ways to come at this question, but I am going to pick an approach that I have found easy to grasp and remember. Our personal orientation to the world and Christ's kingdom can be described in terms of our engagement in self-government, family government, church government, and state government. By briefly exploring each one we will be better equipped to fulfill our role as image bearers in God's world.

| Self-Government | Family Government | Church Government | Civil Government |

Self-Government

Every time I think about the subject of self-government, I think of Michael Jackson's hit song, "Man in the Mirror." Here are the opening lyrics:

I'm gonna make a change
For once in my life
It's gonna feel real good
Gonna make a difference
Gonna make it right

As I, turn up the collar on
My favorite winter coat
This wind is blowing my mind
I see the kids in the streets
With not enough to eat
Who am I to be blind?

Pretending not to see their needs
With so much disregard, a broken bottle top
And one man's soul (and a one man's soul)
They follow each other on the wind ya' know
'Cause they got nowhere to go
That's why I want you to know

I'm starting with the man in the mirror
I'm asking him to change his ways
And no message could have been any clearer
If you want to make the world a better place
Take a look at yourself, and then make a change

Truer words were never spoken—or sung, for that matter. Our redemptive role in the world is tied to our own condition. What impact can we expect to have on our own context if Christ has had no impact on us?

In fact, the apostle James said something quite similar to Michael Jackson's song. He wrote,

But be doers of the word, and not hearers only, deceiving yourselves. For if anyone is a hearer of the word and not a doer, he is like a man who looks intently at his natural face in a mirror. For he looks at himself and goes away and at once forgets what he was like. But the one who looks into the perfect law, the law of liberty, and perseveres, being no hearer who forgets but a doer who acts, he will be blessed in his doing. (James 1:22–25)

We rarely look in a mirror to simply admire ourselves. We usually look into a mirror to make some adjustments to our appearance so that we look presentable. If we looked into a mirror, made no alterations, and then forgot what we looked like, that would be highly abnormal. So it is with reading and hearing God's Word. If it doesn't change us, we have to wonder about our state of mind.

This all sounds straightforward enough, but this is where it actually gets quite tricky. None of us is remotely perfect and all of us tend to struggle with problematic patterns of life and thought that seem almost endemic to our very person. At what point of personal transformation can we expect to be used in kingdom work? Is there some point of maturity we need to attain before we can get into the fray?

On the one hand, I think the answer is no. We are always in the fray whether we want to be or not. Everything we do and don't do carries weight in God's world irrespective of our readiness and intentions. All of our actions and inactions carry meaning because the universe is deeply personal and purposeful. There is therefore no waiting period for people to participate in the extension of God's kingdom.

On the other hand, the answer is a modified yes. The more mature we are as individuals, the more we fruit we can expect to bear in our lives. When our emotions, will, and intellect are aligned to God's ways and purposes, God can use us to move mountains.

Effective self-government and personal holiness matter in public and in private. It is easy to compartmentalize private aspects of our lives as if they have no bearing on our call. But when we realize how integrated we are as people and how interwoven we are into the fabric of the world, we see that all of our thoughts and behaviors have significance.

How great a salvation

What does it mean to be a Christian—to be united by faith to the second Adam and alternate representative for the human race? What actually changes in the life of someone who believes that Jesus is the Lord of lords?

It has to do with our personal identity. Imagine being placed in a witness protection program with a new name, government identification number, address, and career. In one sense, nothing has changed about you. In another sense, everything has changed about you.

Being a Christian means knowing that your new personal history and story extend far beyond your own birth and family of origin. It means that your spiritual union to Christ identifies your very being. But what does it mean to be united to Christ?

I like to think of the application of Christ's redemption to us as akin to a golf swing. A golf swing has different components—the grip, the stance, the backswing—but none of those components, in isolation, is a golf swing. They become a swing only when they all come together.

Theologians often call the components of our salvation the *ordo salutis*, or order of salvation. Don't think of them as pieces of salvation, rather think of them together as a total picture describing what it means to participate in Christ's death and resurrection. There are several places in the Bible where these aspects of salvation can be seen working in tandem, but here is a quick summary of the list:

- *Foreknowledge and Predestination*—Before the creation of the world, God knew humanity would fall, and He planned to rescue a people for Himself. His choice was an act of pure mercy and grace because everyone in humanity deserved justice. God decided to send His only Son to redeem many from the deadly consequence of sin.

- *Calling, Regeneration, Faith, and Repentance*—God calls to faith and repentance those whom Christ redeemed. The Holy Spirit imparts spiritual life so that corrupt and sinful humans can hear God's voice and respond in faith.

- *Justification*—We are mysteriously united to all of the benefits of Christ and his death and resurrection when we trust in Him. One of the first benefits is that we have a right relationship with God. Instead of being condemned, our sins are judicially pardoned and we counted as righteous. More than being declared innocent in the courtroom of God's justice, we are considered holy because we are united to the very person of Jesus Christ.

- *Adoption*—Our right standing with God does not end with a legal declaration. Instead, God presses further by adopting us as His children. We become heirs to all that is His and objects of His love and affection.

- *Sanctification*—God does not merely declare that we are righteous in Christ; He progressively makes us more like Jesus by the power of His Spirit. As we participate in Word, sacrament, and discipline, we are slowly transformed into his likeness.

- *Glorification*—When we are resurrected, our human nature will be perfected, and we will be everything we were intended to be. We will not only be free from guilt of sin, but we will be free from its power and consequences. We will be enabled to work in God's world forever.

The path of morality

Without question, there are positive dos and negative don'ts for God's people. Unfortunately, it is very easy to emphasize one over the other. Fundamentalists tend to focus on the negative don'ts, and liberals tend to focus on the positive dos. But the Bible warns against slipping down either slope by adding or subtracting from God's law. Christ's followers are supposed to be characterized both by what they do and by what they don't do.

This principle seems obvious enough. God's Word negatively teaches that extramarital sex, drunkenness, and stealing are wrong, so we should not do those things. God positively tells us to take care of widows and orphans, feed the poor, and help the sick, so we should do those things. True morality integrates both the negative and positive dimensions of God's plan.

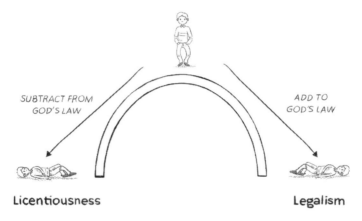

SUBTRACT FROM
GOD'S LAW

ADD TO
GOD'S LAW

Licentiousness   Legalism

By no means do I mean to hold myself up as a standard-bearer of morality who is walking the narrow road of righteousness. In my own heart and life, I have patterns of veering to the right and left of God's program. My goal here is not to point out anyone's foibles, per se, but to stress that true personal holiness does not add or subtract from God's directives. Adding leads to false legalism and subtracting leads to dangerous licentiousness. We do not get to decide what the positive and negative boundaries are. That is God's domain.

Matters of conscience

This gets practically interesting and intellectually difficult when there seems to be a general principle, but the application is in question. For example, in the ancient church there was a controversy over where people bought their meat. The cheapest meat by far came from pagan temples that sold leftover meat from their sacrifices.

Imagine being a convert from one of those pagan cults. How hard and internally offensive would it be to give money to the false religious institution that you had renounced? If you went to a friend's home for dinner, should you ask where they bought the meat? Should you get your neighbors to boycott meat from pagan temples?

The Apostle Paul offered an ingenious solution to this problem. First, he said that in an objective sense, meat is meat, irrespective of its origin. Since false gods are actually nonexistent figments of our own imaginations, there was nothing intrinsically unholy about the meat. Therefore, it was perfectly lawful to eat meat that had been sacrificed to idols.

But Paul added an important caveat. He said that if someone's conscience was offended by eating meat from pagan temples, they should absolutely not eat it. He explicitly declared the meat to be clean in God's eyes, but encouraged them not violate their inner compass regarding the issue. If it felt wrong to eat that meat, then they should not partake. The important priority is to obey your conscience.

This raises an immediate problem. How do we live in close community if each person's conscience sets different boundaries? What happens if your conviction is to abstain from pagan temple meat and you go to someone else's house for dinner? Paul's answer was simple and profound. The people of "weak" conscience that are offended must not foist their conscience on the "strong" who are not offended, and vice versa. Brethren of "weak" conscience should not attempt to discover the origin of meat served at their neighbor's table, and the "strong" should not intentionally provoke. We must acknowledge and respect one another's consciences without legislating or pursuing a morality according to our own judgment.

Our ability to live in unity with each other is directly related to our understanding and practice of these principles. When we drift from them, we tend to create insular communities with extraneous rules and regulations. Instead of displaying an amazing diversity and unity in the bonds of love, we opt for a lame, homogenous subculture that is severely self-limited.

Sincerity

Of course, our batting average as moral actors and patient neighbors will never be as high as we hope. We will continue to battle selfishness and sin that creates division. We can strive after a moral life with special regard to matters of conscience, but we will never live all of our principles perfectly.

The chief way to overcome the communal brokenness we each perpetuate is to continually acknowledge and confess our own brokenness. When we are able to live in the light of God's truth because we are loved in Christ, we don't have to pretend to be who we are not. Our personal pursuit of transparency will work like a salve on the wound of our many offenses.

During my brief stint as a pastor, I remember preaching on this topic using a passage in Philippians. It is a letter from the imprisoned Apostle Paul to a community he was deeply invested in and fond of. He wrote, "And this I pray, that your love may abound still more and more in knowledge and all discernment, that you may approve the things that are excellent, that you may be sincere and without offense till the day of Christ, being filled with the fruits of righteousness which are by Jesus Christ, to the glory and praise of God" (Phil. 1:9–11, NKJV).

During the sermon I spent some time focusing on the Greek word for *sincere*, a term used to describe pottery that had not been painted over to hide cracks. When consumers were shopping for pottery in the marketplace, they would hold it up to the sun to see if it was sincere and not containing hidden flaws. Without thinking I extemporaneously started urging everyone to "show their cracks." With the flourish of an ecstatic orator I repeated it in several ways—"Let your cracks show! Be sincere!"

As people started doubling over in laughter I slowly realized my blunder. My impassioned attempt at preaching transparency had tripped into the absurd and obscene prospect of people lowering their pants. It might not have been my best sermon, but it was probably the most memorable.

Being sincere is not easy because we want people to admire and respect us. It is tempting to conceal our shortcomings and sins as we seek approval and love. But when we pretend to be perfect and do not "show our cracks," we actually encourage self-isolation. People may indeed admire us from a distance, but they will not identify with us and become close to us. True relationships and communities at peace require the humble sincerity that Christ frees us to enjoy.

The pattern and power of prayer

The true source of power in the world and our lives is God Himself. By His grace and His Spirit we have direct and immediate access to Him through prayer. Our heavenly Father delights in our fellowship and is always willing to hear us and strengthen us. Unlike many pagan traditions, we do not have to manipulate circumstances to gain His attention. We always live in His presence, and His throne of grace is always open for business.

Thankfully, Jesus gave us a pattern of prayer. What do we say in the very presence of God? Jesus taught his disciples, saying,

> Our Father in heaven, hallowed be your name.
> Your kingdom come, your will be done, on earth as it is in heaven.
> Give us this day our daily bread,
> and forgive us our debts, as we also have forgiven our debtors.
> And lead us not into temptation, but deliver us from evil. (Matt. 6:9–13)

Many books have been written on Christ's prayer, and I cannot hope to give it the full attention that it deserves, but a number of things are worth noticing briefly.

First, the pronouns are plural, indicating that this prayer is corporate in nature. We belong to a wider community. There is a place for individual prayer, but we need to be ever mindful of our corporate identity as God's people. We do not ultimately come to God alone.

Second, we should approach God with simultaneous confidence and awe. He is at once our loving and devoted Father and He is also utterly holy. We can find comfort and strength in the knowledge that His deep love is matched by His power to do all things.

Third, the overarching priority of our prayers should be for God's will to be done. This point is absolutely critical to internalize. Too many Christians in our day believe that true faith makes "claims" in God's presence. But this is simply not the case. We are never taught that faith makes personal claims on God to meet our own desires. Rather, faith submits our wills to His will and our priorities to His priorities.

God's chief priority is for His kingdom to come to earth. This simply means that God's desire is for His will to be done on earth as it is in heaven. The heart of our prayers should be for God to bring redemption and transformation to this broken world. Even as we ask God to meet our daily needs, we do so in the context of seeking Christ's kingdom.

Our specific personal requests should be addressed in the light of God's kingdom, not with a focus on our comfort or success. When we consider our needs in the light of God's heavenization program, we will approach Him differently. The desires of our hearts are meant to be shaped by God's will. When our requests and supplications align with His program, we can expect amazing things to happen.

This truth is the secret of powerful prayer: bringing our desires into alignment with God's desires. That is not to say that our prayers work only to change us. The Bible teaches that prayer somehow changes God's mind as well. However, the guiding impetus behind our deep longings in life should be God's kingdom agenda. If we want to be happily married we need to consider what that means for our kingdom work. If we want an advanced academic degree toward a particular career we should want it for kingdom-centric reasons. When we strive with God in prayer this way, we will discover the vast power and wisdom of His will.

One of the priorities of prayer is to ask for the forgiveness we continually need to stay in close fellowship with God. Over and over again, we must ask for our Holy Father to have mercy on us because of what Christ has done on our behalf. The puzzling twist is that we are supposed to ask for mercy that parallels the mercy we grant to others. Does this suggest that we are doomed if we have not forgiven the people who have wronged us?

The answer is a sobering *yes*.

Consider a parable Jesus taught on this matter:

> Therefore the kingdom of heaven may be compared to a king who wished to settle accounts with his servants. When he began to settle, one was brought to him who owed him ten thousand talents. And since he could not pay, his master ordered him to be sold, with his wife and children and all that he had, and payment to be made. So the servant fell on his knees, imploring him, 'Have patience with me, and I will pay you everything.' And out of pity for him, the master of that servant released him and forgave him the debt.
>
> But when that same servant went out, he found one of his fellow servants who owed him a hundred denarii, and seizing him, he began to choke him, saying, 'Pay what you owe.' So his fellow servant fell down and pleaded with him, 'Have patience with me, and I will pay you.' He refused and went and put him in prison until he should pay the debt. When his fellow servants saw what had taken place, they were greatly distressed, and they went and reported to their master all that had taken place. Then his master summoned him and said to him, 'You wicked servant! I forgave you all that debt because you pleaded with me. And should not you have had mercy on your fellow servant, as I had mercy on you?' And in anger his master delivered him to the jailers, until he should pay all his debt. So also my heavenly Father will do to every one of you, if you do not forgive your brother from your heart. (Matt. 18:23–35)

The point is fairly obvious, but the perspective is even more poignant when we know what the value of "ten thousand talents" and "a hundred denarii" are. A denarius was worth about a day's wage, and a talent was worth about six thousand denarii. So the first servant owed the king roughly 160 years worth of wages and the second servant only owed about three months worth of wages. To put it in today's money, the king forgave a debt worth billions to the first servant. But the first servant would not show mercy to the man who only owed several thousand dollars.

Jesus is clearly saying that our unwillingness to forgive others is utterly ridiculous in light of the costly and almost infinite debt God has forgiven us. If we do not grasp the magnitude of the mercy that we need and have in Christ, then our faith is false and misguided. True faith so deeply understands the immensity of God's grace toward our individual poverty and brokenness that it cannot help extending mercy to others.

Finally, we are instructed to ask for help in our journey toward personal holiness and preservation. In light of our frailties we need God's guiding hand to protect us from paths that would lead us toward temptation, evil, and destruction. We plead for support and guidance because of our utter dependence on His sovereign grace.

So much more could be said about self-government, but I believe these are the foundational matters that give us the ability to function well in the other spheres of life.

Family Government

The next sphere we are designed for is that of family. I will not belabor the blessing of marriage and procreation here since we spent a fair amount of time on it in chapter eight. Suffice it to repeat that marriage between one man and one woman is the fundamental building block of human community, culture, and civilization. This central relationship is not only the procreative vehicle for perpetuating and establishing God's image bearers on earth; it is the ultimate picture of the way God relates to His people. Marriage is the relationship that most clearly portrays the intense love and sacrificial mutual submission that humanity was made to epitomize.

Duties of parents

One of the greatest privileges and most challenging aspects of life is being a parent. Physical provision and protection are only the beginning of what parenthood entails. When we have or adopt children there is a real sense in which God is actually entrusting us with *His* children. Parents are temporary stewards tasked with nurturing and equipping another generation of image bearers to carry on kingdom work.

There is an interesting Psalm in the Old Testament that reads,

> Behold, children are a heritage from the LORD,
> the fruit of the womb a reward.
> Like arrows in the hand of a warrior
> are the children of one's youth.
> Blessed is the man
> who fills his quiver with them!
> He shall not be put to shame
> when he speaks with his enemies in the gate. (Ps. 127:3–5)

I've always puzzled over the curious notion that children are like arrows in a quiver. What does that mean? The answer is that our children are like offensive weapons for the kingdom of God. That doesn't imply that we put them in harm's way like suicide bombers; it means that we can strategically aim and guide them to fulfill their unique callings according to their gifts and strengths. The future work of our children becomes the legacy that vindicates our own lives.

Of course, parents do not have the direct power to bequeath Christian faith and belief in their children. However, the Bible does teach that the child of at least one Christian parent has a special place in God's program. We know this in part because of an obscure argument the Apostle Paul made while addressing a question about divorce.

In his letter to the Corinthian church, Paul dealt with the question of whether a Christian spouse had to stay married to a non-Christian spouse. His basic answer was that the Christian spouse should stay married unless the non-Christian became unwilling to live in a married relationship. In that case, the Christian was free to divorce and remarry.

The fascinating thing about Paul's teaching on this subject is the way he reasons through it. He writes,

> If any woman has a husband who is an unbeliever, and he consents to live with her, she should not divorce him. For the unbelieving husband is made holy because of his wife, and the unbelieving wife is made holy because of her husband. Otherwise your children would be unclean, but as it is, they are holy. But if the unbelieving partner separates, let it be so. In such cases the brother or sister is not enslaved. God has called you to peace. For how

do you know, wife, whether you will save your husband? Or how do you know, husband, whether you will save your wife? (1 Cor. 7:13–16)

So Paul is saying that when at least one spouse is a Christian, the unbelieving spouse and their children are holy and not unclean. These are technical categories lifted straight from the Old Testament Scriptures. In fact, they are directly related to being included in covenant with God. Paul is saying that the unbelieving spouse and children are in covenant with God by virtue of the Christian spouse.

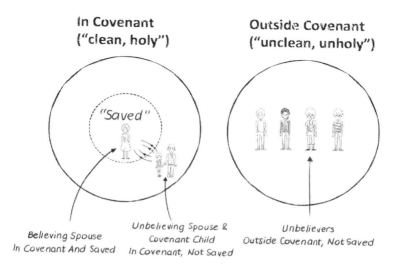

But how can someone be included in the covenant circle of God's redemptive promise without being explicitly converted? Doesn't this contradict the biblical teaching about the necessity of faith and trust? How can a child or an adult be holy without making a confession for Christ?

The heart of the answer is that Paul makes a further distinction between being "saved" and being in covenant. So according to Paul's paradigm, being in covenant is not equivalent to being saved in an ultimate sense. All saved people are in covenant with God, but not all covenant people are ultimately saved.

This is hard for many to understand, but a review of biblical covenants shows that they are often inclusive of all family members. God's covenant of preservation with Noah and redemptive covenant with Abraham included their families and offspring. We know that the same dynamic exists in the New Covenant as well because the Apostle Peter

said, "Repent and be baptized every one of you in the name of Jesus
Christ for the forgiveness of your sins, and you will receive the gift of
the Holy Spirit. For the promise is for you and for your children and
for all who are far off, everyone whom the Lord our God calls to himself" (Acts 2:38, 39).

Being in covenant with God through a spouse or parent brings someone close to salvation and into the sphere of God's redemptive program.
It puts them in immediate proximity to the ministry of Word, sacrament,
and discipline. This gives them the amazing opportunity to taste and see
that the Lord is good. But it also means that whether or not they realize it,
people inside the covenant are called to respond to God's grace. The opportunity and exposure to God's redemption translates to responsibility.

Parents of covenant children are therefore soberly instructed to rear
their children in the "nurture and admonition of the Lord." Notice that
they are not instructed to proselytize their children as strangers and
foreigners to God's covenant promises. Instead of treating children as
"vipers in diapers," as some traditions are prone to do, Christian parents
should appeal to the nearness of God's love.

There is a very real sense in which covenant children are to be understood as God's children. When the church baptizes covenant children it
is with this understanding. Parents are not merely devoting themselves
and dedicating their child to God when a child is baptized. Baptism
of covenant children is a recognition that the child has already been
brought into the family of the church and should be treated accordingly.
Our hope and firm expectation is to see that child mature and blossom
like a plant rooted in good soil.

Duties of young children

As we discussed in chapter nine, the Ten Commandments are organized
in two major sections—loving God and loving our neighbor. Curiously,
the first command about loving our neighbor is not about murder, theft,
or adultery. The first command is actually for children to honor their
parents. God makes it the very first priority of all human relationships.

In fact, the command to honor parents is not only the first law about
how to love neighbors, it is the first command with a promise. God
promised that when children honor their parents they will "live long in
the land." In other words, they will live a life filled with blessing.

But why? Shouldn't laws about murder take priority over the behavior of children? The answer is that when children obey their parents they learn how to obey God and respect others. Childhood is the best time to internalize the reality that freedom and fruitfulness occur within healthy boundaries. It is very dangerous to live life without respect for the authority structures and figures God puts in place. There is a sense in which the other commands about loving our neighbor are first learned by our relationship to our parents and authority.

God reveals Himself as Father because people are created to relate to Him as children living within a family. God cares for and guides His family as a pillar of wisdom, refuge, and strength. He wants His children to look to Him for provision, protection, and direction. When we develop this posture within our earthly families in the context of our earthly parents, the probability of adopting this perspective with God is very high.

Duties of grown children

Of course, there comes a day when children become adults and start their own families. During this phase, men and women have instructions that come from the Garden of Eden itself. The text reads, "...a man shall leave his father and his mother and hold fast to his wife, and they shall become one flesh" (Gen. 2:24).

I have often heard pastors refer to this as the "leave and cleave" principle. In preparation for marriage, adults are instructed to leave their parents in order to cleave to their spouse. Adult children are not bound to a relationship of obedience to their parents in perpetuity.

The leave and cleave principle is especially relevant in our day when so many adults never seem to leave home. And even the ones who physically leave home to begin other families are tempted to maintain unhealthy ties of dependence to their parents. They never truly cleave to their new life partner because of the inability to leave their family of origin.

Sarcastic mother-in-law jokes exist for a reason. Accomplishing a healthy separation to form a new union requires understanding from parents and adult children alike. The departure of adult children is a two-way street that parents must honor and encourage. It can be very hard to swallow, but parents need to embrace the reality that the nature and degree of their stewardship transforms and declines over time.

334 Life in the Kingdom

Another dynamic of the parent-child relational transformation is that adult children inherit a certain responsibility toward their aging parents. We are called to care for and help support our parents as they enter their twilight years. Jesus once chastised the Pharisees for saying they gave their money to God instead of taking care of their parents. Jesus wants adult children to honor adult parents by taking care of them as necessary.

Parents are ideally called to save up enough resources to care for themselves and to leave an inheritance. However, life is not perfect and this ideal is not always achieved. Adult children are therefore called to be the primary social safety net for their aging parents. The burden of social security for aging parents is primarily given to families, not other entities and institutions.

Church Government

Up to this point we have loosely defined the church as the family of God's people. The conceptual challenge of this definition is that the institutional church includes pretenders and self-deceived people with no faith at all. Not everyone attached to the institutional church is really a sincere follower of Christ. Don't we need to be more precise about who the church includes?

The definition of the church

Some have tried to grapple with this reality by thinking in terms of the visible and invisible church. Everyone attached to the institutional church is a so-called visible member, but only those with true faith are included in the invisible church. This approach is not arbitrary. Even Jesus said, "Not everyone who says to me, 'Lord, Lord,' will enter the kingdom of heaven, but the one who does the will of my Father in heaven" (Matt. 7:21).

However, as useful as the visible/invisible conceptual distinction is in some respects, it creates a fairly serious problem. Namely, it plants the insidious seeds of faith-destroying self-doubt and recrimination of others. Is my faith real enough? Am I really in God's family or am I deceiving myself? What about Joe Bob who is a perpetual moral disaster? Maybe he isn't *really* in God's family. Perhaps I should keep my distance and we should treat him differently.

There is a great tension between discernment and charity within the Christian community. We must be vigilant and alert to false teachers and hucksters who live to fleece the sheep, but we must be incredibly patient and generous in light of the brokenness we all bring to the table.

A contemporary theologian has suggested that perhaps a more helpful distinction than visible/invisible is historic/eschatological, i.e., the church as we see it now, changing and growing throughout earthly history, and the church as it will be in eternity. There is a very real sense in which even hypocrites and hucksters are part of the historic church of God. Even without faith, their participation in the sacraments bring them into covenant with God. They therefore owe God their fealty, but they are in fact living unfaithfully. However, not everyone who is attached to the church in history will remain part of the church after the final judgment at the marriage supper of the Lamb.

This nuance is helpful because it leaves ultimate judgment where it belongs—at the judgment seat of God. We must care for the family of God now and protect it by disciplining and sometimes dismissing those who will not live according to the family rules. But we should carefully refrain from strictly personal judgments that destroy faith and community.

Jesus taught this in one of his most famous parables:

> He put another parable before them, saying, "The kingdom of heaven may be compared to a man who sowed good seed in his field, but while his men were sleeping, his enemy came and sowed weeds among the wheat and went away. So when the plants came up and bore grain, then the weeds appeared also. And the servants of the master of the house came and said to him, 'Master, did you not sow good seed in your field? How then does it have weeds?' He said to them, 'An enemy has done this.' So the servants said to him, 'Then do you want us to go and gather them?' But he said, 'No, lest in gathering the weeds you root up the wheat along with them. Let both grow together until the harvest, and at harvest time I will tell the reapers, Gather the weeds first and bind them in bundles to be burned, but gather the wheat into my barn.'" (Matt. 13:24–30)

The institutional form of the church

It is one thing to talk about the responsibilities we have as individuals and families, but another when we wade into communal and institutional waters. Thankfully, God has not left us entirely to our imaginations in these matters. There are principles that shape our thoughts and actions in the corporate contexts that preclude our temptation to invent structures of our own making.

Of course, when it comes to the formation and function of church government, there is wide diversity in practice. In fact, this diversity has been one of the chief issues dividing Christians from one another for centuries. Discernment in these matters does not come easily.

We can think of the organizational diversity along a continuum with hierarchical formations at the top and populist and quasi-democratic formations at the bottom. In between are hybrids that borrow from each end of the spectrum:

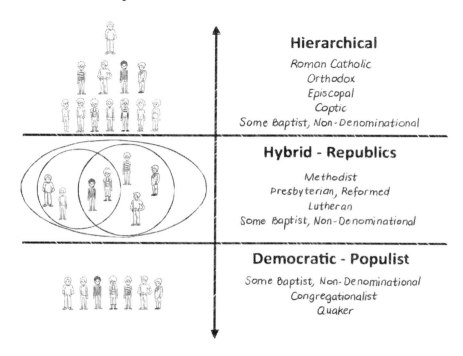

Hierarchical

Roman Catholic
Orthodox
Episcopal
Coptic
Some Baptist, Non-Denominational

Hybrid - Republics

Methodist
Presbyterian, Reformed
Lutheran
Some Baptist, Non-Denominational

Democratic - Populist

Some Baptist, Non-Denominational
Congregationalist
Quaker

You may notice that Baptist and nondenominational churches can appear anywhere on the spectrum. Even though a church may be independent, it may function internally with small and unspoken, but very real hierarchy. A church may not call their leader a pope or a bishop, but can still come close to giving their leader that kind of authority.

Let's begin our attempt to discern God's intent for institutional formation by digesting an episode between Jesus and His disciples just before His crucifixion:

> Now when Jesus came into the district of Caesarea Philippi, he asked his disciples, "Who do people say that the Son of Man is?" And they said,

"Some say John the Baptist, others say Elijah, and others Jeremiah or one of the prophets." He said to them, "But who do you say that I am?" Simon Peter replied, "You are the Christ, the Son of the living God." And Jesus answered him, "Blessed are you, Simon Bar-Jonah! For flesh and blood has not revealed this to you, but my Father who is in heaven. And I tell you, you are Peter, and on this rock I will build my church, and the gates of hell shall not prevail against it. I will give you the keys of the kingdom of heaven, and whatever you bind on earth shall be bound in heaven, and whatever you loose on earth shall be loosed in heaven." Then he strictly charged the disciples to tell no one that he was the Christ. (Matt. 16:13–20)

There are a couple of critical issues that this declaration puts on the table. First, what or who is the rock that the church would be built upon? Second, what does it mean to have the keys of the kingdom of heaven? The answers to these questions are crucial for our practical life in the institutional church.

The majority report throughout Christianity's history on the first question is that the rock is the Apostle Peter himself. That would seem to be an obvious conclusion, but some Protestant exegetes contend that the rock is the content of Peter's confession of faith, not him as a person. I believe this is primarily born out of a concern that if the rock is Peter, that could lead to an inference about the papacy and organizational hierarchy. From their point of view, the church is built upon faith in Christ's identity.

I think the best solution is to recognize that, in fact, the rock was Peter himself. The mental and exegetical gymnastics required to interpret the rock as Peter's confession are laudable, but stretch credulity. Furthermore, recognizing Peter as the rock does not necessarily lead to an inference about the establishment of a hierarchy with a pope.

An alternative way of understanding this is to see that Christ was prophesying about the founding of the church, not about its perpetual organization. As we read in the beginning of Acts, the Holy Spirit was sent to the disciples immediately after Christ's ascension. The apostle who interpreted this event and took the initial lead within the fledgling church was Peter. This historical reality fulfilled Christ's prophecy recorded in the Gospel of Matthew.

If the Acts narrative featuring Peter's initial role ended on this point, the inference about Peter as the first pope and the hierarchical concept of apostolic succession might stand. But the rest of the book of Acts and the balance of the New Testament do not portray Peter's leadership or the functioning of the church in a hierarchical fashion. Instead, it tells the story of a network of individual churches emerging under multiple leaders.

Authority in the church

I say individual churches because each church was set up to be substantially self-governing under the authority of the Scriptures. The Apostle Paul wrote,

> So then you are no longer strangers and aliens, but you are fellow citizens with the saints and members of the household of God, *built on the foundation of the apostles and prophets*, Christ Jesus himself being the cornerstone, in whom the whole structure, being joined together, grows into a holy temple in the Lord. In him you also are being built together into a dwelling place for God by the Spirit. (Eph. 2:19–22)

The phrase "the apostles and prophets" is an idiom for the Scriptures. The personal presence of the prophets and apostles unquestionably helped to establish the community of God, but it is their inscribed message and literature that abides as the lasting foundation.

Each church is constituted with its own council of elders who are jointly responsible for the spiritual care of its people. All elders are pastors in the metaphorical sense that they shepherd God's flock. However, some elders are called to make teaching and prayer their special vocation. Individual congregations are instructed to provide for and honor them well for their work.

While each church is thus independent in one sense, churches are not completely autonomous or disconnected from the whole body of Christ. In fact, the book of Acts highlights a story about a global doctrinal controversy that had an impact on all Christians in the first century—whether or not Gentile converts should be circumcised.

In the Acts narrative we notice two important things that did not happen: Peter was not asked to make an official ruling, and each church was not at liberty to come up with its own decision. Rather, a group of apostles and elder delegates in Jerusalem debated the issue. In the end, the Apostle James appealed to the Old Testament Scriptures to answer the problem. The organizational decision-making process was not hierarchical at all. The wider church looked to a group of leaders who came together to discern the teaching of Scripture.

This early episode during the Apostolic era shows that the organized church is neither a hierarchy nor a pure democracy. It truly functions more like a representative republic with local self-government and organic connections to the wider church for dispute resolution and development. This hybrid elder-led and global council type of organization is usually referred to as *presbyterian* (presbyter = elder). Various churches have a presbyterian type of organization, but do not use the term or label to describe themselves.

Many books have been written about the specific mechanics of Presbyterian government, so I will not develop that here. As someone who has been steeped in presbyterian organizational dynamics for decades, let be the first to say that while this form of organization may be biblical, it is by no means easy or tidy.

Presbyterian government is especially hard because its decision making process is inherently collaborative and connected to other communities. In hierarchical organizations, the buck stops with an empowered individual, and lines of authority are usually clear. In purely democratic organizations decisions are made from a popular vote. This is not the way presbyterian elder-rule works.

The heart of the presbyterian organizational model is representative and cooperative leadership of peers in submission to God's program of Word, sacrament, and discipline. By God's wise design, people striving to serve each other in the context of God's kingdom project will produce maturity and unity.

I had a professor in college who used to say that church organization was nothing and leadership was everything. In other words, the arrangement of the structure was not the underlying reason for corporate achievement or success; it was the dynamism of the people in leadership that mattered. There is a sense in which he is substantially correct. People can be set up with the right structure and offer horrific leadership. But skilled and energetic people in dysfunctional structures can often achieve great things.

The central idea here is not to conceive of organizational form as a panacea for the unity of Christ's church. The critical principle is that we are all called to labor together in an ordered community that is locally organized and universally connected. Absolute local autonomy is not the witness of the Bible any more than a global top-down hierarchy is.

We are called to live in a complex web of local, regional, and universal community that is committed to seeking God's kingdom. When we have internal and external disputes we should come together to discern God's will through His Word.

The keys to the kingdom

But what power did Jesus convey when He gave the church the power of the keys to the kingdom of heaven? What does it mean for the church to loose things in earth and in heaven? Does the church have the power to effectively grant and withdraw salvation from people?

In a limited and nuanced sense, the answer is yes. The church does not make ultimate judgments that belong only to Christ Himself. However, the church does have the authority and capacity to manage the entryway into and continuing membership in God's family through the administration of the sacraments. By regulating access to the baptismal font and the Communion table, the church can effectively open or close the doors to the kingdom of heaven.

God has given the church the high and holy privilege of inviting people to Table fellowship, but it has also given the church the responsibility and the authority to fence and guard the Table as well.

Of course it is possible for the church to exercise discipline in error, and of course God's grace can operate outside of the institutional church, but because the sacraments are God's ordinary means of grace, people who find themselves banned from participating should take sober warning. Disciplinary decisions by the church should not be seen as merely external or perfunctory because of Christ's declaration regarding the power of the keys.

Belonging to and participating in the church carries significant weight. When the church exercises discipline by prohibiting someone's participating in the body and blood of Christ, that person is in grave danger. Being removed from the ministry of the sacrament is a recipe for spiritual starvation and possible disaster.

It must be understood that church discipline and the use of the keys of the kingdom end with the ministry of the sacraments. The church is not authorized to use force or coercive powers to reign in or punish behavior. That would be wielding the power of the sword—and only the civil government is given that power.

Power of the Keys   **Power of the Sword**

Civil government

The Bible is curiously silent when it comes to the recommended form of civil government. It does not explicitly endorse or denounce monarchy, oligarchy, democracy, or any other political structure. Instead, it merely assumes the civil government's role of keeping peace through the power of the sword.

In one of the few New Testament texts concerning civil government, the Apostle Paul wrote,

> Let every person be subject to the governing authorities. For there is no authority except from God, and those that exist have been instituted by God. Therefore whoever resists the authorities resists what God has appointed, and those who resist will incur judgment. For rulers are not a terror to good conduct, but to bad. Would you have no fear of the one who is in authority? Then do what is good, and you will receive his approval, for he is God's servant for your good. But if you do wrong, be afraid, for he does not bear the sword in vain. For he is the servant of God, an avenger who carries out God's wrath on the wrongdoer. Therefore one must be in subjection, not only to avoid God's wrath but also for the sake of conscience. For because of this you also pay taxes, for the authorities are ministers of God, attending to this very thing. Pay to all what is owed to them: taxes to whom taxes are owed, revenue to whom revenue is owed, respect to whom respect is owed, honor to whom honor is owed. (Rom. 13:1–7)

Notice that Paul views the pagan civil rulers of his day as servants appointed by God. Even though the Roman Empire in the first century was anything but Christian, Paul maintained that God granted them authority to punish evildoers. He taught Christians to submit to their rule so that they could live a quiet and peaceful life under the Roman civil authorities.

This is especially poignant in light of the New Testament's repeated use of the word *gospel*. Again, the good news that word implied had to do with new leadership. The gospel is that Christ is King. But the apostles did not engage in rebellion. Instead, they labored and prayed for conversion and reformation of the existing civic leaders.

It is important to point out that Paul's instruction in this text does not completely rule out the possibility of civil disobedience. People do not have to subject themselves to outright tyranny. When governing authorities enact laws that are contrary to God's revealed will, people must obey God instead of man. When Peter and the apostles were imprisoned and told to stop preaching about Christ, they explicitly refused to obey. Civil disobedience is always justified when people in authority make laws that transgress God's law.

Relationship between church and state

Perhaps it would help to contrast the functions of church and state by looking more closely at their respective powers of the keys and the sword:

	Civil Government (Power of the Sword)	Church Government (Power of the Keys)
Means of Influence	Force and Coercion	Persuasion
Discipline	Taxes, Prison, Death	Withhold Sacraments
Money	Mandatory Taxes	Voluntary Tithe
Social Justice	Wrath on Wrongdoer	Grace to Sinners
Social Safety Net	Optional	Mandatory

This is helpful because we can see that the Bible clearly distinguishes the roles and responsibilities of church and state. The church should not use deadly force in pursuit of evildoers and the state should not involve itself in matters pertaining to the Word and sacrament. Each organizational entity has limits to its authority and methods.

While these are useful delineations, they leave some important questions unanswered. Namely, what should the relationship between church and state be? Should they be integrated in some way or completely separate? Is one beholden to the other in any respect?

First, we should understand that the political assumption about the formal separation of church and state is a relatively novel social experiment in the West. For most of human history, there has been a very close relationship between religion and government. The leaders of the state were very often leaders of the state religion as well. And even when the leadership was distinct, the state typically endorsed a particular religion and vice versa.

The fusion of church and state is natural in a religiously homogenous culture. But social diversity and fragmentation of the church make the relationship between the spheres far more complex.

As Christendom began to fade in the West and religious pluralism increased, the close bonds between church and state began to fray and tatter. During the Enlightenment period, various configurations were tried with various degrees of success. But the most successful political experiment arising from this period was arguably found in the United States.

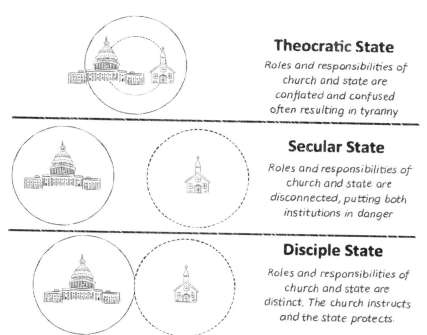

Theocratic State

Roles and responsibilities of church and state are conflated and confused often resulting in tyranny

Secular State

Roles and responsibilities of church and state are disconnected, putting both institutions in danger

Disciple State

Roles and responsibilities of church and state are distinct. The church instructs and the state protects.

The founders of the United States attempted to increase religious and civil liberties by separating the civil and religious spheres from each other. While the formative documents of the United Kingdom explicitly declare fealty to the Lord Jesus Christ, the Constitution of the United

States does not. The founders explicitly understood that social liberty and justice were tied to a common ethical and moral ethos, but they opted for a generic understanding of deity via natural law.

Rather than explicitly tying the Constitution of the United States to the name of Jesus Christ or a particular religious expression of Christianity, they took a new course that depended on the light of reason and nature. They didn't cite scriptural authority to build their case; they endorsed "self-evident" truths. In so doing, they gave birth to one of the largest and most successful experiments in secularism that the world has ever seen.

One could argue whether the success of the United States has been due to other variables outside of its secular formation, but there can be little doubt that the secular Constitutional Republic of the United States has succeeded where others have failed. The atheistic socialism of the former USSR and the quasi-theocratic fundamentalism of certain Arab states are not models most people in the West are rushing to emulate.

The problem with natural law and the secular state

The problem with so-called natural law is that it is severely limited and confused in what it conveys. It may teach that life is precious, but it does not teach when it begins or should end. Natural law may teach that all people deserve equal justice, but it does not teach what activities should or shouldn't be criminalized. Natural law might endorse marriage, but it does not teach its limits and boundaries.

People may object that the government should not legislate morality, but this is nonsensical. All legislation is derived by and for some moral purpose. Speed limits exist to protect life. They have a moral basis. Taxes are levied to sustain systems for the common good. They have a moral basis. The list goes on and on.

Contemporary social controversies in the United States are Exhibit A for the extreme limits of natural law and the light of reason to resolve the most basic moral questions. If the civil government is tasked with punishing evildoers and protecting the peace, evil must be properly defined. Appeals to natural law and reason do not bring self-evidently clear answers. In fact, they often bring strife and political maneuvering. Ironically, secularism ends up creating the discord and minority persecution it is supposed to avoid.

A current case in point involves a small bakery that refused make a wedding cake for a gay couple. In a stunning series of events, the gay couple sued for discrimination, and the civil court ordered the business owners to serve gay clientele. Whatever one believes about this particular conflict and its outcome, it is clear that we have a collision of religious and civil interests that demands attention.

I personally believe the social experiment of the United States has worked for as long as it has because of the borrowed religious capital it has run on for centuries. The assumed matrix of Judeo-Christian morality, rule of law, and heart for social justice have kept the culture largely intact.

But now the secular culture of the United States is wading into dangerous territory. Fights over cultural and civic norms are increasing, and the staggering economic debts caused by the military industrial complex and failed social initiatives have left the nation in an extremely weakened position. Relative to other failed nations, the United States may still be a beacon of light, but a day of reckoning for our joint failures in the civic arena appears to be on the horizon.

Some believe the answers to cultural decline are essentially political. If the right people with the right political platforms can get elected, maybe we can escape cultural doom and reclaim a path toward peace and prosperity. Others believe we need a religious revival to realign our collective civic conscience with the will of God. Perhaps the mere presence of Christians in every walk of life will be transformative outside of any political machinery.

The challenge of conservatism

One of the great challenges of our day is the way Christians get caught up in the conservative versus liberal political paradigm. It is too easy to join the chorus of the culture wars over issues like family values. Thriving families are at the heart of God's program for thriving cultures, so Christians tend to resonate with politically conservative initiatives that are ostensibly family friendly.

The problem is that family values do not exist in isolation from God's Word and God's heavenization agenda. The values on the table aren't owned by conservative political ideology. Rather, they spring from the values of God's kingdom. They are kingdom values, not conservative values.

When Christians too closely identify with conservative political platforms, they give up too much. For example, the kingdom of God is not regressive, austere, or backward looking. It is not conservative in the ways that the word might suggest. In fact, kingdom values are progressive, innovative, and maturing. Why cede these forward-leaning principles and postures to liberals by embracing the conservative moniker?

Of course, there is a place for cultural cobelligerency. Christians can and should cooperate with people of other faiths. It is very right and good for Christians to work with Jews, Muslims, and even secularists who want to promote agendas that leverage kingdom principles. There is no need to stand outside of political processes merely for the sake of ideological purity.

The point isn't about cooperation; it is about holding onto a distinct and nuanced personal identity. Our Christianity and our kingdom values must not be eclipsed by political paradigms. As convenient as it may be to work alongside conservative parties, we run the risk of compromising our full potential and impact if we do not retain and promote the totality of the kingdom of God.

The disciple state vision

We must not conflate the United States or any other civil government with the church or the kingdom of God. The fate of the United States may be bright or dim; I don't know. But I know what the plan for Christ's kingdom is. The plan is for the church to disciple the nations.

And this is the model that I believe the Scriptures want us to pursue. The church and the state are organizationally independent of one another and have different roles. But they are related because they need each other. The state needs the church for its basic moral instruction and guidance, and the church needs the state for protection and peace. They have a symbiotic relationship that brings cultural and civic health and prosperity.

Martin Luther King wrote, "The church must be reminded that it is not the master or the servant of the state, but rather the conscience of the state. It must be the guide and the critic of the state, and never its tool. If the church does not recapture its prophetic zeal, it will become an irrelevant social club without moral or spiritual authority."[50]

Of course, there are at least two major practical barriers to implementing this vision for the disciple state. First, the church is far too divided to speak with one voice to the state. Second, religious pluralism is so pervasive that there would not be the necessary agreement to such a civil shift.

---

50 Martin Luther King, *Strength to Love* (New York: Harper & Row, 1963), 64.

Therefore, the work before Christians is clear. We must work internally for church unity and externally for more converts to Christ. Only as these priorities come together will we have the potential for disciple states to emerge.

In the interim, Christians must become more thoughtful about how to engage in the present context. We must not buy into the naive proposition that the ballot box will cure our social ills. However, we cannot afford to retreat into the Christian spiritual ghetto either.

Our presence and participation are necessary in the civil arena, but we must realistically assess where we stand. The transformational potential of any secular nation will be limited by its philosophical foundations. Until people recognize Christ as King and agree to follow His program, it will be a nip and tuck operation at best.

My hope is that the next generations of Christians will invest more in their civic and political imaginations. Cynicism has overshadowed our vision of Christ's Great Commission. We must repent and become more focused on His worldwide agenda.

I can only imagine that many will shudder in horror at the prospect of a civil government with explicit ties to the Christian church. Will this be a recipe for persecution of non-Christian minorities? Is this a path toward an impure church filled with those jockeying for political favor?

I understand these fears, but I believe they are unfounded. Religious pluralism and liberty can flourish in the context of a Christian disciple state. The love of Christ is not coercive, and the government's role is not to conscript individuals into the church or to punish those outside of it. The arbitrary and dehumanizing nature of secularism alongside the violent proclivities of vast swaths of Islam are far more concerning, in my opinion.

Kingdom living in Babylon

About five hundred years before the birth of Christ, Jerusalem was conquered by Babylon, and many Jews were expatriated. During the Babylonian exile, the Jews in captivity were uncertain how to live their lives. How should they live as God's people in a foreign land? Jeremiah delivered God's word, saying,

> Thus says the LORD of hosts, the God of Israel, to all the exiles whom I have sent into exile from Jerusalem to Babylon: Build houses and live in them; plant gardens and eat their produce. Take wives and have sons and daughters;

take wives for your sons, and give your daughters in marriage, that they may bear sons and daughters; multiply there, and do not decrease. But seek the welfare of the city where I have sent you into exile, and pray to the LORD on its behalf, for in its welfare you will find your welfare. (Jer. 29:4–7)

The Jews were in a strange and pagan land, but God did not tell them to retreat. Rather, He told them to establish a productive presence in the midst of Babylon. He told them to seek the peace of the city so they could live at peace. He told them that its welfare was their welfare.

Christians living in non-disciple states should follow the same pattern. Our job is to be faithfully and productively present wherever we find ourselves. We must not retreat into isolation or into insular communities that await doom and destruction. Instead, we must bring shalom—wholeness—to the places we are called to live. As we demonstrate the garden model for humanity in our fruitfulness and families, we will see cities transform. We will see nations discipled. And then at last we will see the coming of our Lord.

From the beginning of time and before the fall of Adam, God's plan was for His image bearers to glorify the earth. He created us to pursue His agenda in loving communities committed to kingdom work, feasting, and thanksgiving. That was our call from the beginning, and thanks to the Lord Jesus Christ, it is our call today and forevermore. May God help us in His work and bless the feast that He lovingly invites us to enjoy with Him.

Come quickly, Lord Jesus.

Amen.

Acknowledgements

I want to start by thanking a good friend and colleague, Jim Bates, for recommending that I hire a professional writing coach to jumpstart this lifelong bucket-list project. He put me in touch with Stella Togo and she very patiently helped me find a trajectory and a voice. I'm very thankful for both of them.

As the manuscript progressed into potentially more treacherous philosophical and theological waters, Pastor Mark Horne was kind enough to give me candid and constructive feedback. I profited immeasurably from my conversations with him.

During the writing of the book, a small group of men from San Clemente Presbyterian Church met over the course of several months to discuss the contents. I deeply appreciate Brett Knox, Jim Hawkes, Martin Zapp, Tom Dellner, Rick Oliver, and Jim Ciadella, for their willingness to engage with the raw material.

I am also indebted to my editor, Valerie Bost, for her keen eye for detail and discerning theological mind. I can't say enough about the quality of her work.

I must acknowledge and thank the Christian theologians who have contributed so much to my understanding. It would be impossible to list them all, but it goes without saying that my thoughts are heavily derived from Francis Schaeffer, James B. Jordan, Peter Leithart, and N.T. Wright. I feel very much like my thoughts are just a crude reworking of what I have tried to learn from them.

Finally, I want to thank my beloved wife, Gina, for encouraging and tolerating me through this process. It was a sacrifice of time and treasure that I pray will be returned to her by God's grace.

16456867R00206

Made in the USA
San Bernardino, CA
04 November 2014